SHORT HISTORIES

Short Histories are authoritative and elegantly written introductory texts which offer fresh perspectives on the way history is taught and understood in the 21st century. Designed to have strong appeal to university students and their teachers, as well as to general readers and history enthusiasts, *Short Histories* comprise novel attempts to bring informed interpretation, as well as factual reportage, to historical debates. Addressing key subjects and topics in the fields of history, the history of ideas, religion, classical studies, politics, philosophy and Middle East studies, these texts move beyond the bland, neutral 'introductions' that so often serve as the primary undergraduate teaching tool. While always providing students and generalists with the core facts that they need to get to grips with, *Short Histories* go further. They offer new insights into how a topic has been understood in the past, and what different social and cultural factors might have been at work. They bring original perspectives to bear on current interpretations. They raise questions and – with extensive bibliographies – point the reader to further study, even as they suggest answers. Each text addresses a variety of subjects in a greater degree of depth than is often found in comparable series, yet at the same time in a concise and compact handbook form. *Short Histories* aim to be 'introductions with an edge'. In combining questioning and searching analysis with informed historical writing, they bring history up-to-date for an increasingly complex and globalized digital age.

For more information about titles and authors in the series, please visit: https://www.bloomsbury.com/series/short-histories/

A Short History of ...

the American Civil War	Paul Anderson, Clemson University, USA
the American Revolutionary War	Stephen Conway, University College London, UK
Ancient Greece	P J Rhodes, Emeritus, Durham University, UK
the Anglo-Saxons	Henrietta Leyser, University of Oxford, UK
Babylon	Karen Radner, University of Munich, Germany
the Byzantine Empire: Revised Edition	Dionysios Stathakopoulos, University of Cyprus, Cyprus
Christian Spirituality	Edward Howells, University of Roehampton, UK
Communism	Kevin Morgan, University of Manchester, UK
the Crimean War	Trudi Tate, University of Cambridge, UK
English Renaissance Drama	Helen Hackett, University College London, UK
the English Revolution and the Civil Wars	David J Appleby, Nottingham University, UK
the Etruscans	Corinna Riva, University of Erfurt, Germany
Florence and the Florentine Republic	Brian J. Maxson, East Tennessee State University, USA
the Hundred Years War	Michael Prestwich, Emeritus, Durham University, UK
Judaism and the Jewish People	Steven Jacobs, The University of Alabama, USA
Medieval Christianity	G R Evans, Emertius, University of Cambridge, UK
the Minoans	John Bennet, British School of Athens, Greece

| *the Wars of the Roses* | David Grummitt, University of Kent, UK |
| *the Weimar Republic* | Colin Storer, University of Warwick, UK |

A SHORT HISTORY OF

THE BYZANTINE EMPIRE: REVISED EDITION

Dionysios Stathakopoulos

BLOOMSBURY ACADEMIC

LONDON • NEW YORK • OXFORD • NEW DELHI • SYDNEY

BLOOMSBURY ACADEMIC
Bloomsbury Publishing Plc
50 Bedford Square, London, WC1B 3DP, UK
1385 Broadway, New York, NY 10018, USA
29 Earlsfort Terrace, Dublin 2, Ireland

BLOOMSBURY, BLOOMSBURY ACADEMIC and the Diana logo are trademarks
of Bloomsbury Publishing Plc

First published in Great Britain 2023

A catalogue record for this book is available from the British Library.

A catalog record for this book is available from the Library of Congress.

ISBN: HB: 978-1-3502-3340-9
PB: 978-1-3502-3341-6
ePDF: 978-1-3502-3342-3
eBook: 978-1-3502-3343-0

Series: Short Histories

Typeset by Deanta Global Publishing Services, Chennai, India
Printed and bound in Great Britain

To find out more about our authors and books visit www.bloomsbury.com
and sign up for our newsletters.

This one is definitely for Konstantin

Contents

Illustrations

MAPS

1 The Byzantine Empire around 400
2 The Byzantine Empire in the early eighth century with major military commands
3 The Byzantine Empire around 1050
4 The Byzantine world after 1204
5 Constantinople with major Byzantine and Ottoman monuments

FIGURES

(Unless otherwise stated photos are by the author.)

Illustrations

Illustrations

Preface to the revised edition

A Short History of the Byzantine Empire was published in 2014 as one of the first in a new series of books envisaged as 'introductions with an edge'. My aim was to produce a clear account of the long history of the Byzantine Empire based on the latest research in all major European languages. I also wanted to highlight and explain ongoing debates in the field instead of providing a smoothed narrative. Furthermore, contrary to many comparable short histories of the Empire, I gave special emphasis to the economic, social and cultural changes within Byzantium, but also placed its history in the framework of developments in both the Latin Christian and the Islamic worlds.

It was very fortunate that the book was well received and became quite popular. Since its publication it went on to be translated in Estonian (2016), Modern Greek (2016), Turkish (2018), Chinese (2019) and Russian (2020), while a translation in Korean will be published soon. Many of the translators wrote to me with questions that made me rethink some of the book's contents and make changes. At that point I was not expecting that a revised edition would be forthcoming, but I was very glad to take on the task when asked by my wonderful editor at Bloomsbury, Emily Drewe.

In this revised edition small factual mistakes were corrected, and the bibliography was significantly enlarged in order to incorporate more recent publications in English, but also many important studies in other languages that had been left out of the printed reference section in the first edition (and were available at the book's dedicated website). Now the bibliography reflects much more clearly the research of colleagues around the world on which this book is based. Furthermore, I have made numerous changes throughout the text. In some instances, new research made existing interpretations obsolete and these were corrected. The progress of my own research has also made me modify some of my ideas. But perhaps more importantly, I have tried to streamline my arguments and to highlight my own views more clearly and explicitly. The result is, I hope, a better, more readable book; it is now up to you to decide whether you agree.

I would like to thank friends and colleagues whose input helped improve the book: Betsy Bolman, Natasha Constantinidou, Tonia Kiousopoulou, Telemachos Lounghis, Pagona Papadopoulou, Kostis Smyrlis, Vlada Stankovic and Yannis Stouraitis. In the revised edition there are a number of new illustrations and I would like to thank all the institutions and individuals that provided them. My heartfelt thanks go to the Very Reverend Archimandrite Ephraim, Abbot of the Holy Monastery of Vatopedi, for granting me permission to use the image of the stunning late Byzantine icon on the book's cover. I also owe special thanks to Petros Bouras-Vallianatos and Elder Gerasimos of the Monastery of Hagios Pavlos for arranging this. I am also very thankful to all my colleagues at the University of Cyprus for their very warm welcome (amid the pandemic, nonetheless) to my new professional home. Finally, I am grateful to Megan Harris and everyone at Bloomsbury for a brilliant cooperation.

Acknowledgements

For the past three years, give or take a week or two, my life revolved around this book. The journey was long and not always easy, and along the way I incurred many debts which I am very happy to acknowledge here.

Alex Wright at I.B.Tauris trusted me with this project and spearheaded it along the way – this book would not exist without him. The production team, Lisa Goodrum and Ricky Blue, as well as my copy editor Stephen Cashmore were wonderful to work with. At the earliest stage of this book Diana Newall and Barbara Rosenwein gave invaluable feedback on questions of organization and structure; it was Ludmilla Jordanova who helped me crack the key question of structure, effortlessly, over a cup of tea.

I am sure that I have driven everyone around me absolutely mad by always talking about this book in an alternating jubilant or desperate manner depending on whether a particular chapter was progressing or not. And so I am very grateful to all my colleagues and students at King's College London as well as my friends and family for politely ignoring the fact that somehow, regardless of the context, I always brought the discussion back to Byzantium.

Yannis Stouraitis, Kostis Smyrlis, Alicia Simpson, Thierry Ganchou, Alessandra Bucossi, Angeliki Lymberopoulou and Sharon Gerstel will all recognize how a number of discussions we had profoundly shaped some of the key arguments in the book. Vlada Stanković, Dhwani Patel and Alessandra Bucossi read chapters in draft and made numerous helpful comments. Averil Cameron, Ioanna Rapti, Angelina Chatziathanasiou, Judith Herrin, Vaso Seirinidou and Solon Chouliaras all read a full draft of the book and made very valuable comments, corrections and suggestions. Not only did they prevent me from numerous slips and mistakes but more importantly they gave me the confidence to press on.

I would like to thank all my friends and colleagues who gave me photographs for this book. I would also like to acknowledge my thanks to Kay Ehling (Munich), Nadia Gerazouni (The Breeder Gallery, Athens) and Angeliki Strati (Kastoria) for their permission to reproduce works from their collections. Maria Cristina Carile provided me with the images from Ravenna and Petros Bouras-Vallianatos facilitated the permission to include the stunning image from the Monastery of Vatopedi on Mount Athos. Ioanna Rapti deserves my gratitude for her invaluable help in choosing and handling the images in this book.

This short history, however, would never have been written without the support and love of Konstantin Klein. He put up with my frequent tantrums with the patience of a particularly stoic saint; he was the first critical reader and the biggest fan of the manuscript as it was evolving, and so it gives me great pleasure to dedicate the finished work to him.

About the book

The introduction aims to place the Byzantine world in its chronological and geographical context as well as present some necessary background to the reign of Constantine I with which this book formally begins.

The main eight chapters (one to eight) are organized along the same principles. Half of each chapter is devoted to *events* (largely political history which in Byzantium includes matters pertaining to the Church and questions of dogma); the other half is taken up by the exploration of *infrastructures* (important issues of economic and social history) and *environment* (cultural history in the largest sense, dealing both with the material environment and the dominant intellectual trends in each period). Chapter nine picks up the narrative on the day following the fall of Constantinople in 1453 and brings it up to today. The appendices include a timeline of key events as well as a helpful overview of the major peoples that either fought with or against Byzantium through the centuries.

A short history covering more than one thousand years is unavoidably the result of selections and omissions. Consequently, and as a result of the extant sources, this book is top-heavy, dealing mostly with the upper echelons of Byzantine society; furthermore, it is centred on dominant rather than marginal groups and focuses mostly on men. In the annotated bibliography I have made an effort to address some of these implied omissions.

Finally, a note on transliteration: I have used the following system for rendering Greek names and place-names. Standard anglicized forms of personal names (Theodore, George, John, Thessalonica, Constantinople) will be used; all other names will be transcribed as closely to the Greek as possible, avoiding Latinized versions. Thus, Prokopios and not Procopius, Nikephoros, not Nicephorus and so on.

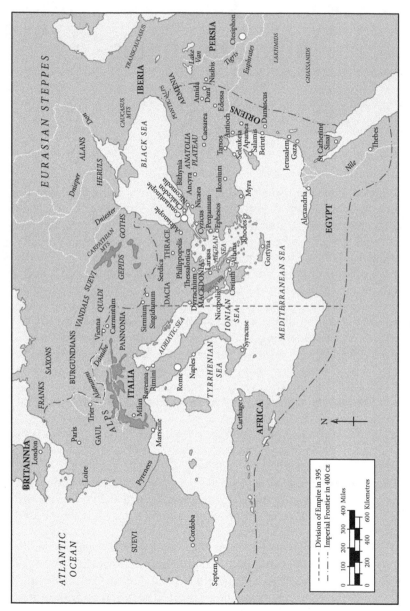

Map 1 The Byzantine Empire around 400.

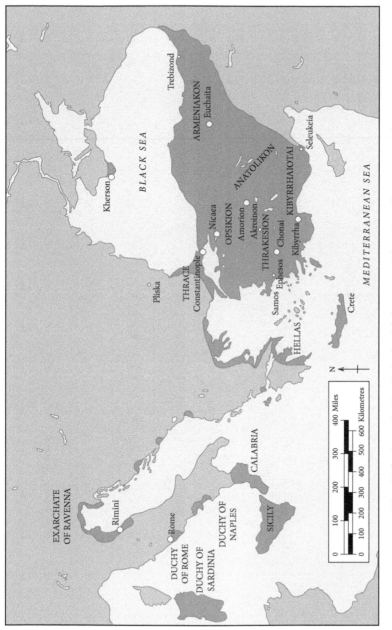

Map 2 The Byzantine Empire in the eighth century with major military commands.

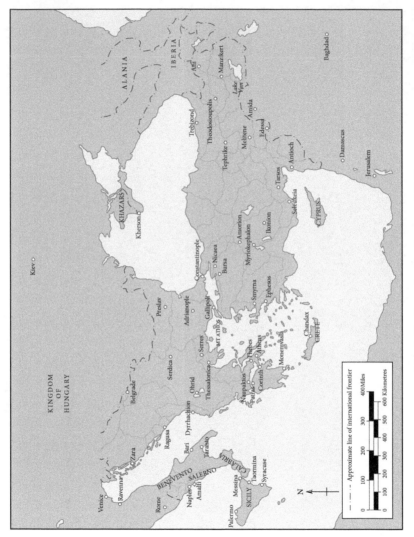

Map 3 The Byzantine Empire around 1050.

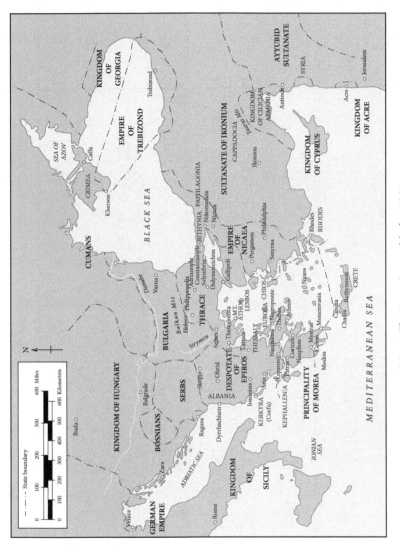

Map 4 The Byzantine world after 1204.

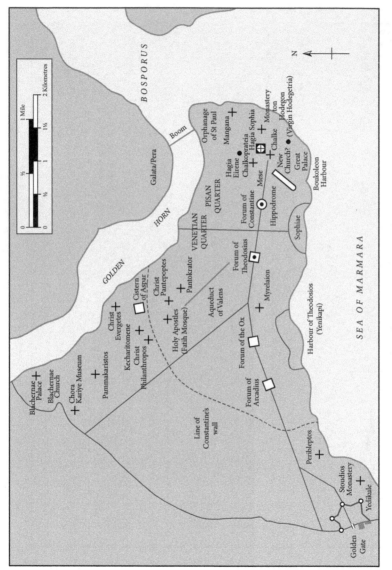

Map 5 Constantinople with major Byzantine and Ottoman monuments.

INTRODUCTION
WHAT IS BYZANTIUM?

For most people Byzantium is not a familiar world. In English the word 'byzantine' is routinely used to characterize something as excessively complicated, while in French the expression 'c'est Byzance' refers to something superb and luxurious. So, words can be misleading, but what about bricks and stones? On the ground the remains of Byzantium fall largely into two categories: churches and walls. Churches are far more numerous and have received far greater attention. Their presence seems to corroborate the notion that Byzantium was a state for which the Church and matters of faith were absolutely central. The often-sumptuous decoration of these churches with mosaics, frescoes, icons and colourful marbles fascinates visitors and transports them to an almost timeless space focused on transcendence. Walls, by contrast, are usually overlooked. They are not very much to look at and they seem almost identical. A closer inspection, however, has its merits. Walls are the signs of a state with a very long history in which constant warfare against enemies from all directions was a defining trait. They were erected to protect important cities, torn down when these urban centres grew to make more space and they were constantly repaired and adorned with inscriptions to commemorate those who built them. Walls remind us of the history of a state and its people that did a lot more than just pray.

The aim of this book is to put together a basic body of knowledge about this state, to challenge stereotypes about it by providing a straightforward and sober account and to place it firmly in the context of both the European and Middle Eastern Middle Ages. Because Byzantium held for most of its existence a position between East and West, partaking of both, but still following a different path, it is easy, even convenient, to overlook it. But, as I hope to show, Byzantium is an indispensable and fascinating part of European history. It needs to be taken seriously.

Even in this short opening section we are faced with a problem. Names are extremely important, even if we sometimes fail to question them as a result of convention and habit. The problem, in our case, is the name Byzantium. It refers to an ancient city (Byzantion in Greek), a colony of Megara. It was founded in the seventh century BCE on the spot of Constantinople and modern-day Istanbul. The actual term 'Byzantine' began to be more widely used in the sixteenth century (see Chapter 9) to denote the historical state that is the subject of this book. But this was a name that the citizens of that state would have understood very differently, namely as referring to someone from or living in Constantinople, never as a designation for their state. The people we call Byzantines called themselves Romans. In their minds, there was no break in the political existence between Augustus' empire and their own state, and this was true in many ways. This self-designation can be found, for example, in the way that the rulers of the state called themselves emperors of the Romans in an unbroken line between the fourth and the fifteenth century. The eastern neighbours and enemies of this state adopted the term: both Seljuqs and Ottoman Turks referred to the state and its areas as Rum. In modern Greece, the self-designation *romios* (Roman, but meaning Greek) was current until at least the late twentieth century. However, a significant number of other states – both in the West as well as in the Balkans – termed the Empire 'Greek'. As far as the West is concerned, it is easy to see why. Once an emperor of the Romans was crowned in Rome in 800 (see Chapter 4), the other empire could no longer be termed Roman as well; it was therefore called Greek or Constantinopolitan. Calling the Byzantine Empire 'Constantinopolitan' is quite straightforward: it is meant to reduce the potential sphere of authority and influence onto its capital, and to deny it the more universal claims that the adjective 'Roman' would entail. The term 'Greek' is much more ambivalent. It is true that Greek was the dominant language in the East since the Hellenistic period, but in the early Christian centuries the word itself had acquired negative connotations: it had come to mean pagan. In the last centuries of the Empire, when its territories were largely limited to regions in what is geographically modern Greece, most people embraced the self-designation of Greeks.

The term 'Byzantine' began to be universally employed as a designation for this state in the nineteenth century, completely replacing the designation 'Greek Empire' or 'Empire of the Greeks' to the effect that such terms would seem incomprehensible and confusing to us today. The self-designation of 'Roman' was thought, mainly by Western historians, to be misleading when applied to the period, say, after 300. Adjectives were introduced to make the distinction clearer – East Roman, for example, which suggests a focus on the Eastern Mediterranean world and the Levant and, therefore, excludes the long Byzantine presence in Italy. More recently, the term 'Medieval Roman' has been gaining momentum. It is true that changing an established name for a historical state and the disciplines that study it may seem difficult or awkward. There are those who propose sticking to the term 'Byzantine', but injecting it with new meaning, namely acknowledging that far from being merely a neutral early modern invention, it became an orientalist derogatory term that keeps its object distant and foreign. The debate is raging at the moment and it is very possible that the next edition of this book may carry a different title. But for now, the familiar term 'Byzantine' or 'Byzantium' will be used, but readers should be aware of its problematic and contested nature.

Once the question of the name is settled, we are faced with another important problem: chronology. It is simpler to start from the end: in May 1453, Constantinople was captured by the Ottomans, marking the end of the Byzantine Empire. Its beginnings are not as easy to pin down. Those who adopt a long-term perspective (as I do) set the birth of the Empire in the reign of Constantine I (324–37). In this we are following the self-perception of the Byzantines. Constantine is connected with two aspects that came to have a fundamental importance in the life of the Empire: he was the first Christian emperor and he founded Constantinople, the city that grew to become the capital of the Empire, remaining in this role until its conquest in 1453. Therefore, I see little reason to place the conventional start of Byzantine history at a later date – as long as it is clear that it is a convention and that no perfect or universally accepted alternative exists. This by no means implies that the state of the fourth century remained unchanged in its millennium of existence – nothing could be further from the truth. In my mind, however, the changes that the Empire underwent were never as radical as to produce a completely different state: until the end of the Empire, for example, the legal system was largely based on law going back to the Roman imperial period. The capital, its monuments, the imperial office, its institutions and ceremonial always consciously retained core elements that linked them to the past. If Constantine I embarked on a time machine and visited the last Byzantine emperor, his namesake Constantine XI, he would certainly be startled with the sad condition of the state and his capital, but he would still have been able to find plenty of familiar elements, not least a number of landmarks in the city he had founded.

States exist not only in time but also in space. The geographical extent of the Byzantine Empire underwent considerable fluctuation during its long history. We can compare its broad outlines to the movement of a wave. From a vast Roman Empire encompassing an area of almost four million square kilometres and extending from Britain to modern-day Algeria and from Portugal to Mesopotamia, it was divided administratively into an eastern and western part in 395 with the eastern part encompassing an area of around 1.4 million square kilometres and stretching roughly east of a line going from Belgrade to modern-day Libya (see Map 1). The division became permanent due to political developments, but it was reversed for a short period under Justinian I in the sixth century when the Mediterranean became an internal lake once more as a result of the wars of reconquest which re-integrated Italy, a strip in southern Spain and the areas of modern-day Tunisia, Algeria and Libya. This was a period of demographic and economic expansion in the East. In the period following Justinian's death in 565, large parts of northern Italy as well as the holdings in Spain were lost, and from the second decade of the seventh century so were Egypt, Syria and Palestine – first to the Persians and after the 630s permanently to the Arabs – while the southern Balkans and especially Greece had largely slipped out of the effective control of Constantinople. By the end of the seventh century North Africa had been conquered as well, leaving the Empire with some areas in Italy (Sardinia, Calabria and Sicily, Naples and Rome with their hinterland, and a thin arch of land from Rimini all the way to the Dalmatian coast; see Map 2) and otherwise a clear focus on both sides of the Aegean – the Empire had effectively lost more than half of its territory. In the course of the following three centuries, Byzantium gradually managed first to stem the Arab onslaught and more or less fix a frontier zone, then to recover its dominion in the Balkans and finally to push towards the east and south in Anatolia and Syria. The territorial gains were neither spectacular nor very stable (see Map 3). The emergence of two formidable enemies from the second half of the eleventh century, the Normans in Italy and the Seljuqs in the East, ate away at the margins of the state, forcing it once more to a core in the southern Balkans and parts of Anatolia. The First Crusade (1096–9) changed the landscape in the Levant and on its coattails Byzantium managed to expand in Anatolia and Syria, but this was definitely checked in 1204, when the armies of the Fourth Crusade captured Constantinople and fragmented the territory of the Byzantine Empire into dozens of smaller states. Reconquest came fairly fast in 1261, but for the last two centuries of its existence the Byzantine Empire was constantly shrinking: Anatolia was the first to go, most of it captured by the Ottoman Turks in the first half of the fourteenth century; the Balkan provinces quickly followed suit and by the last fifty years of its existence Byzantium merely consisted of a few city states, disjointed and connected to each other only by sea (see Map 4).

THE PHYSICAL WORLD

It is clear that some areas (modern Greece and Turkey) belonged to the core of the state, while others either formed part of it for prolonged periods of time (southern Italy) or became marginal within the long history of its existence because they were lost at a fairly early stage (Egypt, Palestine, Syria and North Africa). The landscapes in all these regions obviously shaped a variety of aspects in the life of the Byzantine state: its defence, agricultural regime and production, networks of exchange and communications.

Mountains come first: the long mountain ranges of the Pontic Alps and the Taurus–Anti-Taurus range flanking Anatolia in the north and the south, respectively; in the Balkans, the Pindos range and the Dinaric Alps in the west, Rhodope and the Balkan range in the north-east. The more or less protected corridors between the mountains formed the usual entry points of invaders from the east and the north, respectively. The Caucasus and its Christian nations, Armenia and Iberia (modern Georgia), were only rarely under direct Byzantine lordship, but the Empire often extended its influence there through the use of diplomacy and the establishment of client rulers. This was the primary field of conflicts between Byzantium and first Persia, then the Caliphate and ultimately the Turks, over interregional jurisdiction and control of neighbouring areas.

Rivers were important as natural barriers (the Danube, between Roman territory and the various nomads of the steppes), as passageways (the systems of the Danube, the Dniester, the Dnieper and the Don providing links to central and northern Europe and to Scandinavia) and as the life force of agriculture (the Nile, whose rich alluvial deposits made Egypt the single-most-productive Roman province; to a significantly lesser extent the rivers in north-eastern Greece).

Agriculture foremost and animal husbandry were the driving forces of the economy and as such plains were crucial, if rare on the whole. The western and southern parts of Anatolia were the most fertile and densely populated, with a number of rivers providing water for agriculture as were the western shores of the Black Sea. Much smaller and fragmented plains were to be found in the Balkans. The Anatolian plateau, the largest area that remained part of the Empire almost down to its fall, is for its most part semi-arid which did not hinder settlement, agriculture and animal husbandry. Bithynia, across the water from Constantinople, and the hinterland of the capital in Thrace, on the European side, formed a large metropolitan area as a result of the pull of the capital. Bithynia linked Constantinople to the plateau, and Thrace and the Roman highways linked it to the inner part of the Balkans and Italy. The Via Egnatia cut across Macedonia to the Albanian coast, providing an easy link to Italy across the water. The Via Traiana, the military highway, connected Constantinople with Adrianople/Edirne, Serdica/Sofia and Singidunum/Belgrade. Constantinople itself was strategically placed with connections to the Aegean via the Sea of Marmara, and to the Black Sea through the Bosporus.

The Aegean Sea was always an internal lake for Byzantium. The very large number of islands fostered close connections to the mainland on either side. The Adriatic provided an easy connection to southern Italy, largely Calabria and Apulia, which remained under Byzantine control for long periods up to the last quarter of the eleventh century as well as to Rome through an ancient network of roads. Finally, deserts separated settled populations with their practice of agriculture from nomadic peoples in Syria, Palestine and North Africa.

When it comes to the demography and settlement density of the Byzantine Empire it is important to stress from the outset that we can only operate with guesswork; for no time of its existence is it possible to produce exact figures. Demography, obviously, followed territorial fluctuation, but there were other important factors affecting it such as the outbreaks of plague pandemics (from 541 to 750 and again from 1347 to 1453 and beyond) and warfare – which both directly claimed human lives, but also created confusion and insecurity, significantly affecting reproduction rates as well as sparking migration. Roughly speaking, we may begin with a positive demographic trend in Late Antiquity in the Eastern Mediterranean: urban centres and the countryside were both flourishing. Constantinople became the biggest city in Europe, reaching a population of 400,000 or more up to the outbreak of the plague. Other cities were equally populous: Antioch (150,000–200,000), Alexandria (200,000–300,000); by contrast, Rome suffered a severe demographic breakdown in the fifth century, remaining a shadow of its imperial self at around 100,000 – and yet it was still the largest city by far in the West. The combination of plague and warfare (against the Persians and then the Arabs) from the late sixth century onwards led to demographic decline – the population was most probably halved by the late eighth century. There was an influx of Slavic populations settling south of the Danube from the late sixth century onwards; with the exception of Bulgaria, these populations were gradually assimilated (i.e. they became Christian and adopted the Greek language in large numbers). The same period saw specific population groups (e.g. Armenians or Slavs) moved around either for political or military reasons or to repopulate certain regions. Recovery from around 800 was initially slow, but steady, and sustained a positive trend up to the early fourteenth century. Despite the loss of territory, the Empire experienced a demographic and economic boom, particularly visible in the twelfth century, with the proliferation of cities – perhaps reaching a stage comparable to the conditions before the sixth century. Certainly, Constantinople had become again a vast metropolis. The traumatic events of the Fourth Crusade in 1204 did not stop this positive trend, but the combination of plague and warfare – both civil wars and widespread enemy incursions – in the fourteenth century led to demographic breakdown; by then the state was in rapid decline anyway. The last centuries of the Empire saw the influx of various ethnic groups: after 1204, a significant number of Westerners (mostly French and Italians) settled in various parts of Greece, but their overall presence paled in comparison with the Albanian and then Turkish migrations to Greece after the mid-fourteenth century.

These demographic changes had clear repercussions in the linguistic landscape of the Empire. Up to the loss of the eastern territories in the seventh century, Byzantium was a clearly multilingual empire. Greek was the dominant language on the ground, but large areas had their own languages that were not just spoken among the inhabitants but were also used to produce a wide variety of literary genres: Syriac in Syria and Palestine, Coptic in Egypt. Latin was dominant in the West but remained important in the East in the imperial administration, especially in law and the army, until the seventh century. It was equally the principal language in Italy, although Sicily and southern Italy had important communities of Greek speakers. When the Empire was on its way to becoming an increasingly homogenous state after the seventh century, the supremacy of Greek was almost absolute. However, this must be nuanced: at least from the eleventh century onwards numerous foreigners settled permanently in Byzantium – especially in the large urban centres and particularly in Constantinople. Though their numbers were never very large, they formed communities (often with their own churches and mosques) and contributed to the cosmopolitan character of their place of residence.

As in most pre-modern societies, the majority of the Byzantines lived off the land. Agricultural production and animal husbandry provided food and fiscal revenues for the state. The agricultural regime was defined by a command of natural resources in breadth and not in depth – climatic fluctuations could have extremely negative results on production especially if prolonged (i.e. affecting more than one harvest cycle) or combined (e.g. drought followed by excessive rainfall). Roughly speaking, the climatic conditions in the Byzantine world were not very different from those of today. The coastal areas were characterized by temperate climates with hot, dry summers and moderate winters without snow or frost, while the mainland, where more often than not mountains acted as barriers to the sea, experienced colder winters with snowfall and more precipitation. The most densely settled areas over time were those with coastal climates that favoured agricultural production; marginal areas were settled in times of demographic expansion when the need for more land made populations eager to engage with more taxing environmental conditions.

Finally, we should recognize that a number of landscapes of the Byzantine world have changed considerably and look quite different in our times. Erosion, deforestation, the silting of ports and modern large-scale hydrological projects (such as the dredging of lakes and marshes or the creation of dams and artificial lakes) have made a major impact. Classe, Ravenna's port, for example, dried up by the eighth century. The large-scale building of dams in southern Turkey submerged a number of important Byzantine frontier cities, while deforestation as a result of the use of timber for shipbuilding, mining, smelting and heating has changed the coastal areas of Dalmatia, Cyprus and the modern Lebanon.

FROM CRISIS TO CONSTANTINE I

The reign of Constantine I (sole emperor: 324–37) must be placed within the context of the period that preceded it. This can be divided into two main phases: the so-called 'crisis' of the third century (235–84) and its successful termination, which brought about some major transformative changes in the Empire (284–337).

The term 'crisis of the third century' is conventionally applied to the troubled era between 235 (the usurpation of Maximinus, an army officer of equestrian rank) and the ascent of Diocletian (another army officer) to the throne in 284. During this short period more than twenty individuals were proclaimed Roman emperors, of which the majority either fell in battle or most commonly were killed by their own armies when the tide was turning towards one of their adversaries. The period is generally marked by constant warfare, often on many fronts at the same time: in the east against Persia, in the south against nomadic raiders in North Africa and in the west and north against Germanic tribes on the Rhine and Danube. Dealing with multiple enemies stretched the capacities of the Empire almost to breaking point: campaigns were very expensive and often prompted rulers to increase taxation (as expected, an unpopular and much-resisted measure). The coinage was constantly debased, leading to hoarding and inflation. Furthermore, as the majority of these short-lived emperors came from the military, they faced an almost impossible task: to effectively counter enemy threats at the margins of the Empire while not neglecting the powerful centre, Rome and its Senate. The city was obviously still very important; its millennium was celebrated in 246 and emperors, as a rule, tried to control it and be acclaimed and recognized in it. However, the constant campaigns made it necessary to spend considerable time in various other cities that were much closer to the theatres of war: for example, Sirmium (in northern Serbia) for the Danube front, Trier (in modern Germany) for the Rhine or Antioch (Antakya in southern Turkey) for the Persian front.

It is clear that most of these emperors intended to counter the Empire's problems and to revert to a pacified state, ruled by a strong monarch. A fair number of measures designed to address previous shortcomings were taken. These included sharing power (mostly with one's sons), the development of more flexible army commands and more permanent field armies, as well as a growing emphasis on the person of the emperor, often linked with deities chosen to demonstrate power and security. The period was also marked by the outbreak of a pandemic from the early 250s onwards, which claimed many victims, even some emperors. The overall dire military situation and the ravages of the disease prompted some rulers (such as Decius) to favour a metaphysical understanding of this critical phase: the current troubles were perceived as being caused by angry gods displeased at the abandonment of traditional worship. The solution was the imposition of religious uniformity and one of its side effects became the persecution of the growing Christian community for almost a decade in the 250s.

The major change took place in 284 when Diocletian came to power. Initially it seemed a repetition of the usual mode: he was an army officer who was made emperor by the troops. But this time change came about as he disrupted the vicious cycle of the past generations with a bold programme of all-encompassing reforms that gained momentum. Diocletian ruled alone only for a short period of time; he chose Aurelius Maximianus as his Caesar in 285, naming him Augustus in the following year. Both rulers placed themselves under a protective deity: Jupiter for Diocletian and Hercules for Maximianus. In 293 the ruling team expanded to two more, junior, members Constantius Chlorus and Galerius, thus providing a designation for the period – Tetrarchy (rule of four) (Figure I.1). Territories were divided among them and each controlled a vast area of the Empire,

Figure I.1 Porphyry statue of Tetrarchs embracing from Constantinople, fourth century, looted in 1204 and built in the façade of San Marco in Venice.

making it possible to react more swiftly to enemy incursions and to deal with administrative problems on the spot: Diocletian controlled the East from Nikomedeia (Izmit, in Turkey), while Galerius resided in Sirmium and Thessalonica and was in charge of the Danube frontier, Maximianus' residence was at Milan and his territory was Italy and Africa, while Constantius resided in Trier and was responsible for the Rhine border, Gaul and Britain.

The new members were linked to the older emperors by each marrying one of their daughters and becoming adopted by them. For the first time power was shared not with one's blood kin but with men chosen for their leadership qualities. Diocletian naturally remained the driving force of the project and his programme focused on securing the Empire, both externally and internally, with a strong emphasis on traditional Roman values. The system proved its worth quickly: the Empire was successful against the Persians and at the same time managed to restore order and Roman rule in Britain while protecting the Rhine and Danube frontiers. The military was one of the key areas of Diocletian's efforts, especially the strengthening of the Empire's defences: city walls and fortresses were built and the provincial armies enlarged. By the end of the century, this respite of security allowed the Tetrarchy to focus on internal changes. The control of the state over the Empire and its inhabitants was tightened. The number of the provinces doubled to around 100, but new intermediary structures were placed between them and the government: twelve dioceses and above them three or four praetorian prefectures – all with the aim of improving administrative control and the collection of taxes. The latter was crucial to finance the most important expenditures in the state, the payment of the large armies which reached some 400,000 men. Diocletian abolished the privileged fiscal status of Italy and Egypt and imposed a uniform taxation throughout the Empire, most of which was now to be paid in cash. A regular census, first every five, then every fifteen, years was introduced to ensure that the tax registers were accurate, although the complexity of such processes and the frequent lack of cooperation at local level meant that censuses were never frequent and that tax registers were as a rule inexact. The impetus to record and streamline taxation was combined with a reform of the desperately debased currency (Diocletian simply doubled its face value) and an edict fixing maximum prices for commodities and services – all measures destined to curb inflation. To ensure that revenues and production would remain as stable as possible and given that agricultural slaves were rare and thus expensive, the free labour force increasingly became tied to the land (colonate) and would gradually become hardly different from slaves in terms of their social status.

To keep the momentum going divine favour was crucial: it is perhaps in this light that the persecution of oriental cults deemed as subversive can be best understood. First the dualist sect of the Manichees and then in 303 the Christians were singled out as dangerous to the welfare of the state. The Great Persecution as it came to be known, though not uniformly practised throughout the Empire (Constantius seemed to have been quite mild in its application in the West), signified a concerted effort to uproot and destroy the Christian community, attacking both the material property of the church and practising individuals. A large number of martyrs perished in the period, hailed by the Christians as athletes of Christ, their new heroes.

The successful Tetrarchic regime came to a crucial point in 305 when the senior emperors had reigned for twenty years and the junior ones for a decade. As envisaged by Diocletian, the senior emperors resigned – unheard of in Roman history – and the junior ones took their places, while their own positions were filled not by their sons (Constantine, son of Constantius and Maxentius, son of Maximianus) but by two new individuals: Maximinus (a nephew of Galerius) and Severus. If the first two decades of the Tetrarchy had proven little short of miraculous for their efficacy towards the enemies of the Empire and the concord among the four rulers, given the troubled period that preceded them, the next twenty years were nothing like that. In fact, one way of looking at the period 305–24 is to see it as one man's efforts to restore the rule of the Empire to one person: Constantine I (Figure I.2).

Constantine I was the son of Constantius and a woman called Helena – probably low-born and perhaps a mere concubine. Upon his father's death he was declared emperor – whether junior or senior matters little at this point – by his father's troops in York in 306. In any case, with Severus killed in 307, Constantine married Maximianus' daughter Fausta and was elevated to Augustus. A year later current and former members of the Tetrarchy met at Carnuntum, outside Vienna, to take stock of the situation and plan for the future. Licinius was added to the ruling team and a little later all four Tetrarchs were named augusti. But the second recasting of the imperial college was not to be as stable as the first. Civil wars between the leaders became again endemic: first Maximianus made a brief reappearance and rose against Constantine only to be swiftly defeated. His son, the shunned Maxentius, followed suit and barricaded himself in Rome;

Figure I.2 Head of colossal statue of Constantine, perhaps recut from an earlier
imperial monument, originally in the Basilica of Constantine in Rome.

Constantine defeated him in 312, earning the gratitude of the populace
and the Senate, as preserved to this day on the Arch of Constantine in
the city. In 311 Galerius died after officially ending the persecution of
Christians and offering them freedom of worship; posterity wrongly
attributed this to a supposed edict in Milan, issued by Licinius and
Constantine in 313. Maximinus rushed to capture Galerius' territories
in Asia Minor, subsequently renewing Christian persecution. In 313 he
was defeated and killed by Licinius, who in the same year married
Constantine's sister and thus reinforced the bonds between the two
surviving emperors. But peace between them would not last. Between
316 and 324 Constantine waged war against Licinius, twice invading
his territories, and he was successful in both instances using the
religious card (Licinius had persecuted Christians and Constantine
portrayed himself as their liberator). Constantine's final victory against
Licinius in 324 at Chrysopolis (modern Üsküdar), on the Asian side of
the Bosporus, marks the end of the Tetrarchy and the beginning of
his sole rule. The choice of a new residence to mark this momentous
event fell on the Ancient Greek colony of Byzantion at the intersection
of Europe and Asia, which was renamed Constantinople, city of
Constantine, just across the water from Chrysopolis. The emperor
began an ambitious building programme to adapt the city to its new
ceremonial and political function.

He also initiated a series of administrative reforms, in a way completing and pushing forward Diocletian's agenda. In fiscal terms, his most important and lasting reform was that of the currency. In 309 or 310 a new gold coin of great purity, the solidus, was created with a weight of about 4.5 grams and a fixed relation to the silver coin (which quickly declined in importance) and to the bronze coinage that was the common currency for everyday transactions. The metal reserves required for it came from some of the areas previously ruled by now-defunct Tetrarchs, but also from the sometimes vast confiscated properties of disgraced officials and rulers as well as the fortunes of pagan temples (see Chapter 1). The solidus was from the start a very stable coin and it remained so until the eleventh century. Taxes and imperial office holders were now paid in it, which suggests how its flow operated: the state demanded taxes paid in gold, which it then used to remunerate those in its pay. Because of its success and stability it reflected positively on Constantine's project of uniting the Empire under his reign, and also fostered trade. The introduction of the *chrysargyron*, a new tax on commercial transactions in this period, suggests that revenues from trade were significant. The state had its own factories for essential commodities such as arms, and it ensured the provision of raw materials either on its own properties or, whenever something was lacking, through contributions in kind and compulsory purchases in the provinces.

The army was another sector that Constantine reformed. He increased its size slightly, but also changed the structural emphasis from that of the Diocletianic era by putting together a sizeable field army, headed by the emperor himself, who would be able to intervene wherever it was necessary. Furthermore, he took measures to cement state support for the military, for example, by donating abandoned lands to veterans and granting them tax exemptions. This way he could ensure undisrupted agricultural production and curb any discontent among the military ranks. Finally, he made the imperial guard that was stationed in Constantinople the recipient of free food rations.

But perhaps the aspect of Constantine's reign that has received most attention has been his relationship with Christianity. He certainly died a Christian (see Chapter 1), but the question is: when and why did he begin to favour this religion? During the onset of the Great Persecution in 303 he was already about thirty years old – contrary to later propaganda that claimed he was a young boy at the time – and seemingly did nothing to oppose it. The Christian sources record a decisive turn and link it to his victory against Maxentius in 312: Constantine supposedly saw a vision in the sky that was read as the monogram XP, the first letters of the name Christ in Greek (ΧΡΙΣΤΟΣ). Pagan sources on the other hand speak of a solar vision of the emperor linked to Apollo already in 310. Most probably Constantine experienced the celestial phenomenon known as a solar halo, originally linked to Apollo or the Sol Invictus (the Invincible Sun, a deity that was very current in Tetrarchic circles and which had been revered by his father) only to reinterpret it a little later within a Christian context. If Constantine did not come up with this interpretation himself, Christian authors certainly were unambiguous about it: Eusebios of Caesarea, writing about the vision, records that it was accompanied by the Greek phrase *En touto nika* (in this [sign] conquer) (Figure I.3).

From 312 at the latest onwards Constantine's support of Christianity was quite straightforward and consistent and can be seen, among other things in his foundation and endowment of churches, especially in Rome. The Christian response to Constantine was overwhelming. During periods of persecution Christians had feverishly expected the end of times to come – the old and weary world full of toil and suffering would give way to the eternal reign of Christ. The Roman Empire, identified with the worst enemy of God and its emperor as the Antichrist, was transformed in the Constantinian period into something radically different: the Empire and its universal peace made the dissemination of the Christian faith possible and became the vessel of salvation, while its emperor was seen as the last bulwark against the dreadful reign of the Antichrist. The reign of Christ and the reign of the Christian Roman emperor were gradually fused.

Figure I.3 Silver medallion of Constantine I from Ticinum, dated to 315. The emperor wears a helmet bearing the Christogram (XP).

Now that Constantine was the one Roman emperor believing in the one true God, the keeping of peace within the community of the believers was all the more crucial. Already in the 310s he had actively intervened in the affairs of the Church in North Africa that was bitterly divided over those priests who had bowed to the pressure of persecution and had recanted. Their restitution after 313 caused a serious rift and the emperor tried to heal it by encouraging councils of bishops to debate the question and end the schism. Donatism (as the movement came to be called) was to have a long afterlife. But Constantine's most spectacular involvement in the affairs of what he saw now as his church came in the 320s. An Egyptian priest, Areios expressed the complex relation between the persons in the Trinity in a way that seemed to deny Christ's divinity: the Son was not eternally coexistent with the Father, since He had created Him. There were those who sided with Areios (termed Arians), but a vigorous resistance to what was seen as heresy was mounted by the forceful and outspoken patriarch of Alexandria, Athanasios. As the rift kept growing it was again Constantine who summoned a general council in Nicaea in 325 for the matter to be debated. For the first time Christian bishops learned what it meant to enjoy the privileges of imperial favour, but at the same time the emperor also sowed the seeds of a particular Byzantine power dynamic between the emperor and the Church by not only attending the church council but also taking on a rather active role in its proceedings. In a celebrated saying Constantine allegedly declared to the summoned bishops that he was 'the bishop of those outside'. Areios' doctrine was rejected at Nicaea: Father and Son were seen as consubstantial, sharing the same essence (*homoousios*; the novel term was coined to express this relationship). The disagreement was declared terminated, but it was only the start of a very turbulent period in Christian politics.

1

BECOMING THE EASTERN
ROMAN EMPIRE, 330–491

In May 330 Constantinople was officially inaugurated to mark
Constantine's final victory against Licinius. Apart from that, Constantine's
last years were relatively uneventful. Despite his arduous quest to be sole
emperor he clearly did not intend for power to pass into the hands of a
single heir. Instead, he seems to have envisaged a new tetrarchy of blood
with power shared between his three sons, Constantine II, Constans
and Constantius II, and two nephews, Dalmatius and Hanibalianus, in
more minor positions. Gradually all of them were sent to the field as the
emperor retreated from campaigning. There was some success against
the Goths on the Danube frontier. In the East there was a direct Persian
provocation as the Christian king of Armenia was replaced by a Sasanian
client. War was on the horizon and in fact Constantine embarked on the
campaign towards Persia himself. Early into the campaign he died in
Nikomedeia, baptized on his deathbed by Eusebios, the Arian-leaning
bishop of the city, in May 337.

The aftermath of Constantine's death was bloody: all his male
relatives but his three sons and two other nephews, Gallus and Julian
– still children at the time – were killed and so the three heirs quickly
divided the empire between them in 338. The following period up to
353 saw bouts of civil war and numerous usurpations that ended with
Constantius II being the only surviving heir and sole emperor, while his
cousin Julian held an important military command in Gaul.

The growing military success of Julian meant that a showdown
between him and Constantius, the man he probably considered as
responsible for the murder of his closest relatives, seemed inevitable.

Acclaimed by his armies as emperor in 360, Julian began to march against his cousin, who, however, died in 361 while on campaign against Persia. The new emperor made an unexpected and spectacular public about-face by declaring his support for the old religion, winning him Christian scorn and the epithet 'the apostate'. Julian's embrace of paganism went against the grain and was certainly deeply personal. He did not, however, lack a degree of pragmatism: he identified key aspects of Christian success (charitable behaviour, for example) and urged important pagan religious leaders to emulate them. Furthermore, he attempted to wrestle back for his religion the privileges granted to Christians by his two predecessors.

After purges at court and in the army, Julian embarked on the Persian campaign, and gathered his army in and around Antioch in 362. He spent almost a year in the city and managed to indirectly provoke a food shortage becoming the hated object of ridicule of the Antiochenes (his satirical reply, the *Beard-hater*, is one of the most lively and humorous texts of Late Antiquity). He was mortally wounded in combat – according to Christian legend by the lance of a dead holy man – within a month of leaving the city. His successor Jovian, who reigned less than one year, hastily withdrew his remaining troops and agreed to peace with Persia on entirely unfavourable terms for the Romans; he died en route to Constantinople in 364. As with Jovian, it was the army that again proclaimed the new emperor, Valentinian I, who quickly elevated his brother Valens as co-emperor in the East, while Valentinian ruled the West from Milan. The following years were replete with usurpations and revolts as well as the effort to stabilize the Danube frontier that was frequently menaced by barbarian peoples – with some success. When Valentinian I died in 375 his sons Gratian and Valentinian II, both still minors, were proclaimed emperors. The following year a sizeable group of Goths, who were pressured to move westwards by the Huns at their rear, requested and were given permission to cross the Danube and settle within the imperial realms. This massive movement of people was badly mismanaged and led to open hostilities. Valens rushed with his army to contain them but suffered a great debacle at the battle of Adrianople in 378: around two-thirds of the army perished while the emperor himself was killed – the first Roman emperor to die in battle since Decius in 251. Some months later Theodosius I, a Spanish military commander, was raised to the throne in 379 and recognized by the Western emperor Gratian. Theodosius I initially suffered defeat against the Goths in 380, but brokered a peace treaty in 382, whereby significant numbers of

Figure 1.1 Bust of Arcadius, found in the Theodosian Forum Tauri in
Constantinople; the upward gaze towards God is meant to suggest piety.

Goths under their own rulers were settled along the Danube frontier on
imperial territory.

In 383, Gratian was murdered by troops in the midst of a rebellion
which was put down by Theodosius in 388. In 383 the emperor had
his son Arcadius (Figure 1.1) proclaimed co-emperor in Constantinople,
while his younger son Honorius was raised to the same position for the
western part of the Empire in 393.

THE EMPIRE DIVIDED

When Theodosius died at Milan in 395 power was to be shared between
his two sons with the seniority accorded to the East. What came to be
a real division was certainly not meant as such at this point, but merely
continued the practice of sharing power that had by then been in place
for the best part of a century.

Many important positions in the military were increasingly occupied
by Germanic officers. Barred as a result of their ethnicity and Arian faith
(see later) from claiming the imperial throne for themselves, they had
to exercise power through a number of Roman puppets, a development
that characterized almost the whole of the fifth century. It is therefore
appropriate to speak of the Germanization of power structures and
especially the army. One such figure was Stilicho, a Vandal, with a very

successful career begun under Theodosius I, who was married to the emperor's niece, Serena, and thus came as close to the imperial centre as was possible for a non-Roman. Unlike their father, both Arcadius and Honorius were not outstanding emperors (Arcadius was likened to a jellyfish by a contemporary philosopher and bishop, Synesios of Cyrene), but their reigns were long, though dominated by others: in the case of Arcadius, by his powerful eunuch minister Eutropios or the Gothic military commander Gainas, while Honorius was clearly dominated by Stilicho. Animosity and even outright conflict characterized the last years of the century between the two parts of the Empire. As a backdrop to these political developments were population movements that occurred beyond the imperial frontiers of the Danube and the Rhine. Like a deck of dominoes, the westward movement of the Huns from the area of the Don and Volga set in motion forced mass migrations of other peoples (as the Goths), inevitably pushing them into imperial territories. None of these peoples represented a unified ethnic body (therefore, when we speak of Goths it would be more appropriate to speak of *some* rather than *the* Goths), but the pressure against the Empire gradually increased as the numbers of enemies crushing through the frontiers swelled. In some cases, the chosen strategy was to allow several of these groups to settle within imperial territory and to make use of them in the army. At the time, they were still content as their service brought them considerable benefits, both economic and social. Furthermore, the Empire was occasionally able to use some of the Hunnic tribes to pressure some of the Germanic newcomers into submission. It is telling that throughout this period non-Romans in the Empire's pay were used to fight other non-Romans.

In this troubled era the figure of Alaric can be an illustrative example of the complex interplay between the state and the Germanic newcomers. He appeared on the political scene in the early 390s, a little later threatening Constantinople in 395. Since his army was not equipped for a siege, he turned towards Greece, ravaging and pillaging a number of cities including Athens and Corinth. On two occasions Stilicho came close to destroying his army, but both times Alaric escaped, prompting rumours of Germanic conspiracies. Alaric's men, which were later termed Visigoths, began a series of campaigns in Italy from 408 onwards. This coincided with the execution of Stilicho in that same year. Without a powerful military defender, Rome was threatened and besieged three times. In the course of the third siege in 410 the city was captured and sacked, sending ripples of panic throughout the Mediterranean. The

Visigoths moved to southern Gaul and from there to Spain, which they would eventually conquer.

In the East, Arcadius died in 408 leaving his infant son, Theodosius II, as his heir. The dynastic sentiment was strengthened as Theodosius had been made co-emperor while his father lived. It was obvious that others would govern in Theodosius' stead as regents: his elder sister Pulcheria was certainly an important power broker, but real power lay with a number of officials, both civil and military. The earliest years of Theodosius' reign were dominated by Anthemios, the praetorian prefect of the East. Safety was of paramount importance and the impressive land walls in Constantinople and Thessalonica (both of which still stand) date from this period. The growth of Constantinople also meant increased pressure on food security and Anthemios took measures to ensure that shortages would be avoided. When Rome was sacked, the East sent troops to Ravenna, the new capital of the Western Empire, a practice that was followed in the next decades.

In 414 Pulcheria was named Augusta and assumed the regency for her brother. Her actual grip on power has often been exaggerated, but the means of assuming her position was to swear an oath of virginity and so to refuse to be controlled by a potential husband. Theodosius himself followed in the footsteps of his father and the defining features of his reign clearly lay in the expression of imperial piety and charity through public displays and foundations of churches and their endowment with relics by him, his wife Eudocia and his sister. The more worldly aspects of government were seemingly left to others: a succession of influential eunuchs at court and a number of foreign military commanders, especially the Alans, Ardabur and his son Aspar. Eunuchs, usually men who had been castrated as boys, were a fixture of the Byzantine court since the beginning. Many attained important and influential posts at court, not least because they were barred from actually ascending the throne themselves since emperors were expected to be intact.

When Honorius died in 423 the Western Empire plunged into tumult and again the East duly sent armies and restored the rightful heir, Valentinian III. The real power behind the throne, however, was Flavius Aetius, a Roman military commander, who was quite successful in stemming the tide of barbarian invasions. The players were known, but the constellation of power shifted when the Huns gradually moved again westwards towards the Danube in the 420s. After sporadic attacks and stints as allies against usurpers in Italy, the Huns under Rua launched a serious attack in Thrace, the hinterland of Constantinople, in 434.

The leader was struck by lightning, effected as the sources tell us by the prayers of Theodosius. Rua was succeeded by his nephews Attila and Bleda and under their leadership the Huns entered a new period of their history with much more consolidated power structures and clearer political aims. When the joined forces of East and West launched a major campaign against the Vandals, who had managed to capture the important North African provinces in about a decade (429–39), the Huns timed their invasion on the Danube. The Eastern forces had to withdraw, the acknowledgement of the Vandal occupation of Africa became official while the Eastern Empire for over a decade suffered a number of defeats by the Huns and had to buy its security very dearly in the form of tribute. Attila was left the sole leader after Bleda died in 447, and the raids continued.

Theodosius II died in 450 without a male heir and it was again the army, and more specifically the powerful Aspar, who chose his successor Marcian, an older army officer. Pulcheria agreed to marry him – in a chaste marriage compatible with her vow of virginity – thus giving the transition of power a modicum of dynastic continuity. The Eastern Empire reached an accommodation with Attila and the Huns turned westwards in 451. The Western Empire had to adapt its policy: instead of using Huns against Germanic and other intruders it now did the opposite and managed to stand its ground without, however, preventing Attila from capturing and looting a number of important cities in Italy. Attila's death in 453 proved a blessing, as fierce conflicts arose over his succession, leading in less than a decade to the breakdown of the Hunnic Empire as the patchworks of peoples that constituted it reached for their independence. Echoes of these events found their way into the popular *Nibelungensaga*, a cornerstone of Norse and Germanic mythology. In the West there were important consequences as the (chiefly) Germanic peoples had emerged strengthened from this crisis. It increasingly became impossible to exclude them from power and this realization, coupled with the dwindling resources of the Western Empire, led to a new approach: the empire was no longer seen as something worth preserving because one could profit from it. Instead it seemed no longer extraordinary to the German military leaders to actually rule the conquered territories themselves; neither were many of the remaining great landowners horrified at the prospect of a Germanic ruler. The competition for power was fierce and it led to the actual dissolution of the Western Empire in the two decades that followed.

In the East the reign of Marcian and Pulcheria is connected to an event whose repercussions resonate to this day, the council at Chalcedon in 451. This was the first council which was designated as ecumenical, that is, seen as representing the Universal Christian Church and therefore able to define matters of faith. Christological debates had been a staple of the Christian Church from the moment the persecutions stopped. Arianism, despite being condemned at Nicaea, had made a comeback under the support of Constantius and Valens, resulting in the exile of many members of the Church hierarchy for their adherence to Nicene orthodoxy. Another important side effect was the consecration of an Arian bishop, Ulfila, sent to evangelize the Goths. His translation of the Bible in Gothic had a lasting impact: the majority of the Germanic peoples adopted his Arian Christianity.

Theodosius I, who was keen to promote his piety and support for orthodoxy, chose Gregory of Nazianzos, one of the most learned and well-known theologians of his day, as patriarch of Constantinople and in 381 helped to summon a new general council in the city to address Arianism once more. This council, held in Constantinople, added clarity to the Nicene creed through substantial additions (and some omissions), mostly on defining the Holy Spirit. Furthermore, it tampered with the established order of precedence within the Universal Church by placing Constantinople, the imperial capital and New Rome ahead of the more ancient sees of Alexandria and Antioch and second only to Rome, which enjoyed the primacy of honour as it housed the tombs of the two leading figures of Christendom, Peter and Paul. This step would create endless antagonism in the centuries to come.

While the councils of Nicaea and Constantinople had removed the danger posed by Areios the conflicts did not stop. They only spread to different aspects of the same problem: how to reconcile the human and divine within Christ without drifting into the dangerous waters of dualism. The compromise that the term *homoousios* represented did not achieve the universal acceptance that the emperors desired. All kinds of positions followed to explain the consubstantiality of Father and Son: the Son was like or utterly unlike the Father, of the same or of a similar essence. Basil of Caesarea, a celebrated bishop and theologian of the period, likened these debates to fighting a naval battle at night while a storm was raging. A new term, *hypostasis* (essence, in practice almost synonymous with *ousia*), was introduced to achieve clarity, but to no avail. In 428, Nestorios, an Antiochene, was chosen as patriarch of Constantinople and very soon attracted controversy by denying the title Theotokos (Godbearer) for Mary, insisting that a human cannot bear God. The Alexandrian response followed hard on the heels and made clear the power politics in the background between the ancient and powerful Oriental sees (Alexandria and Antioch) and Constantinople, seen as a newcomer whose views did not have the gravitas of tradition. The third general council held at Ephesos in 431 duly condemned Nestorios and cemented Mary's status as Theotokos. In 449 a second council took place in Ephesos, this time utterly dominated by the Alexandrine side: the council vehemently condemned what was presented as the Antiochene implications of stressing two (separate) natures in Christ. The Roman Pope Leo I sent a text, the *Tome*, which he considered the definitive pronouncement to these Christological problems, but it was ignored.

When the ecumenical council arranged by Marcian and Pulcheria gathered at Chalcedon it was clear that the situation was dangerously explosive and divisive. Chalcedon overruled the second council of Ephesos and pronounced that Christ was consubstantial with the Father regarding His divinity and consubstantial with humans regarding His humanity. In retrospect the councils of Nicaea, Constantinople and Ephesos were regarded as ecumenical as well. The *Tome* of Leo I was read and accepted, Nestorios once more condemned, but the council's agreed formula was in fact much closer to the two-natures theology advocated by the Antiochene school, rather than the one-nature version of the Alexandrines. The aftermath of Chalcedon produced a deep rift between the churches that has never been bridged. The group known as Nestorians wished more emphasis to be placed on the two natures – they began to migrate to Persia and from there spread to India, Central Asia and China. This is today the Assyrian Church of the East. Those who believed that the true doctrine involved only one nature in which human and divine are mixed, were called Monophysites. The term derives from the two Greek words *monos* (only, alone) and *physis* (nature) and is polemical (Christ had *only* one nature); in more recent years scholars prefer to use the term 'miaphysites' instead (*mia* = one), which is descriptive and neutral (Christ had one nature). A significant number of Christians in Egypt and Syria and the Armenian Church all embraced this interpretation. To this day both Nestorian and Miaphysite Christians are not in communion with those who accepted the Chalcedonian decisions, the Greek and later Slavic Orthodox, the Roman Catholic and later the majority of Protestant Churches. It is almost ironic that the council that fixed the Pentarchy, the rule of all five patriarchates (Jerusalem was added to the four existing ones), as the guiding principle for all matters of Christian faith was to be the last one before the permanent splintering of the Universal Church.

Chalcedon brought turbulence to the religious life of the Empire, but political matters were uneasy as well. Marcian's government depended heavily on Aspar and his son Ardabur the Younger. Despite being Arians – and therefore despised on these grounds by a considerable number of people in Constantinople – these military commanders managed to assuage such views with important works of benefaction (e.g. the building of Aspar's cistern in 459, direly needed in a city that to this day has problems with its water supply). The Alan domination continued into the reign of the following emperor, Leo I (457–74), who like Marcian was a mature ex-army commander from the Balkans; he had worked for Aspar and the latter was again the kingmaker. Leo, however, soon began to try to disentangle himself from Aspar's hold. He did so by investing others with power as a counterweight, members of his family and an Isaurian, Tarasis, son of Kodisas. The Isaurians, a people from the mountainous areas of south Asia Minor, were notorious for being rugged bandits. Tarasis rose through the ranks in the late 460s: he brought about the downfall of Ardabur by linking him to an alleged conspiracy with Persia, married the emperor's daughter Ariadne, adopted the Greek name Zeno and was invested with a series of important military commands. After the costly fiasco of a serious expedition against the Vandals in 468 (it almost used up the state revenues for one entire year) for which Aspar was blamed, the time was ripe for his disposal. Both Aspar and Ardabur were murdered in the palace in 471 and when Leo I died in 474 Zeno succeeded him, though initially only as regent for his infant son, Leo II, who died a little later.

Zeno's hold on power was tenacious as he often had to deal with a number of insurrections during his reign, including some by fellow Isaurians. The overall promotion of Isaurians met with growing distaste and there were bouts of violence against them that would reach their high point in the last decade of the century. It was under Zeno that Odoacer, an east Germanic king, deposed the last Western emperor, Romulus Augustulus in 476 and pledged to rule in the emperor's name in Italy. When Odoacer, however, began to extend his reach towards Dalmatia and thus threatened eastern territories, Zeno sent Theoderic against him. He was the king of the Ostrogoths and had grown up as hostage in Constantinople before gradually uniting all Ostrogoths under his rule in the early 480s. He successfully invaded Italy in 489 and would soon unseat Odoacer and inaugurate a very successful reign in the region, while the Ostrogoths would leave the Balkans and thus make eastern frontiers safer. Further to the west and south-west, the Empire had to accept the status quo through treaties. Roman control had slipped away entirely:

the largest part of Spain and Gaul was controlled by the Visigoths, while North Africa was held by the Vandals.

In theological matters, Zeno made attempts to heal the rift that Chalcedon had produced by issuing the *Henotikon* (Decree of Unity) in 482: Nestorios was condemned, but any discussion of Christ's natures was avoided – and that included ignoring the *Tome* of Leo. In the short term the Eastern churches seemed less displeased with this arrangement, but the Roman Church saw its teachings (and by implication its status as the head of all patriarchates) challenged, resulting in a schism with Constantinople that lasted until 518. Zeno died in 491 without a male heir.

SOCIAL STRATIFICATION IN THE EARLY BYZANTINE EMPIRE

Roman imperial society is usually depicted as a pyramid: the emperor represents its summit, and below him are situated those elites who share rank, office, wealth, prestige and political clout, while the broad base of the pyramid is made up by the vast majority with access to none of the above. The form remained the same in the period, but the constitution of the elites did change. When Constantine inaugurated a senate in Constantinople his aim was to attract members of the old senatorial aristocracy to his new residence. This did not come to pass; instead, the Constantinopolitan senate was gradually peopled with new men from the provinces of the Greek East. As with the city in which it was housed, this Senate had little in common with its Roman mother institution, no history and no independent power as it owed everything to the emperor who created it. Developments that had begun with the tetrarchy, or even earlier, but crystallized with Constantine, put the emperor in a particularly exalted position. Christianity might have actually curtailed the longstanding divine status of emperors (since for Christians there is only *one* God), but the ritualization of court ceremonial acted as a barrier between the emperor, God's representative on earth, and his subjects.

The army remained the major factor behind the making of emperors throughout almost the entire period, although dynastic continuity certainly played an important role on a number of occasions. Each new emperor was raised on a shield in the midst of acclamations and the waving of banners. Unlike in Rome, the Senate initially played no part whatsoever in this process, even less the people of Constantinople. Gradually, however, when emperors no longer left the city and did not lead military campaigns, their distance from the armies in the field and their proximity to court and Senate began to affect these power dynamics. A senatorial share into power brokering was slow in the making, even if it appears quite suddenly: while the choice and acclamation of Marcian was still dominated by the army, his successor, Leo I, was elected by the Senate, only for this election to be sanctioned by the army through acclamation.

There was a new element in elite formation in the period: the Church and its leaders, the bishops. From the early period of Constantine's reign they emerged as not just spiritual leaders but also as managers of a growing set of assets that obviously differed between the various sees. Many of them came from the landowning classes; a career in the Church must have been a viable alternative path to one of office at court. The Church became one of the greatest landowners in this period, as a result of both imperial favour and private donations. Ecclesiastical and senatorial elites had therefore common sources of income and status; in the fifth century they gradually converged on the project of promoting and defending Chalcedonian orthodoxy. This brought into sharper focus not just a theological, but also a social polarization which meant that in the regions of Miaphysite domination the clergy enjoyed and instrumentalized the support of the lower socio-economic strata against what was perceived as the representatives of the persecuting and tax-extracting (Chalcedonian) state.

At the lowest end of the scale were urban and rural populations – though the former are much more visible in our sources. The people of Constantinople, again unlike the people of Rome, who could look back at a long history of involvement in political developments, played only a minor and rather decorative role in the ceremonial, mostly in the guise of circus factions who chanted ritual acclamations before the emperors in the Hippodrome. There were instances when the people did not follow the script, but voiced dissatisfaction or dissent, following it up with bouts of violence often connected to theatrical performances, chariot races or food shortages. But such instances were as a rule met with particularly harsh retributions, as when Theodosius I ordered the violent suppression of an insurrection in Thessalonica that had been sparked by the arrest of a popular charioteer in 390.

STABILITY AND ECONOMIC EXPANSION

The dominant trend that characterizes economic and social life in this period in the East is one of expansion. Its demographic aspect is the most obvious and easily identifiable, reflected in the growth of cities (both in absolute numbers and in the size of existing ones) and the proliferation of rural settlement, illustrated by archaeological surveys that suggest the spread of communities into marginal landscapes – always an indication that more easily cultivated land was already sated. Some areas suffered more than others in the turmoil of barbarian incursions and were therefore less prosperous, but all in all, the East experienced a boom that would last – with regional variations – until the sixth century.

Those who profited most from this expansion were the social elites. These included now a growing aristocracy of service to the imperial government (gradually supplanting the older, senatorial aristocracy), the Church and certain monasteries and shrines as well as the imperial fisc (the sum of the revenues of the imperial state). The majority of the labouring population worked the land. Slaves no longer constituted the most important part of the workforce, their role being gradually taken over by *coloni*, dependent farmers who from the early fourth century were increasingly tied to the land they cultivated. Free peasant smallholders and middle-sized landowners were equally part of the mix in what should be seen as a fairly variegated countryside, in which, no doubt, the great estates played the most significant role.

The tax and coinage reforms of Diocletian and Constantine had produced a firm system of taxation and, through the solidus, a stable gold coin that structured exchange. The players and parameters may be thus defined, but there is still a lively debate on how the two aspects interacted. The state stimulated production, for example, by requiring huge amounts of grain that fed the growing population of Constantinople (who enjoyed free state-sponsored bread rations since 332) as well as the armies. This in its turn encouraged the production of those staples required for these purposes. It is still debatable, however, whether the great landowners preferred to produce only what was required for this transaction and their own consumption and drew a large part of their revenues through renting land, or whether they were pursuing additional revenues through other means of exploitation (cultivating cash crops such as grapes, for example) and indirect investments in trade and agricultural production through loans. The extent of elite investment in amelioration projects (for procuring water, for example) or agricultural machines (such as water mills) and their potential impact on production is another open question. To put it very roughly, the issue is whether one should consider those large estate owners as conservative rentiers or as forward-looking protoentrepreneurs. The importance of trade, especially over long distances, is another matter of debate. The state subsidized the grain trade, but this also meant underwriting transport costs for further cargo (ships that brought grain to Constantinople would not travel empty back to Egypt). Elite consumption, especially that of the court at Constantinople in its wider sense, was a key driving force in this process, but one should not underestimate the production and consumption of the lower socio-economic strata: very modest when viewed individually, but significant in its cumulative effect. Obviously, local and regional trade was important, suggesting a close relationship between cities and their hinterland, and also the good state of communications throughout the Empire, both at sea and on land. Constantinople is a telling example: under Julian and then Theodosius I, two vast artificial harbours were constructed on the south shore of the city along with granaries and other storage facilities. The total capacity of the city's ports reached its apogee around 400 with some 4 kilometres of quays, which suggests a thriving commercial hub.

BECOMING A CHRISTIAN EMPIRE

The fourth and fifth centuries saw the Empire transformed in a number of ways, the most pervasive and lasting of which was surely its Christianization. The process obviously began more visibly with the general end of persecutions in 311 and accelerated immensely so that by the end of the fourth-century Christianity became the state religion. Since, with the exception of Julian, all emperors were Christian, the new religion was favoured with privileges and it was inevitable that this would lead to a cultural domination that would change the outlook of life both externally (the emergence and dominance of Christian churches in the landscape, public Christian art and rituals) and internally (attitudes towards the body, family, ideals of life and ultimately the perception of the cosmos). Emperors legislating in favour of Christianity meant necessarily doing so against all other religions, especially the until then prevalent ancient cults. The legal evidence suggests a constant but also gradually intensifying set of prohibitions and exclusions: withdrawal of imperial support for pagan cults, stripping temples of property, bans on sacrifice, first in public, then also in private, closure of temples to any ritual actions. The reality on the ground was more ambiguous as enforcement of the letter of the law was practically impossible. There were bouts of violence, as in the case of Alexandria where in 389 public clashes between Christians and pagans in the city (as it seems provoked by the former) claimed many victims and ultimately led to the destruction of the famous temple of Serapis. Even before that event, Libanios, the famous orator and teacher in Antioch, had written a spirited defence of temples in a very practical fashion (temples are beautiful buildings that can be put to different uses by the state if they are not allowed to be destroyed). A generation later, in 415, saw the brutal lynching of the philosopher and mathematician Hypatia by a Christian mob in Alexandria and the involvement of the city's bishop. Such events should not, however, lead us to believe that there was a comprehensive and orchestrated attack on pagans throughout the Empire, but rather that the role of the ancient religion in public life through rituals and the meaning and structure they provided it with was gradually being actively eroded. Ancient institutions were dying out: the Olympic Games ceased in the 390s, partly due to Theodosian prohibitions of pagan activities, but also as a result of the devastation of Greece by Alaric. Towards the end of the fourth and the early fifth century there were many figures in public life who were unequivocally pagan without this fact diminishing their career prospects or their visibility. What was long thought of as a pagan revival among the senatorial aristocracy in late fourth- and early fifth-century Rome has been now persuasively reassessed: Roman elites were increasingly adopting Christianity; those who did not, accepted that the tide had turned and hoped – at most – for tolerance and coexistence.

The growing confidence and economic prosperity of the Christian Church and the leading role its bishops came to play in the life of their sees also brought about the emergence of a number of new forms of urban buildings: charitable houses for the sick, the elderly, orphans, the poor or widows. These began to emerge in the 360s, initially sponsored by the then dominant Arian clergy, but instantly adopted by the Orthodox Church. Though none survive archaeologically there is ample evidence of their presence and their overwhelming popularity, both as visible proofs of the Church's growing presence and also as a genuine source of relief for the urban poor and destitute masses who did not partake of the economic boom of the period.

If urban landscapes were increasingly dominated by Christian buildings, the countryside was equally transformed through the emergence of Christian monasticism. Initially solitary, charismatic, ascetic figures, termed hermits, withdrew to the deserts in Egypt and Syria following Christ's example of retreating to the desert for forty days (the word hermit comes from the Greek word for desert). Such individuals attracted followers and disciples who sought them out and often made them retreat even farther away from the civilized world. At the same time, as numbers grew, so did the impulse to organize the life of solitary ascetics and the first communities emerged under the leadership of Pachomios in mid-fourth century Egypt, not quite in the desert, but in a liminal space between it and the inhabited world. The Pachomian communities were very successful and soon this model of life – defined by hardship, manual labour, rejection of worldly goods and values, celibacy and communal prayer – gained momentum and spread throughout the late Roman world. From these rural monasteries built in or near deserts (or at least desert-like places on mountains, woods and generally uninhabited regions), it was not hard to see how monasteries could be then transplanted to places either near or inside villages and cities. The symbolic element of the desert was created through the separation of inside from the outside world through walls and rules that were meant to regulate contact and access between them.

The transformation of ancient ideals into Christian ones was internalized as well. New attitudes towards the body and the shape and function of families that had emerged around the second century now became dominant. Constantine repealed the punitive Augustan legislation against childlessness making chastity, virginity and abstinence socially acceptable. The disdain for the flesh and the world as practised by ascetics and monks helped to propel these special citizens to the status of new heroes and role models, whose prayers and intercession were sought after by the communities of the faithful. Christians – increasingly those born in the decades after the end of the persecutions – assumed key positions in the imperial government and the Church hierarchy and began to produce a new literature by and for Christians. Classical literature – though teeming with pagan gods – was not rejected wholesale but was accommodated within a new Christian curriculum in education where Homer and the Book of Psalms were equally valued. This sealed the preservation of a large body of Greek texts that would otherwise have perished from neglect or rejection. New literature was written, both adapting older genres and creating new, hybrid forms such as the lives of saints (the model for which became Athanasios' life of Anthony, the prototype of the Christian hermit) or edifying and exhortatory sermons, which owed a lot to ancient rhetoric, its powers harnessed to promote Christian ideas and ideals.

THE MAKING OF CONSTANTINOPLE

The fusion of Christianity and empire was nowhere clearer than in the imperial capital. Its layout and function in this formative period are particularly important because these factors set the tone for the centuries that followed. So much of what we know and discuss about Byzantine history relates to Constantinople that it often appears as if the two are one and the same.

The huge building project initiated by Constantine was certainly not finished by the time of his death but continued into the next decades. The city was modelled on Rome (even down to its seven hills); it came to be called the Second or New Rome (the Patriarch of Constantinople still holds the title to this day). It was clearly a huge imperial project of unprecedented scale: not just because of the new buildings and enlarged public works but also because of the hundreds of statues and works of art from around the Empire that were brought to adorn it and also to create a history and prominence that Byzantion simply lacked. Some pagan monuments in the city were preserved (perhaps also as a kind of historical decor); equally some aspects of the city's inauguration ceremonies must have evoked the pagan past, albeit in a way that emphasized their traditional Roman imperial elements. Nevertheless, Constantinople was from the start a city that owed everything to its re-founder, the emperor and since that emperor was a Christian, the city was intended for all practical purposes to be a Christian city. Its basic shape goes back to this early period with an imperial residence in close proximity to the Hippodrome (present in all Tetrarchic residences), some (rather few) churches and shrines and of course public buildings such as the Senate and ceremonial spaces such as the Forum of Constantine with a naked statue crowned with the radiant diadem of the sun atop a porphyry column at its centre. The city grew both in size and splendour in the late fourth and fifth centuries and was provided with a wide array of landmarks: ports, cisterns, fountains, an aqueduct, granaries, new land and sea walls, new fora, honorific columns, a multitude of churches and monasteries. The link to Rome was still clearly important as suggested by Theodosius I's erection of an obelisk (Figure 1.2) at the Constantinopolitan Hippodrome (as many emperors had done in Rome) even when voices from the West contested the *Romanitas* of the new capital and perhaps by association of the Eastern Empire.

The most lasting of Constantine's church buildings in the city was certainly his mausoleum, the Holy Apostles. Though it no longer survives

Figure 1.2 Egyptian obelisk (1400s BCE) erected at the Hippodrome of
Constantinople in around 390 by Theodosius I.

the written evidence makes it quite clear that Constantine intended to
be buried in a sarcophagus made of porphyry in a domed space flanked
by twelve sarcophagi that would come to contain relics of the apostles
– the first time that relics of holy persons were moved from their
actual graves to a different location. If Constantine did not intend to
be perceived as Christ-like surrounded by his apostles, then the choice
of layout in his mausoleum would have made little sense. Constantine's
funeral, that of the first Christian Roman emperor, was bound to have
a lasting impact. The army dominated one part of the proceedings,
while another was distinctly Christian and liturgical and ended with the
burial of Constantine in his mausoleum. Again, pagan elements were
not entirely absent (posthumous coinage showing the deified emperor
was issued), suggesting the transitional aspect of Constantine's reign in
which innovations were introduced while ancient traditions had not yet
been fully extinguished. It seems that on his death Constantine suffered
a demotion of sorts: instead of the decisively Christ-like position of
his tomb, he was ultimately presented as equal to the apostles. This

Figure 1.3 Pedestal of obelisk, north side. The Emperor Theodosius I sits at the imperial box at the Hippodrome flanked by his co-emperors and guards. Below are barbarian peoples offering tribute.

point serves to emphasize the fluidity of categories and the transitional character of the period in which a Christian emperor could no longer be God, but nevertheless as chosen by God did have a privileged relationship to the divine (Figure 1.3).

Gradually the city grew as a sacred landscape, both through the proliferation of churches and also through the import of relics that were deposited in major shrines. In the mid-fifth-century Constantinople even enjoyed the honour of having a living holy man, Daniel the Stylite, in its proximity. The ascetic, who lived atop a column, was duly visited and consulted by pilgrims, including the emperor and his courtiers. Constantinople still had to import talent rather than produce it, as with the case of the learned patriarchs Gregory of Nazianzos and John Chrysostom, or the pagan orator and statesman Themistios who occupied an eminent position at the court from Constantius II to Theodosius I. This would gradually change as the concentration of power and money – and thus of patronage – shifted in favour of the capital. In 425 the foundation of a state-funded school of high education (anachronistically termed a university in older scholarship), where grammar, rhetoric, philosophy and law were taught in both Latin and Greek, suggests a move that was aimed at making Constantinople an important centre of education alongside much older and established ones such as Beirut for law, Alexandria for medicine and Athens for philosophy. The major project of collecting all laws issued between Constantine I and Theodosius II took a decade to complete (429–38). This was an antiquarian kind of collection (laws were included regardless of whether they were in force), but it stands at the beginning of the lasting Byzantine engagement with Roman law: collected, codified, translated and adapted many times up to the end of the Empire; it never ceased to be a living fount of tradition and legitimacy.

In the fifth-century Constantinople became de facto not just an imperial residence but a capital and then *the* capital of the Empire, a city that emperors now would rarely leave and whose infrastructure and buildings provided them with the ceremonial backdrop of reflecting on earth the order of heaven.

2

MASTERS OF THE MEDITERRANEAN, 491–602

After the death of Zeno the crowds gathered at the Hippodrome compelled the Empress Ariadne, widow and daughter of emperors, to select the next ruler, demanding an orthodox emperor and a Roman – that is, not an Isaurian. She chose Anastasios, an elderly civil official from Dyrrachium in the Balkans, whom she later married. Although acclamation by the army was still the most important element in the ascent to the throne, Anastasios was crowned by the patriarch – with the very unusual detail that he was forced to sign a declaration of adherence to Chalcedonian orthodoxy prior to the ceremony. He was successful in dealing with the problematic Isaurian influence in the state: Zeno's brother, Longinos, was exiled, all Isaurians were expelled from Constantinople following a riot and beginning in 492, war was brought to Isauria itself; at its end in 498, Isaurians would never again dominate the political landscape of the Empire. This allowed the emperor to embark on a wide range of reforms that proved both fiscally beneficial in the short term as well as having positive long-term implications.

When it came to external enemies Anastasios' reign was characterized by efforts to consolidate alliances and to extend Byzantine influence. In Italy, Theoderic the Ostrogoth had murdered Odoacer in 493, and ruled the land as its king, a fact reluctantly recognized by Anastasios, who could not hope to unseat him by force of arms. Theoderic's reign saw a peaceful and flourishing period in Italy, evident in the buildings he sponsored in his capital Ravenna, many of which survive today. While not making the decisive step of declaring himself emperor in the West, Theoderic secured his position by pursuing a number of marriage alliances with the other major powers in the West (the Franks, Visigoths and Vandals) and by following a policy of accommodation with the remnants of the Roman senatorial aristocracy. To counter this, Byzantium was pursuing a diplomatic rapprochement with the Chalcedonian Franks (who were gradually becoming the major power beyond the Alps) against the Arian Goths, aiming to kindle enmity between them. Relations with the Vandals were normalized, given that it had proved impossible to dislodge them from Africa. In the northern Balkans, the Turkic Bulgars launched a number of incursions into Byzantine territory; in particular Thrace, the hinterland of Constantinople, suffered repeatedly.

In the East there was a bout of warfare with Persia between 502 and 506. After an incursion by king Kavadh into Armenia, followed by the dramatic siege and capture of Amida in Mesopotamia, Anastasios sent a vast force to repel the Persians, which was ultimately successful in regaining lost ground. Before agreeing to peace, the Byzantines strengthened the frontier with Persia by constructing the fortress of Anastasioupolis (better known as Dara) and repaired the fortifications of numerous cities. At the outset of the war Anastasios sought alliances with the Arab tribal leaders of the Kindites and Ghassanids (or Jafnids): they would receive payments and privileges to defend the frontier with Persia and fight alongside the Empire.

Anastasios died in 518 at the advanced age of ninety without an heir, although his three nephews had been promoted to various important offices. His divisive religious legacy – he was a supporter of Miaphysites – was probably the factor that propelled Justin I to the throne. He had been the commander of the imperial guard and was a man who had made a career from a very modest background (our sources stress the fact that he had been an illiterate provincial from Dalmatia). The Senate was key in this decision and we are informed that the acclamations of the people praised this political body as holy and most glorious as well as linking the new emperor's orthodoxy with God-granted protection. Justin's foreign policy continued along the lines set by Anastasios: in the West by isolating the Arian Ostrogoths, in the East by continually, if often covertly, strengthening defences against Persia. Furthermore, under Justin the extension of Byzantine influence through new alliances continued: in the Caucasus the Empire was quite successful in attracting the allegiance of Lazica and Iberia, while in the South it supported the campaign of the Christian kingdom of Axum (modern Ethiopia and Eritrea) against the persecution of Christians in the Himyarite kingdom in Yemen that adhered to a Judaizing monotheism and was the dominant force in the Arabian peninsula.

THE AGE OF JUSTINIAN

Despite Justin's achievements his reign is completely overshadowed by that of his nephew and successor, Justinian I (527–65). Justinian's reign officially began in 527, but scholars tend to count Justin's rule to what has been termed the 'Age of Justinian' (Figure 2.1). This impression is strengthened by the availability of a particularly rich source record. Brought to Constantinople and adopted by his uncle, Justinian is presented as the real power behind the throne. During Justin's reign he headed negotiations with Rome and had a number of buildings erected in Constantinople. At some time before 527 he had his uncle change the law that forbade senators from marrying actresses, so that he could marry Theodora (Figure 2.2). She was the daughter of a bear keeper in the Hippodrome and a performer herself. Even sources friendly to her do not deny that she was a prostitute, or a concubine. When Justin died in 527 she was made Augusta and ruled in close connection with her husband.

Figure 2.1 Mosaic panel with Justinian I, the Bishop of Ravenna Maximianus, courtiers and soldiers, north wall of the apse, San Vitale in Ravenna (540s).

Figure 2.2 Mosaic panel with Theodora and courtiers, south wall of the apse, San Vitale in Ravenna (540s).

Justinian I is perhaps the most famous Byzantine emperor for a variety of reasons: his long reign saw the biggest territorial expansion of the Empire, won at a hard price through constant warfare; he sponsored both administrative projects and buildings that survive to this day, recording his vision of what it meant to be the ruler of this Empire. This is the Justinian as he would have wished us to see him: all-powerful and all-present, entrusted with a mission from God to lead the Empire to salvation and investing all his energy and the state's considerable resources to achieve this. One single text, however, has been the fly in the ointment. The *Anecdota*, or *Secret History*, penned by the court historian Prokopios, who is otherwise known for his eight books on the wars of Justinian and a panegyric on the emperor's building programme, reverses and twists all that we know about Justinian into a wonderfully readable invective. The Justinian of this text is the spawn of a demon and a demonic creature himself, seen wandering without his head in the palace at night. His sole mission: to destroy everything and everyone. Those closest to him fare no better. His Empress, Theodora, a former prostitute – so much is true – is presented with an amount of attention to her sexual depravity and altogether evilness that can only be understood as misogynistic banter. Finally,

Belisarios, Justinian's key general, Prokopios' long-time employer and the actual hero of the author's books on the wars, is reduced to the status of a weak marionette of his ever-cheating and scheming wife, Antonina, a close friend of Theodora. The text's aim is clear: to further discredit Justinian by association not least by employing a typical Byzantine gender construction: by presenting Theodora and Antonina as depraved, but also as 'manly' in their strong and decisive actions and their hold on their husbands, the latter are implicitly characterized as 'womanly' in their weakness. Between the two extremes of absolute praise and absolute condemnation it is hard to find a middle ground. In what follows I will review the long reign of Justinian looking first at developments within the Empire and then discussing interactions outside its frontiers region by region.

Upon Justinian's ascent there was ongoing tension with Persia in the Caucasus and the Syrian border as well as a potentially critical phase in Italy, but overall there was no major conflict to demand attention and resources and so the emperor focused on a series of reforms. His closest associates, the civil officials John the Cappadocian and Tribonian owed their careers to the emperor's patronage. Tribonian was made head of a commission entrusted with the task of collecting, collating and updating existing laws since the time of Hadrian – an infinitely bigger project than that of Theodosios II (see Chapter 1). The first collection was promulgated in 529 (and does not survive); some few years later, in 534, a second edition was put together as Justinian himself had legislated extensively during that period. This edition was accompanied by additional collections of legal texts: the *Digest* (pronouncements of Roman jurists) and the *Institutes* (a textbook for students of law). These texts played an immensely important role in the preservation and transmission of Roman law; they are still studied today as they form the backbone of numerous continental legal systems. Justinian would base his self-perception as the 'animate law' on this ambitious programme.

As the programme of legal codification was underway, at the very start of 532, a popular riot broke out in Constantinople. This was nothing new as such. It was prompted by the unwillingness of the authorities to pardon certain members of the circus factions who had been condemned to death after a spell of violence. The encounter between the people and the emperor at the Hippodrome did not resolve the conflict, which resulted in the outbreak of a serious urban uprising, when the usually warring factions united and, chanting 'Nika' (victory), went about burning and looting in the city. The emperor and his court were safe within the palace as large parts of the city's monumental centre burned. The mob soon demanded the demise of Justinian's closest associates, which the emperor granted, but without the desired result. Nobody led the crowds – when certain senators were sought to undertake such a role, they declined or hid. Ultimately the emperor brought armies over from Thrace who entered the city and massacred the rioting masses: our sources record more than 30,000 dead, although such a figure is surely exaggerated, given that it represents almost 10 per cent of Constantinople's assumed population – how would one be able to dispose of the dead bodies? Two of Anastasios' nephews who had allowed themselves to come too close to the rioters were executed and a purge of some other senatorial aristocrats followed. Fear reigned in the city and it seems that Justinian's resolve and attitude hardened after this episode.

Another key aspect of Justinian's reign lies in the various wars he waged. Although it seems that most military campaigns under Justinian were constantly underfunded and understaffed, some achieved impressive results. The first target was Vandal Africa in 533. The timing was important: the memory of the Nika riot was still fresh and Justinian needed to display his resolute will as well as indulge a part of the Senate who favoured an aggressive policy towards the barbarian kingdoms. Once the East was pacified after the conclusion of 'Eternal Peace' with Persia in 532, the Empire was free to pursue other targets. The Vandal campaign was headed by Belisarios and proved to be successful very quickly: where the costly and gigantic campaigns of the previous century had ended in fiascos, within a year the rather modest Byzantine armies had crushed the Vandal forces and spread their authority. Belisarios returned to Constantinople laden with the considerable treasures that the Vandals had accumulated. Although there was no shortage of problems in the region in the coming decades – for example, through the raids of the Berbers from the south – North Africa remained a stable and prosperous part of the Empire and the Vandals more or less vanished from history.

It seems that the same was hoped for – and expected – when Byzantine forces faced the Ostrogoths in Italy. Political instability was prevalent in that region already during Theoderic's last years and even more so after his death as his successor was still a child at the time. When a new king removed Theoderic's line, a surprisingly small force under Belisarios was sent against him. The war that began in 535 was not to be a short affair: it would last for two decades and would see the leadership change a number of times (Belisarios was victorious, then recalled, then sent again, then replaced by the actual victor, the eunuch general Narses). By 552, with the help of Franks and Lombards, a Germanic people who had been recruited as mercenaries, the war was won, but at a very high price: Italy was left devastated and depopulated. In 554, the emperor issued the *Pragmatic Sanction*, a document that was to regulate Italian matters by more or less pretending that the Goths had never been there: it gave the confiscated lands and slaves back to the senatorial aristocracy and imposed imperial rule and Byzantine administration.

The clear victories of Justinian in Africa and Italy should be contrasted with the military and political developments in two areas where the outcome was much less positive – against Persia in the East and in the Balkans.

The Eternal Peace with Persia in fact lasted only until 540, when Khusro attacked and sacked Antioch, carrying off a large number of citizens to Persia. More raids followed, together with a Byzantine military response. The two empires were not in a position to neutralize each other and so warfare continued, after 545 mostly in the Caucasus where it was centred on the expansion or curtailment of influence over Armenia, Iberia and Lazica, and where shifts of power were frequent as regions passed under the authority of one empire or the other. The war officially ended with a stalemate and a peace treaty in 562; it was signed for thirty years, but again it only lasted for about a decade.

The situation was equally uncertain in the Balkans. Justinian held on to an alliance with the Gepids against the Goths during the Italian warfare. However, when the Gepids expanded their reach in the 540s (mostly against the Lombards, to their north), he decided to support the latter as the Gepids had started to represent a destabilizing effect on the region, by facilitating the crossing of the Danube of a new people, the Slavs, who had begun raiding in the area in the last years of the 540s. The Slavic raids into Thrace and Macedonia continued in the 550s, while towards the end of the decade they joined the Turkic Kutrigurs to mount a serious attack against Constantinople. The aged Belisarios was brought back into service and managed to ward off the threat, but this made clear that the Danube frontier was fragile. At around the same time, another group made its first appearance in Byzantine sources: the Avars. A nomadic Turkic people, their arrival to the region north of the Black Sea was a result of inner Asian population movements caused by the expansion of the Göktürk Empire (between northern China and Mongolia and southern Siberia). There were embassies to Justinian from the late 550s and, although the Avars were denied official settlement within the Empire, they received payments from Byzantium to secure their alliance against Slavs, Lombards and Gepids.

THE EMPIRE AFTER JUSTINIAN

It was fitting that the cloth that covered the emperor's coffin was decorated with scenes from the military victories won in his name. He was succeeded by his nephew Justin II who was married to one of Theodora's nieces, Sophia. Any potential dissent was suppressed through purges, but it is revealing that from the outset of his reign the new emperor seemed keen to follow a different path than Justinian. Part of this was down to necessity, as the Empire was no longer thriving, neither economically nor militarily. The tribute to the Avars was stopped; that this would unleash a snowball effect was not anticipated. The Avars sided with the Lombards against their common enemy, the Gepids. Once these were crushed, the Avars moved to occupy their territory in Pannonia and began their push southwards and westwards; the Lombards fled westwards invading Italy in 568. The country, ravaged by decades of warfare, presented little resistance: while the northern Italian regions fell one after another in the 570s, the Lombards pushed southwards as well in the next two decades and managed to establish a principality in Benevento. The costly reconquest of Italy had been all but lost (though Rome and Ravenna remained), since Byzantium was not in a position to seriously oppose them, as it faced the resurgence of war with Persia, beginning in 572 after Justin had refused to pay the agreed tribute. The Persians managed to take two key cities, Apameia and Dara, forcing the Empire to sue for peace at a very high price. At the same time, the Byzantine holdings in Spain and Africa were also being attacked.

Justin developed serious health issues, both mental and physical (our sources single out a mental breakdown after the loss of Dara), and was deemed unfit to rule on his own. At first the Empress Sophia took over, but she soon shared power with Tiberios, the head of the imperial guard and a close associate of Justin. He was made Caesar in 574 and adopted by the emperor, de facto ruling the state until Justin's death in 578 and then seamlessly ascending the throne.

The downturn to the Empire's military prospects continued: war with Persia went on in Armenia, but a successful campaign led by Maurice, an important military commander from Cappadocia, improved Byzantine prospects. However, before a treaty could be signed, the Persian king died in 579 and his son and successor, Hormizd pushed on for war. The Byzantine campaigns led by Maurice and al-Mundhir, the chief of the Ghassanids, inside Persian territory were fairly successful in 580 and 581, but neither side could claim a clear victory. In the Balkans, despite the payment of a heavy tribute to the Avars, raids by the Slavs – nominally under Avar domination – south of the Danube continued, while in 582 the Avars captured the key city of Sirmium.

Tiberios died unexpectedly in the same year but had made Maurice his designated heir. To respond to the threat posed to the overseas Byzantine holdings in Italy and Africa, Maurice reorganized their administration and created two exarchates, one based in Ravenna (584) and one in Carthage (591). These were territories under the command of an exarch, an officer with both military and civil authority and therefore able to react swiftly and effectively to enemy challenges. This seems to have brought the desired result in Africa; in Italy, however, the exarchate only managed to postpone the disintegration of Byzantine control, although the Empire with the help of its Frankish allies did score some victories against the Lombards in the North. In Rome the Church was caught in the middle, officially protected by the armies of the exarchate, but in reality, constantly harassed by the Lombards. Under Maurice relations with Rome deteriorated as the Roman Church began to negotiate directly with the Lombards, especially under the leadership of Gregory the Great (Pope 590–604), a Roman aristocrat. He was keen to keep rulers out of the affairs of the Church (the Justinianic meddling was still very fresh, see later in the chapter) and objected to Maurice's legislation in such matters while also vehemently opposing the title ecumenical patriarch that had been adopted by the patriarchs of Constantinople since the late fifth century. The title suggested a jurisdiction over the Universal Church which was seen as a challenge to the traditional Roman primacy.

In the East the danger from Persia took an unusual turn: in 590 the Persian king was overthrown in a coup; his heir, Khusro II, who was supposed to succeed him, lost the throne and appealed to Maurice who decided to help the young prince back to power. This must appear as odd and yet it shows that despite ancient enmities and more or less constant warfare, the two empires – said to be the two eyes of the world – had a vested interest in preserving the status quo. Khusro was back on the throne in the following year and the two states sealed this with a peace treaty that pretty much reversed the Byzantine losses of the past: Dara was returned and the Empire regained control over Iberia and the Persian parts of Armenia.

Once the armies were free to move from the eastern frontier, Maurice began to confront the Balkan problem. In a number of campaigns – some headed by the emperor himself – the Byzantines pushed back the Slavs to the Danube frontier. These campaigns put a great strain on the soldiers as the emperor refused to let the fighting cease in the winter, as was customary, but was also trying to impose cuts on army pay, which sparked mutinies. In the winter of 602 a rebellion became much more dangerous: headed by Phokas, a middle-ranking officer who had been proclaimed emperor by the army, it reached Constantinople, already in turmoil against Maurice because of a severe food shortage. Phokas was crowned emperor by the patriarch and had Maurice executed together with his sons and many of his male relatives and close associates – the first instance of a bloody change of regime since the massacre of Constantine's male relatives in 337.

A PROCESS OF CENTRALIZATION

The expanding phase of the early Byzantine state reached its apogee in the sixth century, at the same time as its limits were also becoming clear. In terms of its demography – the necessary basis for economic prosperity of all pre-modern societies – the period witnessed a watershed: in 541 the bubonic plague, the first pandemic of the disease in recorded history, broke out in the Mediterranean and went on to engulf the entire known world. This was to be the first of a total of some eighteen waves of the disease, which struck once every decade until 750. It was a serious catastrophe: in major urban centres – above all, Constantinople – it inflicted a mortality rate of 20 per cent or more in its first outbreak in the 540s and was somewhat less severe in its subsequent visitations. In addition, both before and after the plague a number of particularly damaging earthquakes occurred. Combined with the prolonged warfare in Italy and Africa, as well as the bouts of raiding in the Balkans, Mesopotamia and Anatolia, it cannot be denied that the Empire faced a serious demographic challenge with some chronological and geographical variation.

The basic structures of the economy did not change in this period. State revenue came almost exclusively from land. Anastasios abolished the *chrysargyron*, the Constantinian tax on urban mercantile transactions, to the great relief of mostly low-income craftsmen and merchants who were liable to it. Furthermore, the land tax was commuted to cash (apart from emergency cases), rather than kind, which had a very positive effect on the logistics and cost of paying for the army (commodities collected in kind needed to be transported wherever needed and often had to be turned into cash – both measures now becoming redundant). Anastasios also introduced stability into the bronze coinage with a fixed relation to the solidus and a steady output flow: each bronze coin now bore a mark of its value which had a stabilizing effect on common transactions for the majority of Byzantines, for whom bronze was the only coinage they were actually using for their everyday lives. The system was clear, straightforward and proved quite popular; it remained in use until the eleventh century.

The relationship of the state to its fiscal basis was restructured in the period. It is obvious that since the state's main asset was income from taxation, it had a keen interest to ensure it would be collected in a timely and reliable fashion. The collection of taxes at provincial level had been entrusted to the local city councils; Anastasios removed this responsibility from them and gave it to new state officials, the *vindices*. This resulted in a clear rise in fiscal revenues for the state, but it was also the first step in an increasingly interventionist and centripetal approach. Furthermore, under Anastasios free peasants who leased land were tied more strongly to it, which suggests that the state desired a stable and reliable outflow of agricultural production and fiscal revenues. The combination of Anastasios' measures brought fruit: it is perhaps with some exaggeration (and as a covert criticism of Justinian) that our sources inform us that on Anastasios' death there was a surplus of some 320,000 pounds of gold (23 million solidi) in the treasury – an indication that his fiscal policies had been quite successful.

From 535 to 538 Justinian and Tribonian produced more than ten new laws (termed 'novels' and written in Greek) which dealt in great detail with the administrative organization of the Empire. Despite regional differences, there is a clear motif common to all: unity and uniformity of practice are at the heart of his reforms, continuing a trend already clear in Anastasios' reign. The aim was to make the imperial administration more efficient, curb corruption and injustice and regulate the balance between the civil and military authorities. Provincial governors appointed by the emperor were given additional authority and significantly higher wages to be effective in their fiscal duties against any efforts by provincial elites to withhold tax income. A series of other measures was also taken to curb the excessive power of these elites, such as the prohibition of maintaining private militia (as they could be used for extortion), of issuing exemptions from taxes and forbidding state officials to acquire land in the provinces during their tenure of office – not even as a gift. It was evident that the state was pulling back privileges and ensuring that all power radiated from the emperor and should not be taken for granted. Frequent confiscations served to underline this point. Once new areas were brought back under imperial control, they were linked to the state by being provided with the administrative structures reflecting these unitary principles – this was the case in Africa, Italy and parts of Armenia. Most of these measures date to the 530s and are linked with the tenure of John the Cappadocian in the praetorian prefecture, an office strengthened in this period, until his fall from grace in 541. The combination of natural catastrophes and expensive warfare in the 540s, however, slowed the reform zeal to a halt.

EMPEROR AND ELITES

Some scholars see a conflict between Justinian and the senatorial aristocracy. If Justinian had indeed wished to curb the power of the aristocracy then he clearly failed. The senatorial reaction to the strengthening of the imperial office by Justinian was hardly direct – if we leave aside their role in the Nika riot, which, in any case, was secondary. To attack the emperor directly was dangerous: the draconian measures taken after the riot, and also a number of purges instigated by the emperor were meant to inspire fear and prevent dissent. Instead, the criticism was expressed in more subtle and indirect ways; the clearest example of this is found in a number of texts written by authors with an elite background, for example, Prokopios. The newcomers favoured by Justinian – John the Cappadocian (the Thomas Cromwell to his Henry VIII) was key among them – were singled out for fierce criticism. What the imperial propaganda presented as its efforts to curb corruption and ensure a steady flow of fiscal revenues, for example, the senatorial opposition represented as the rapacious effort to rob the wealthy of their fortunes out of pure greed. Two sides of the same coin present Justinian as the restorer of Roman glory and God's powerful Viceroy on Earth, and a demonic, parvenu innovator who caused innumerable casualties and irreversible damage. And yet it seemed that there were other areas in which the two sides appeared to agree, one of them being the quest for orthodoxy. The failure to find common ground after Chalcedon had been quite clear; despite repeated efforts, both through debate and violence, the two sides embraced their interpretation of

Christian faith as an important aspect of their identity. It became clear that the Constantinopolitan people and the senatorial elites embraced Chalcedon; an emperor like Justinian who actively sought to promote it was therefore harder to reject than, say, Anastasios, who may have supported the vested interests of the senatorial elites, but was clearly a heretic. Once Justinian, who was both interventionist and prone to adopt administrative changes regardless of whose privileges he disturbed, died and his successors saw no reason to antagonize the senatorial aristocracy, the convergence of the elites and the imperial office in the defence of orthodoxy became a central trait of Byzantine political practice.

Overall in this period the stratification within the elite became more pronounced, as the wealthiest of its members became wealthier and more powerful by acquiring high office – which again provided them with additional means to accumulate more wealth and power. As early as 569 it was decreed that provincial governors would be exclusively chosen from the great landowners and bishops of the province in question. There was continuity of some old aristocratic clans, like the Apion family in Egypt, attested from the fifth to the seventh centuries with extensive estates throughout the province. The Church was another big winner, its property rendered inalienable and constantly growing as a result of donations (many of which were imperial). The Church of Rome, for example, emerged as the biggest landowner in Italy in this period, with extensive estates in Sicily and Calabria.

PREPARING FOR THE END OF THE WORLD

One of the keys to understanding this period is eschatology, the study of last things. Perhaps the reason why natural catastrophes are so meticulously recorded in the sources is because the years around 500 coincided with what was thought to be the end of times. According to various chronological systems current in Byzantium, the world began around the year 5500 BCE. The completion of the sixth millennium therefore was expected to usher in Judgement Day. Every natural catastrophe, enemy incursion or unusual event was seen as a sign of the imminent end of the world and corroborated this reading of history. The Chronicle of Pseudo-Joshua the Stylite, a Syriac text from the time of Anastasios, reads like a list of catastrophes: famines, epidemics, plagues of locusts, enemy incursions, floods. Justinian's demonization in Prokopios' *Secret*

History and the emperor's propaganda that clearly apportioned blame on others (it is our – which means your – sins that brought on plagues and earthquakes, he wrote in a law of 559 on immorality) are sides of the same coin.

Justinian's reaction to religious dissent was particularly harsh. Those labelled as pagans were repeatedly persecuted. Two general instances are known, in 545 and in 562, and even members of the elites were not spared. It is all the more remarkable that some very prominent authors from Justinian's immediate circle are seen by some scholars as (crypto-) pagans, who chose to voice their dissent through covert and coded ways. These include Tribonian and Prokopios. Whether these prominent men were in fact not Christian may be beside the point; the key aspect is that they could not perform their otherness in public – they could only hope not to be detected, or to be silently tolerated, with the threat of persecution looming large. The year 529, in which the Academy in Athens, the leading school of (pagan) Neoplatonic teaching ceased to operate, is also seen in this context of enforced religious uniformity, but again we should probably regard it as a long overdue development: a state that defined itself through its adherence to Christianity, an exclusive religion, could not accommodate religious pluralism. Non-Christian religious groups such as the Samaritans – who rose twice in rebellion and were punished severely (in 529 and 556) – did not fare any better. Other forms of deviance were persecuted as well – homosexuals, for example, were singled out for punishment in 528 (those named were all bishops) and 559. Within the Christian community the period saw the division of the Universal Church after Chalcedon become more entrenched and permanent. It was becoming impossible to reconcile Chalcedonians (supported by the Church of Rome and the people of Constantinople) with the Miaphysite populations and churches in the East. Some emperors chose sides and alienated their opponents, while others tried (and failed) to come up with another formula of compromise. Anastasios, who had the making of a popular ruler as a result of his achievements in fiscal, administrative and foreign policy, was in fact resented and hated because of his religious policy. He upheld Zeno's *Henotikon* and chose to appease the Miaphysites, removing patriarchs of Constantinople and Antioch who opposed his stance. Matters came to a head when in 512 he had the Trisagion, an ancient Christian prayer (Holy God, Holy Mighty, Holy Immortal, have mercy on us), altered with the addition 'who was crucified for us'. This was seen as a Miaphysite affront as it blurred the clear Chalcedonian distinction between Jesus' two natures by suggesting that God had been crucified. Riots engulfed Constantinople and the emperor was forced to back down, appearing without a crown to the assembled crowds in the Hippodrome. The calm was temporary, for in 514 the revolt of Vitalian, an influential army commander, used opposition to Anastasios' religious policy as a pretext in his quest for the throne. Although Vitalian was defeated in 515, the fact that he had gathered considerable support from a variety of social groups and managed to mount two serious attacks against Constantinople testify to the deep tensions that Anastasios' anti-Chalcedonian position unleashed.

Justin reversed these religious policies and restored good relations with Rome. Remarkably, Justinian, who otherwise showed great resolution in crushing religious dissent, proved much more accommodating – though in an ambiguous way – towards the Miaphysites, perhaps because they were too numerous, and he could not hope to eradicate them by force. Most sources agree that Theodora was a clear supporter of Miaphysites; furthermore, we are informed that she openly protected and even fostered them. According to Prokopios this seemingly contradictory behaviour was deliberate; it was the imperial couple's way to divide and rule, as the emperor would project the image of the defender of Chalcedon, while indirectly – since everyone knew how close he was to his Empress – not alienating the Eastern populations. To secure wider acceptance Justinian promoted a theological formula that implied that Jesus had suffered in the flesh (Theopaschism) or posthumously condemned theologians who were deemed Nestorian, but again it failed to work: the Miaphysites were little moved while Western theologians distanced themselves from this policy as tampering with Chalcedonian orthodoxy. An ecumenical council in 553 summoned by the emperor merely functioned as another reason for a rift with Rome. As the attitudes were hardening it was with imperial support – or at least toleration – that the Miaphysite cause was strengthened: Justinian entrusted the Miaphysite bishop John of Ephesos in the 540s with missions of mass conversions in Anatolia. Furthermore, by the ordination of Jacob Baradaeus as the Miaphysite bishop of Edessa in 543 the path was opened for the emergence of a parallel hierarchy in the Miaphysite and Chalcedonian churches that continues to this day. This respite from persecution for a generation laid the foundations for a strong Miaphysite Church and this may have been one of the reasons why all efforts to reach common ground between Chalcedonians and their opponents failed at every single instance from the mid-sixth century onwards.

BUILDINGS AND TEXTS FOR A CHRISTIAN EMPIRE

Emperors were ideally expected to make their mark also through erecting lasting monuments and both Anastasios and Justinian I were known as great builders. Anastasios' most-celebrated project is his construction of the long walls, a protective system with a ditch, 45 kilometres in length, constructed at around 65 kilometres west of Constantinople. It was meant to seal the peninsula from the Black Sea to the Marmara from enemy attacks. Although it failed to protect the city, together with the numerous forts erected both by Anastasios and Justinian, this reflects a growing trend: the world around the Empire was becoming dangerous and unsafe – even close to the heart of the state. Justinian may be more famous for the religious buildings he sponsored, although in fact the majority of his building projects were civil and secular. After the destruction of large parts of Constantinople in the Nika riot he took care to furnish the palace with a granary and a large cistern for cases of emergency. Much of what had been destroyed was restored and, in most cases, enlarged and enhanced, especially in the ceremonial core of the city between the palace, the Hippodrome and the Forum of Constantine.

The most characteristic example is the majestic Hagia Sophia (Figure 2.3), built in a record time of just five years after the destruction of the Theodosian cathedral during the Nika riot. Easily the most iconic Byzantine building, it still dominates the skyline of Istanbul. The Hagia Sophia continues to amaze as a feat of engineering that allowed the vast dome, rising to 55 metres from the ground, to seem, as contemporaries described it, as if hanging from a chain from heaven. The church was lavishly decorated with coloured marble slabs, finely chiselled capitals carved with the emperor's monogram atop marble columns gathered from around the Empire, and golden mosaics with geometric and floral patterns. Images of saints in gilded silver – that no longer survive – covered a screen before the altar. Furthermore, the emperor completely rebuilt the church of the Holy Apostles (originally built by Constantius II adjacent to Constantine I's mausoleum) into a cruciform church with five domes (widely seen as a model for the church of San Marco in Venice) as well as adding another mausoleum. This became the main burial place for Byzantine rulers until the twelfth century. Theodora, who died in 548, was the first person to be buried in it. Outside the capital, several buildings mark Justinian's achievement. The main church and the fortifications surrounding the monastery of St Catherine's at Mount Sinai – still a flourishing centre today – go back to Justinianic sponsorship. In

Figure 2.3 The church of Hagia Sophia. Despite later additions (e.g. the Ottoman minarets or the buttresses on the right of the photograph) the building largely survives in the form erected under Justinian I in 537.

Jerusalem, Justinian built the vast Nea (new) Church in honour of the Mother of God, both linked to and competing with Solomon's temple.

Under Justinian's successors in the sixth century imperial-sponsored building naturally continued, albeit on a more modest scale. Justin II reportedly rebuilt two important churches dedicated to the Virgin in Constantinople, at Blachernai and in the Chalkoprateia. Later traditions suggest that Marian relics, her robe and girdle, were deposited in them. The importance of Mary was further emphasized by the official adoption of two feasts in her memory under Justin II and Maurice, her Nativity and Dormition. Justin II, furthermore, is credited with bringing to Constantinople two exceptional relics connected with Christ: a fragment of the True Cross from Apameia and a miraculous icon from Kamuliana (in Cappadocia), considered an *acheiropoietos*, that is an image not made by human hands. These relics enhanced the sacred topography of Constantinople; the presence of objects that had been touched by Christ and His mother suggested their actual presence in the city and offered protection. Later in the century the two relics of Christ would be taken into battle to defend the imperial armies. The importance of religious ritual and its increasingly central role in the understanding and performance of imperial rule can also be seen in the gradual transformation of the coronation rituals: the role of the army and the raising of the new emperor on a shield were first accompanied and later replaced by a coronation by the patriarch and acclamations by the circus factions, as the latter became integrated and thus much more controlled and subdued within the ceremonial proceedings.

The Christianization process within the Empire was largely complete by the sixth century. Yet much of the high-brow literary and cultural output of the period was still coined in classic language and style evident, for example, in a chain of historians from Prokopios to Theophylact Simocatta, who wrote a history of the Emperor Maurice in the early seventh century. More generally, the period was characterized by a trend towards the collection and codification of past knowledge – most clearly expressed in the Justinianic collection of laws, but also apparent in other fields of knowledge such as medicine and philosophy. But it was clear that things were changing. Justinian may have collected Roman law in Latin, but he chose to issue his new laws (after 534) almost exclusively in Greek. Latin was gradually disappearing from most aspects of everyday life, but it was preserved in some areas: inscriptions on coinage, military commands and acclamations. In literary production new texts emerged that would prove particularly popular. Such new literary types include the Christian chronicle, a mostly chronological account of history from Creation to the present, filled not just with imperial deeds but also with records of natural catastrophes and various oddities (the dog who could tell adulterers by smell and identify emperors by their coinage is a characteristic example). The first and one of the most influential chronicles was written by John Malalas during the reign of Justinian. Another new textual form that emerged during the period was the *kontakion*, a long liturgical poem set to music and sung during service. Romanos the Melodist, a sixth-century Syrian writer who was active in Constantinople under Anastasios and Justinian I, is seen as its key proponent. Justinian commissioned Romanos to produce some *kontakia* – for example, the one entitled 'On Earthquakes and Fires' performed after the Nika riot to praise the emperor, while making clear that the riot had been a punishment sent by God to chastise the Byzantines for their transgressions. The use of liturgical poetry as propaganda should not detract from its craft and beauty, nor should its powerful effect on people be overlooked.

3

NEGOTIATING RETRACTION, 602–717

The brief reign of Phokas proved catastrophic. In the East, Khusro launched a war to avenge Maurice, giving him a pretext for a show of strength to his own elites. This war would last more than two decades. The Persians seemed unstoppable as one key city after another was captured in the span of a few years: Theodosioupolis (Erzurum in Turkey), Dara, Amida, Edessa bringing about the loss of fiscal revenues, produce and prestige. In Italy too, the unchecked Lombards expanded their hold over the North. Within his empire Phokas did not enjoy broad support. The only backing he received came from Pope Gregory in Rome, perhaps hoping for accommodation in the question of the ecumenical title and help against the Lombards that Maurice had withheld. Most of Phokas' reign saw a number of rebellions against him, most supported by the senatorial elites, as the emperor had taken particularly harsh measures against them. The most serious of these uprisings originated in Africa. The Exarch Herakleios, a veteran of Maurice's Persian warfare, supported the joint campaign of his son (also called Herakleios) and his nephew. Phokas was to be toppled by land and by sea. This was no ordinary coup: the rebels commanded great support – for example, by the powerful and fabulously wealthy family of Apion in Egypt; they minted coins (including in gold) and the effort to overthrow Phokas quickly became a full-blown civil war. Herakleios was greeted enthusiastically en route wherever his fleet stopped and the same happened when he arrived at Constantinople, carrying with him an image of the Virgin. Phokas' supporters deserted him and in 610 Herakleios the younger entered Constantinople and had Phokas executed.

The army was purged of Phokas' supporters and the pockets of resistance of those loyal to him were gradually cleared in the first two years of Herakleios' reign. In political terms the Empire was in a dire situation in both West and East. The Balkans had been left largely undefended because of the need to mobilize troops on the Persian frontier and as a result of the civil war. Consequently, in the last years of Phokas and the first of Herakleios there was a second wave of Slavic migration and settlement in Greece. This was a slow process, but it led to the de facto loss of Byzantine sovereignty over the region, apart from coastal strips that could be defended by the imperial navy and some major fortified towns that the Slavs could not capture. The Slavs were organized in *sklaviniai*, settlements around strongholds, each under their own leaders, though occasionally a confederation of some sort also occurred. They were not, however, unified in a state-like structure and this meant that they did not pose the type of threat that larger and more centrally organized polities did.

In the East, the victorious Persians showed no signs of accepting a proposed truce coined in rather humiliating terms by the Senate and Herakleios. In fact, in the first five years of his reign, the Persians – despite some military opposition – captured a series of important cities: Damascus and Caesarea, in 613, and Jerusalem, in 614. The latter was accompanied by massacres and to the shock of the Christian population, the removal to Ctesiphon, the Persian capital, of the relic of the True Cross together with numerous prisoners. In 615 the Persian raids reached across the water from Constantinople, while the conquest of Palestine was achieved by the following year, opening the way to Egypt, which was captured in 619. The loss of this province brought the distribution of free bread in Constantinople to an end. Faced with these disasters, Herakleios is supposed to have hatched the plan to abandon Constantinople and instead establish his capital at Carthage, still safe and familiar to him, but he did not go through with it, whether as a result of counsel or, as legend has it, because a ship laden with the state's treasures sunk ominously.

The Byzantine defeats found an echo in a religious community that was forming in Arabia: in a chapter (*sura*) of the text that was to become the Qur'an, the leader of this community, the prophet Muhammad, recorded the Byzantine defeats, but was assured that they would be reversed. It was a positive message: a monotheistic empire crushing a pagan one, the Sasanians. Muhammad was right, but it is quite ironic that those in his community (who came to be known as Muslims – those who adhere to Islam) would be responsible for another dramatic reversal of the events shortly thereafter.

In the international context, Byzantium had to ensure that it was not attacked on two fronts at the same time as rumours of a rapprochement between the Avars and Persia suggested. After an initial failed attempt to come to terms with the Avars – the emperor was ambushed and barely escaped with his life – a peace treaty along with the payment of a heavy tribute was signed in 620. Furthermore, Herakleios seems to have made contacts with the Turks beyond the northern frontiers with Persia to broker an alliance against the Sasanids. The material means to finance his campaign against the Sasanids came from melting down sacred vessels and turning them into coin in 622. The emperor personally took over the training of his armies in Asia Minor and embarked on a campaign, taking along a miraculous icon of Christ not made by human hands. His risky plan was to surprise the Persians by attacking the empire itself from the North. Initial success must have prompted a move of retaliation from the Persian side: in 626 a joint attack by Avars, Slavs and Persians moved to take Constantinople, largely undefended at that time. The siege was supposed to divert Herakleios from his campaign, but the emperor sent some troops and did not move the bulk of his army. Almost unexpectedly, the capital was saved: according to contemporaries this was only possible through divine aid. Images of Mary had been fastened to the city gates, while an image of Christ was carried in procession on the walls; witnesses record that they saw Mary destroying the Slavic boats in a violent storm. One of the most famous pieces of Byzantine poetry was composed to honour her aid on that occasion, praising Mary as a general and defender of her city, Constantinople.

On the Persian front Byzantine success became more evident, prompting Herakleios to encourage dissent among the Persian high command. The combination of warfare and diplomacy bore fruit: in 628, some six years after the start of the campaign, Persia sued for peace and accepted the frontiers that had been agreed under Maurice in 591. The emperor was triumphant – reflected in the title he adopted from that moment on: 'faithful in Christ *basileus* (Emperor) of the Romans'. The triumph was completed in 630 when Herakleios restored the True Cross to Jerusalem, ending more than 20 years of warfare.

But this was to prove illusory. In the same year Muhammad's community of believers captured his hometown, Mecca, from which he had been driven out in 622 – a year that marked the start of Islamic reckoning of time, which begins with the hijra (flight, or migration). Muhammad died in 632, and his followers took the central message he had brought them from God to convey the religion of Islam to all mankind. First, they successfully imposed the message on the tribes in Arabia and then proceeded in 634 to attack Byzantine, Palestine and Syria. The Byzantine armies resisted in Syria, but the province was lost after a sound defeat at Yarmuk in 636. Jerusalem was once more captured in 638. Warfare then spread into Egypt, on the one hand, and Mesopotamia and Persia, on the other: Alexandria fell by 642, Ctesiphon in 639, while the Arabs then pushed to the northeast and conquered Armenia as well. They were prevented from penetrating beyond the Caucasus by the Khazars, a Turcic people formerly part of the Turkish confederation who had helped Herakleios against the Persians and who had settled in the area east of the Black Sea and north of the Caucasus.

In less than a decade the reconquests of Herakleios were lost and this turned out to be irrevocable. It is a detail of great symbolic significance that the Muslim leader Umar received Egyptian grain at the port of Mecca in 644; Egyptian grain would not be delivered again to Constantinople until after 1453, when the Byzantine Empire had been conquered by the Ottoman Turks.

The success of Islam seemingly caught Byzantium and Persia by surprise. Their interest in what was happening in Arabia had been limited, as they had been delegating the protection and oversight of the frontier to the Ghassanids and Lakhmids (or Nasrids) – their respective allied Arab tribal confederations. While Persia as a state would not resurface until the sixteenth century, Byzantium did survive, having lost more than half of its territories, including its wealthiest and most productive regions.

Herakleios died in 641, and in the last decade of his life he had to witness not only the destruction of his life's work by the advent of Islam but also the squandering of his popularity as a result of his personal life and his religious policies. His second marriage to his niece Martina proved scandalous. His goal of healing the rift caused by Chalcedon failed. The formula that was chosen, this time through the doctrinal formulations of the Patriarch of Constantinople Sergios and the Pope Honorius in the 630s, was that of one will or one *energeia* (operating activity) in Christ despite two natures. Monothelitism, as it came to be called, was adopted by the emperor in 638 and, as previous imperial attempts at dogmatic solutions, failed to achieve unity despite some initial success in Armenia and Syria. In fact, it would become a reason for further bitter disputes in the decades that followed. The consequences of his incestuous marriage came to the fore forcibly after Herakleios' death. His second wife obviously favoured her own offspring, but an attempt to rule together with one of her stepsons ended in his death and brought about the disgrace and exile of the Empress; instead, Constans II, Herakleios' young grandson, ascended the throne in 641.

From the 640s to the mid-650s the Arab pressure on the remaining Byzantine territories continued without cease: there were raids in Anatolia, a slow expansion towards North Africa as well as – and this was perhaps the most alarming aspect for Byzantium, which had enjoyed at least naval hegemony up to that point – the construction of an Arab fleet and the first naval raids against Rhodes, Kos, Cyprus and Crete. In 655, in the so-called 'Battle of the Masts', the Byzantine fleet commanded by the emperor suffered a crushing defeat off the Lycian coast. Byzantium was only granted a respite due to the outbreak of the first Islamic civil war (*fitna*) over the succession from 656 to 661. The murder of the Caliph Ali, a cousin and son-in-law of Muhammad, eased the path of Muawiya to the caliphate, the first ruler of the Ummayad dynasty, who established Damascus as his capital and would prove a formidable adversary. The inexorable drive of Islam lay in its fundamental division of the world into two zones: the House of Islam, where the true religion was already prevalent, and the rest, the House of War (*dar al-Harb*). The latter was there to be attacked in the course of holy war (*jihad*: literally struggle) with the aim of subduing it into accepting the true faith; only then would the scope of Islam be complete.

Within the Empire the quest for uniformity continued. Monothelitism was still the official dogma and it received further support in 648 from Constans II, but opposition to it had been growing, mostly among theologians in the West. The most vocal of these, Maximos, joined forces with Pope Martin I in Rome, where a synod held in 649 declared Monothelitism heretical. Constans had Martin and Maximos arrested by the Exarch in Ravenna. They were brought to Constantinople, where they stood trial for treason and were ultimately exiled to the Black Sea – Maximos was mutilated as well. First Maximos and then Martin died in exile; both were later venerated as confessors, having defended the true faith. This episode serves to highlight a development that would reach dramatic proportions in the following centuries: the estrangement between the Church of Rome and the Empire. As Byzantine efforts were chiefly focused in the East, the western parts of their dominion were considerably weakened. The role of the Exarch of Ravenna was still crucial, but the encroachment of the Lombards could not be reversed. Despite the signing of some peace treaties between the Lombards and Byzantium in the early decades of the seventh century (a de facto recognition of the end of the Justinianic ecumenical Empire in East and

West) and the conversion to Chalcedonian orthodoxy of the Lombard king Adaloald, by the middle of the century, the Lombard-controlled states had reduced Byzantine holdings to a thin corridor that linked two zones on either side of Italy, from Naples to Rome in the West and from Ravenna to the lagoon of Venice in the East.

In 662 Constans II moved to Italy, received the homage of the Pope in Rome, signed a peace treaty with the Lombard duke of Benevento and set up his court in Syracuse, in Sicily, in the following year. Given that the Eastern Mediterranean seemed doomed, it is not surprising that the emperor would choose to recoup his forces in the West – both Sicily and the opposite north African coast were still quite safe. Constans quickly became deeply unpopular in Italy and beyond – mostly for his fiscal policies; he was murdered in 668 and was succeeded by his son, Constantine IV.

The political situation that Constantine had to face in the 670s was very difficult as Muawiya aimed to take Constantinople. An Arab base was established in the peninsula of Cyzicus in the Sea of Marmara at which the army could winter and unleash renewed attacks and blockades of the city in the spring, though the return of Constantine from the West, where he had gone to put down the rebellion that had killed his father, made the Arabs withdraw. They launched further raids in the following years, culminating in a joint attack by land and sea. It was only with the help of Greek fire, a secret weapon of the Byzantines, that the attacks could be repelled (Figure 3.1). For obvious reasons Byzantine texts are silent on how Greek fire was either made or projected, but it seems to have been a flammable liquid that could not be extinguished by water. It probably consisted of petroleum oil and naphtha, among other ingredients, was heated and then hurled on enemy ships through special devices – probably a bronze tube that was at the end of a force pump. Combined with a successful Byzantine counterattack in northern Syria the repelled naval expedition of the Arabs made Muawiya sign a peace treaty for 30 years in 678. This was the first time that the Islamic juggernaut was seriously obstructed, and it clearly harmed the caliph's standing, leading ultimately to another bout of civil war from 682 to 692.

Though the danger from the East was assuaged, another enemy appeared at the northern frontier of the Empire. The political situation around the Danube had been in uproar in the second half of the seventh century. The failure of the Avars to take Constantinople in 626 had weakened their grip on the peoples they controlled. One of those, the

Figure 3.1 Miniature from the twelfth century depicting a Byzantine ship using Greek fire against enemies.

Turcic Bulgars, fled westwards under pressure from the Khazars in 680 and settled near the mouth of the Danube. A joint Byzantine force by land and sea dispatched against them was defeated and the Bulgars settled in what is now the Bulgarian Black Sea coast, subjugating the Slavs who lived in the region – much as the Avars had done. Byzantium could do little else at the time but recognize the settlement through a treaty.

Constantine was succeeded in 685 by his son Justinian II in the same year that Abd al-Malik became caliph while the *fitna* was still raging. Justinian's first move was to send an army to the Caucasus to help the Christian populations against the invading Khazars. This show of strength and the fear of another attack in Syria prompted the caliph to sue for another peace treaty – this time with rather unfavourable terms for the Arabs: on top of a very large tribute, a condominium was agreed over Cyprus, Armenia and Iberia. Justinian was therefore free to turn to the Balkans. He mounted a campaign against the *sklaviniai* in Greece in 688 during which he took many prisoners and settled them as soldiers in Bithynia.

In 692 the second Arab civil war ended and Abd al-Malik prevailed. It was natural for the Muslims to resume their plans to conquer Byzantium, although in the first years the battle was waged over propaganda and symbols. It seems that Abd al-Malik was the first Islamic ruler to issue coins with a religious inscription, the *shahada*, or declaration of faith: 'There is no god but God alone, and Muhammad is the messenger of

Figures 3.2 A&B Solidus of Justinian II, issued between 692–5. The front shows
a bust of Christ, the reverse the emperor holding a cross and the Latin inscription
'servant of Christ'.

God.' As these coins were used to pay the tribute to the Byzantines, they
obviously found little favour in Constantinople.

It is not clear whether it was in response to this – the dating is
contested and varies between *ca*. 692 and 695 – but Justinian issued
coins with a new iconography: for the first time the front side showed a
bust of Christ, while the reverse held a portrait of the emperor with the
caption 'servant of Christ' making clear that God and emperor were, so
to speak, two sides of the same coin (Figure 3.2). To this Abd al-Malik
seems to have responded after 693 by issuing a unique coin showing
him standing, clutching his sword (Figure 3.3). Towards the turn of the
century the caliph reformed the coinage completely; from then on Islamic
coins would bear no images, but exclusively texts such as the *shahada*
and *suras* from the Qur'an.

The spiritual aspect of the Byzantine–Islamic struggle is also evident
in some other events. In 680–1, Justinian's father had convoked an
ecumenical council that duly condemned Monothelitism. A decade
later, in 692, Justinian summoned another council that was to collect
and codify ecclesiastical canons – something which the previous two
councils had failed to do. The canons collected at this council, termed
Quinisextum (fifth–sixth), touched on a variety of topics, but some key
themes emerged: uniformity of practice through the exclusion of those
deemed as heretical, identification and suppression of customs perceived
as pagan and the pastoral needs of Christian communities that had either
been displaced by the Islamic conquests or that now lived under Islamic
control. In addition, there were canons about religious images (Christ
was to be depicted in his human form, not, allegorically, as a lamb, nor

Figures 3.3 A&B Gold dinars of Caliph Abd al-Malik. Left: issued in 694/95 and showing a standing caliph clutching his sword; right: issued in 697/98 containing only the *shahada*.

should there be images of the cross painted on floors). Previous canons that upheld equal privileges for the sees of Old and New Rome and the positioning of the latter ahead of the three Oriental patriarchates that were now all under Islamic rule were confirmed (needless to say, this canon was not accepted by Rome). All in all, this should be seen as an effort to ensure divine favour through correct faith and practice, which makes sense in a climate of spiritual antagonism. At the same time (in 691/92) Abd al-Malik built the Dome of the Rock in Jerusalem, decorated in the Islamic aniconic style with passages from the Qur'an, most prominently the *sura* 112 (He is God the One, God the eternal. He begot no one nor was He begotten), which is seen as a succinct rejection of the Christian belief in the Trinity.

Justinian II seemed a successful emperor in many ways at the time and yet he was violently overthrown in 695, mutilated (he had his tongue and nose slit, earning him the nickname Rhinotmetos, slit-nosed) and exiled to the Black Sea. The coup had aristocratic, senatorial backing, and the new emperor came from this social group, the general Leontios. This ushered in a period of instability: Leontios was himself quickly replaced by a naval officer, Tiberios III, in 698, as a result of the defeat of the naval campaign against the Arabs in Africa during which Carthage fell into their hands in the same year. In 705 the disgraced Justinian II came back to power with the help of the Bulgars, unleashing a second reign in which anti-aristocratic purges added to the climate of uncertainty and violence. The Byzantine armies and navies suffered a number of defeats in this period leading to yet another coup against Justinian who was deposed and executed in 711. His Bulgar allies attacked the Empire to avenge his death, causing devastation in Thrace until a treaty was signed in 715 granting them very favourable terms.

In fact, the whole period from 711 until 717 saw a quick succession of three emperors against a backdrop of constant mutinies of the provincial armies terminated only when a military commander, Leo, managed to establish himself bloodlessly in the capital after the Senate had persuaded the reigning emperor, Theodosios III, to resign.

MAKING THE BEST OF REDUCED RESOURCES

The seventh century was a period of important changes for the Byzantine Empire; some were already under way but became more pronounced in the period. For the most part, however, they were the consequences of political events that were new. Resources – or, rather, their lack, and their management – was a key theme. First of all, the Empire had to deal with a new demographic reality. The population was hit by several waves of the plague during the period. Although it is impossible to calculate the exact number of people who died of the plague, it must have been considerable. Normally, pre-modern populations tended to recover demographically from such catastrophes after several generations, but any positive trend would have vanished in the great upheavals caused by the Islamic conquests: both the significant territorial losses (Egypt, Palestine, Syria and later North Africa) as well as the displacement (and hence, the disruption of normal patterns of marriage and reproduction) of populations that were harassed by constant Arab raids in certain areas of the Anatolian frontier. These demographic losses were significant in many ways, resulting in manpower shortage for agricultural production and army recruitment as well as in a diminished tax basis. The policy of large-scale population transfers of specific ethnic groups into either depopulated or sensitive areas, though not new as such, was practiced very frequently from the late seventh to the ninth century and was certainly a response to these problems.

The state had to adapt fast to the shrunken resources at its disposal. Constans II began to put in place a taxation system based on manpower (poll tax), rather than land, as was the case before, with the aim of funding the construction of a fleet against the Arabs. The emperor seems to have adapted this system from a similar tax newly introduced in the Islamic world. Byzantium was on the defensive throughout the whole century; the state's single-largest expenditure and priority was the army. Since voluntary recruitment in the army was never a major component in the Roman world – the State had to pay its soldiers both in cash and kind – it is obvious that one of the main preoccupations of the state must have been both to secure the system and to progressively lighten the burden on state finances. Under Constans II some steps in this direction seem to have been undertaken regarding the organization of a war fleet that would be able to counter the danger of Muawiya's newly emerged navy, by making the building and operation of such a body part of the fiscal obligations imposed on populations in Italy and Africa. The *Karabisianoi*, as the fleet came to be called, constituted a novelty in the state's fight to restructure resources. The organization of the territorial armies was undergoing changes as well. As a result of the Islamic conquests the field armies of the East retreated into what was left of imperial territory, namely Anatolia. Their names Anatolikon (Eastern) and Armeniakon (from Armenia) bear the names and reflect the structure of the late Roman army commands. In the 680s, when large parts of Thrace were under Bulgar control, the imperial armies of the area were moved to western Asia Minor and termed the Thrakesion. Finally, during Justinian II's first term in office, a new elite mobile army termed Opsikion (from the Latin obsequium, obedience) emerged; situated in Bithynia, close to the capital, it became the imperial army par excellence. All these large armies, termed *strategiai* (commands of a general), were headed by generals (*strategoi*) selected and appointed by the emperors. Equally, provisioning the armies with food and weapons was managed from Constantinople at this early stage through a system of warehouses (*apothekai*) and officers (*kommerkiarioi*) stationed throughout the Empire: the *kommerkiarioi* collected and redistributed produce, either through taxes paid in kind or through compulsory purchases by the state. The *strategiai* were spread throughout Anatolia in a layout that was not necessarily the best for strategic reasons, but it made their provisioning more feasible. Pitched battles were to be avoided and, instead, efforts were focused on localized defence, on holding back the Islamic armies from Anatolia through a chain of fortresses. It was a modest strategy, but it worked.

A SOCIETY UNDER SIEGE

It seems obvious that during this period of fighting for the very survival of the Empire the army was a particularly important institution and a powerful and growing force in society. This becomes particularly clear in a letter sent by Justinian II in 687 to the Pope in which all the armies of the Empire are represented through the signatures of their commanders: the commands of the Anatolikon, Opsikion, Thrakesion, Armeniakon, the fleet of the Karabisianoi as well as the armies of Italy, Africa and Sardinia. The effect is impressive, and it suggests the unity of the emperor and his armies, which are often termed God-protected or beloved by God in the sources. The aggression against the senatorial aristocracy that Phokas and Justinian II had unleashed may be linked to those rulers personifying (in the case of Phokas) and championing (in the case of Justinian) the armies and the new elites that their commanders – often individuals of humbler origins – tended to stand for.

In a way, the treatment of Justinian II represented the senatorial aristocracy's last stand. This was a social group that was dealt a decisive blow by the Islamic conquests – obviously many aristocrats lost their estates to the new lords of the East, although some remained in the area and found ways of accommodation and survival in the new regime. In the first century of Islam jihad was the key and only acceptable activity for Muslims; conquered lands were not to be destroyed, nor was ownership transferred to Muslims. The conquered people were to continue cultivating the land and pay their taxes to the conquerors. In post-conquest Egypt for example, most of the landholding patterns remained as they were until the eighth century; in Syria and Palestine, however, already during the Persian occupation, elites had been stripped of their estates to a significant extent. Some of them probably moved into imperial territory and gradually occupied important positions in the administration and the military. Another important influx of elites fit for important positions came from Armenia, from which our sources record the migration of a significant number of aristocrats to Byzantium after their land had been largely conquered by the Arabs in the 640s.

The senatorial aristocracy struggled to assert its power, but it was a losing game since, in many ways, the structures that had sustained it were eroded and becoming gradually extinct. The Constantinopolitan senate would continue to exist until the end of the Empire, but its composition was changing: the new elites owed their wealth and status to office either at court or in the military.

A dearth of sources means that the evidence for such changes in the seventh century is fairly weak. However, a number of trends are clearly discernible. First, there was a growing concentration of power around the court at Constantinople and the immediate circle of the emperor, to the detriment of a more centrifugal organization that gave the provinces and important urban centres and those that controlled them – mainly senatorial landowning aristocrats – some degree of control, as well as local authority through political and economic networks of power. This was perhaps the result of necessity: the urban centres in which these elites resided and from where they managed the assets of their estates in the surrounding countryside contracted sharply in the aftermath of the Islamic conquests. Many cities disappeared; they were either abandoned or their appearance, shape and their function dramatically changed. Furthermore, the state gradually removed the control of resources from the local level to the imperial centre in order to better oversee and control its dwindling assets.

The culture of open, public spaces, colonnaded streets, theatres and baths was no longer fit for a society under siege. Fortified and smaller towns, the *kastra*, centres of military and ecclesiastical administration, protected by walls and able to sustain much smaller populations under adverse conditions gradually became the norm. The remaining territories were less densely populated. Although all this was neither a chronologically nor geographically homogenous process (the Balkans, for example, were affected long before Anatolia), it was largely true for most of the Empire's territories. In these new and much more modest towns the elites were largely new as well – bishops and military commanders – and their outlook was not directed towards monumental public buildings of display. However, demonumentalization does not, as previously believed, signify merely decline, but rather a reorientation in use, for example, in changing the focus of city centres towards more commercial and manufacturing functions. There was little for the old elites to do in their traditional strongholds of power; the state now provided much more lucrative – if not the only – opportunities for wealth and power, and so gradually the surviving provincial elites of the late Roman Empire either moved to the capital to work at the court or found their way into the military or the ecclesiastical administration. A remarkable aspect of the latter migration saw the election of several popes from the East – mostly Syria – between the 680s and the 730s. Eastern monks are equally attested in important numbers in Rome, while in 668, a man from Tarsos in Cilicia, Theodore, was sent by the Pope to become the Archbishop of Canterbury. Eastern migration to Constantinople was less conspicuous.

It is clear from all this that Constantinople became an even more exceptional city in this period. Despite repeated outbreaks of the plague, it remained a fairly populous city – certainly the largest in Christendom – and the seat of the emperor, his court as well as the patriarchate and its clergy. It still could not feed itself and as such getting provisions into the city – if for no other reason than to prevent food riots that could jeopardize the emperors' rule – was an important task. The only regions that could provide grain for Constantinople after the loss of Egypt were Sicily and Africa, and it was there that Constans II sought to install a functional system of compulsory purchases and transportation of grain through state coercion – this was another important function of the *kommerkiarioi* and the *apothekai* that was later enlarged to assume more generalized fiscal duties. Constantinople would receive its grain, but it was no longer subsidized by the state, much less free, except for the army units stationed in it.

In general, the economy of the Byzantine Empire in the seventh century showed clear signs of successfully adapting to its diminished circumstances. In 615 a new, though quite short-lived, silver coin called a hexagram was introduced; salaries were to be paid in it at practically half the rate of the gold coinage. It is revealing that the copper coinage, the kind of currency that enjoyed the widest circulation for its everyday use was continuously devalued (their weight dropped from 12 grams to a little over 3 grams within less than a century) and its production curtailed, as its absence from coin hoards in the period suggests. Even the gold currency was slightly devalued. In the *Farmer's Law*, a collection of legal rules on agriculture and animal husbandry dated to between 650 and 750 and reflecting rural life in an Anatolian or Balkan milieu, payments in cash are very rarely recorded and play a marginal role. Although some scholars have suggested that the economy and the tax system were completely demonetized in the seventh century, this cannot have been the case. In areas with a strong imperial presence – above all Constantinople, but also Sicily in the 660s – the monetary economy was still active. Equally the tax system of the Empire was still functioning, although payments in kind probably represented an important part of it.

COPING WITH DISASTER

The dramatic political events of this period must have baffled those who lived through them. To interpret them they often resorted to an eschatological reading of history; this helped to make sense of them and was in its turn fuelled by them. First the Persian conquests, the massacres of Christian populations, the abduction of the relic of Christ's True Cross and then the Islamic conquests and the constant fight for survival – all this must have seemed a sign of the end of times. Contemporaries certainly understood them in this way, as a number of texts and objects attest.

The silver coin that Herakleios issued in 615 carried the inscription 'God, help the Romans' which already by the late sixth century had been one of the battle cries of the army. In fact, Herakleios' long campaigns against the Persians and their culmination, the triumphant return of the True Cross to Jerusalem, were presented in many contemporary texts as a just war against the enemies of God and it is clear that this is the message that the emperor intended to convey. The widespread use of the cross in the period (e.g. on Constans II's coinage of 642 with the Greek legend *en touto nika,* an allusion to Constantine I), Herakleios' use of the miraculous image of Kamuliana in his campaigns, as well as the emphasis placed on the Virgin's protection of Constantinople in 626, all point to the link between the fate of the Empire and the divine. Equally telling is the fact that three emperors in succession, Maurice, Phokas and Herakleios, courted and consulted the powerful and very popular holy man Theodore of Sykeon (a small town in western Anatolia), receiving prophesies and blessings. The association of an emperor with someone recognized as a saint even in his lifetime underlines the importance of supernatural support.

During Herakleios' Persian Wars, there were numerous voices (mostly expressed in hagiography) that expected this to be the last war, at the end of times. Herakleios' victory was therefore presented as an important event in this cosmic scenario with the emperor in the role of saviour. The adoption of the title *basileus* in this period – a term with clear Old Testament allusions (as it is the word used to refer to the kings of Israel) – as well as the association of Herakleios with David served to emphasize this interpretation, which is nowhere clearer than in the epic poems of George of Pisidia, a deacon of Hagia Sophia in Constantinople, who commented on the events of his time (up to 632) in verse. The victorious emperor of the Persian campaigns is celebrated in a triumphalist style, laced with both classical and biblical allusions: Herakleios is likened to both Heracles and Perseus as well as to Noah and Moses. This glorious moment was also perhaps captured in a set of nine exquisite, classicizing silver plates (now shared between the Metropolitan Museum and Cyprus) which depict the life and triumph of David and date to this period. The confidence of a new and thoroughly Christian art celebrating Christian heroes – both of the past and the present – is reflected in these examples.

But the confidence was misplaced, as we know with hindsight. The 630s brought the explosion of Islam into the landscape and the victories that were perceived as God's gift to the Romans were reversed. The reaction, as expected, was coined in theological terms and took a number of forms. There was the quest for unity, or rather uniformity of faith as expressed in the imperial endorsement of Monothelitism and the persecution of its opponents from the 630s onwards. Herakleios' forced conversion of the Jews in Africa that is attested in 632, though it occurred before the Islamic conquests, also points in the same direction of striving for uniformity. The councils of 680 and especially of 692, with their emphasis placed on correct faith and behaviour, also make sense as efforts to regain divine favour and be once more worthy of victories. The imperial ceremonial through its use of titles and rituals emphasized the connection between the person of the ruler and the divine source of his authority. The use of the term '*basileus*', the placing of the imperial coronation in the Hagia Sophia (for the first time in 641), and Justinian II's use of the image of Christ on his coins and the emperor's designation as Christ's servant make the same point.

The eschatological reading of contemporary events found its clearest expression in a very popular text that was written in Syriac in the late seventh century and was quickly translated to Greek: the apocalypse of pseudo-Methodios. The anonymous author, who assumed the persona of a fourth-century martyr, tells the story of humankind, from Adam to the Arab conquests. According to the text the Arabs will conquer both the Roman and the Persian empires, but the ultimate message the author brings is one of hope: the Byzantine emperor will rise and defeat the Arabs, who will flee before him until they are themselves conquered. The empire of the Romans would prevail and last until the end of times.

But life on the ground went on, and especially for those Christian populations now living under Islamic rule this meant finding ways of accommodation. The monastery of St Catherine's on Mount Sinai is a characteristic example of such a process. It was kept safe from any invasion by a letter of protection that had been allegedly issued to them by Muhammad – it is not important whether this was authentic or not; the important issue was that it was recognized as such. (A copy of the document made in the sixteenth century still exists today, suggesting that its authenticity was always trusted.) Sinaite monks were exempt from taxation and although ties with other Christian centres were not quite as strong as before, the monastery displayed a significant cultural presence in the seventh century and beyond. The most important figure in this respect was Anastasios of Sinai, a Cypriot monk who joined the monastery in the second half of the seventh century. Of his many works, it is useful to single out his *Questions and Answers*, a collection of 103, mostly short texts that seem to be actual answers to questions put to him by either individuals or groups. The texts deal with important questions of faith and practice, but also reveal contemporary realities and anxieties: can one be saved from the plague by fleeing? (only if a particular plague is a result of natural causes and not sent by God as punishment); is it wrong to eat camel flesh if starving either in the desert or in captivity? (if you keep Christ's commandments, this will not be held against you in the Day of Judgement); are all rulers assigned by God? (worthless rulers are not); what should one think about those women who sleep with Arabs while in captivity? (if it happens under duress, it is less of a sin); did all the evil perpetrated by the Arabs against the Christians occur with God's will? (emphatically no!).

Beyond these kinds of exchange that focused on conflict, there were other, peaceful ones as well. Under the Caliph al-Walid I (705–15) the church of St John in Damascus was demolished and on its site he constructed the Umayyad Mosque, one of the oldest monumental and extant Muslim sanctuaries in the world. It is quite remarkable that Justinian II allegedly sent a large number of gold tesserae (blocks of glass) and skilled craftsmen to execute the mosaics that adorn its façade. It is not known whether this was part of a tribute agreed in a treaty, but in any case, it does show that although the two states were constantly at war with each other, this did not prevent the appreciation of the enemy's artistic accomplishments.

4

FROM SURVIVAL TO REVIVAL, 717–867

Once more an emperor with a military pedigree, Leo, born of Isaurian parents in Syria, was called to save the Empire. He had been made *strategos* of the Anatolikon around 713 and had allied himself with Artabasdos, the *strategos* of Armeniakon, in the bid for the throne. He was hardly established in Constantinople in 717 when he had to face an Arab campaign to take the city led by Maslama, the caliph's brother. A land force had surrounded the city on the Thracian side and a fleet lurked in the Sea of Marmara. Contrary to expectations the Byzantines were victorious. Greek fire was used to destroy Arab ships, the Bulgars were incited to attack the rear of the land army in Thrace, but perhaps most importantly, the Byzantines were able to disrupt the provisioning of the Arab army and in combination with the harsh winter of 717/18 this led to the outbreak of famine and then an epidemic disease, decimating its ranks. This was the last Arab siege of Constantinople and a major blow to the project of total Arab conquest. On the other side of the Mediterranean, after crossing over from North Africa and conquering Spain, the Islamic juggernaut was stopped by Charles (nicknamed Martel, 'the Hammer'), a Frankish aristocrat and the grandfather of Charlemagne, at a battle near Poitiers in 732. The two Christian victories marked the limits of Islamic expansion, reconfigured its policy and more or less fixed the status quo of the Mediterranean world for centuries to come.

The immediate danger might have been averted, but Byzantium was in a critical state. Leo III took a number of measures to address this. In the mid-720s there was another effort to collect more revenue by instigating a census of the population and raising a poll tax – as under Constans II. This time, however, the patrimonies of the Church were targeted seemingly more than had been previously the case. Perhaps a number of bishops complained, but the pope apparently withheld the payments demanded from Constantinople. Although the evidence is scarce and tangled, it seems that Leo tried to have the pope removed or even murdered, but this time the arm of Constantinople was not long enough. The revenue from the papal patrimonies in Sicily and Calabria was collected by the Byzantine government – it was probably used to fund a fleet that was successfully employed against Arab raids in Sicily in the early 730s.

Arab forays against Byzantine targets continued: by 725 Ikonion had fallen and Nicaea, Caesarea and Cyprus had been raided or besieged. Leo and his son Constantine campaigned together in 740 and managed to inflict a major defeat on the Arabs at Akroinon in central Anatolia, which was important both for strategic and symbolic reasons after decades replete with Byzantine defeats. When Leo died in 741 the succession seemed clear enough, but Artabasdos challenged Constantine. In the ensuing conflict the loyalties of the major commands were divided but ultimately Constantine prevailed. Either as punishment for the disobedience of the Roman Church, or as part of fiscal restructuring, the diocese of East Illyricum (from Dalmatia all the way to the south, including Greece) was transferred in the 740s or the early 750s from the jurisdiction of Rome to that of Constantinople, a particularly thorny issue of contention between Rome and the Empire that would be raised numerous times in the centuries that followed.

As the 740s were drawing to a close a number of events, though unconnected as such, brought about new dynamics in Europe and the Middle East. Starting in 743 the plague broke out in Egypt and was soon disseminated to East and West: Syria, Iraq and Tunisia were hit in 744/45, Sicily, Calabria and Rome in 745/46, the disease spreading from there eastwards through Greece to Constantinople and hitting the city's population hard in 747/48. Up to the end of the decade the disease had spread to Armenia and returned to Syria, Mesopotamia and Iraq. This was to be the last outbreak until the fourteenth century, but the plague went out with a bang: the major cities (Basra, Damascus, Rome, Constantinople) suffered badly. At the same time in the Islamic world an uprising was under way against the ruling Umayyad dynasty. It ended in 750 with their demise and the establishment of a new house: the Abbasids, who claimed their descent from Ali Abbas, an uncle of Mohammed, and who soon transferred their capital to Baghdad, removed from the Mediterranean.

In Italy the Lombard encroachment on Byzantine holdings took a serious turn when they captured Ravenna in 751, the seat of the exarchate. There was no dynamic Byzantine reaction given that the eastern frontier with the Arabs represented the gravest danger and required the bulk of the troops. Coastal areas (Venice, Dalmatia) were still safe, protected by the Byzantine navy, but on the mainland the Roman Church was left threatened and undefended. In the same year Pope Stephen II lent his authority to a regime change in Francia that saw the dynasty of the Merovingians, which reigned since the fifth century, replaced by the Carolingians (as Charles Martel's family came to be called), an aristocratic clan that had effectively ruled the state for the last few generations. Two campaigns in 754 and 756 by the Carolingian king Pepin secured former Byzantine territories captured by the Lombards, which were now, however, restored not to the Empire, but to the see of Saint Peter. Neither diplomacy nor an alliance with the Lombards bore fruit, while in 774 Charles, nicknamed the Great (Charlemagne in Old French), Pepin's son and heir, conquered the Lombard kingdom and assumed the Lombard crown for himself. Within less than a generation the Byzantine presence in north Italy had been wiped out and the Church of Rome emerged as the clear winner, supported by its Frankish allies.

On the eastern and northern frontiers Constantine V met with more success. Confrontations with the Abbasids continued throughout the 750s and 760s, but with no clear winner. The result was the gradual emergence of a no-man's land between the two states from Seleukeia in southern Anatolia to Trebizond on the south coast of the Black Sea: sparsely inhabited and the target of raids from both sides, it functioned as a buffer and a dynamic frontier. The serious threat of the Bulgar state in the Balkans was countered with numerous campaigns – some of them victorious. The question of the Slavs that had settled in Greece was tackled by forays to impose imperial rule (and taxation) and through large-scale transfers of population that were meant to alter the demographics of regions and re-introduce a culturally Byzantine element to them. There was movement of Miaphysite Syrians and Armenians to the eastern border and to the depopulated region of Thrace, and Slavs from the Balkans to Anatolia – all occurring within a generation under Constantine V, from the 740s to the 770s.

The first two Isaurian rulers were successful in modestly reversing the downward turn of the Empire, yet in most Byzantine sources they are demonized and hated. The reason for this lies in one of the most well-known (and misrepresented) Byzantine disputes, iconoclasm (literally:

breaking of images), the conflict over the use and value of images portraying sacred persons. In what is a complex and contested historical topic, there are four dates that are indisputable: the council of Hiereia in 754 that officially imposed iconoclasm, the seventh ecumenical council of Nicaea that reversed it in 787, the council of Hagia Sophia that reinstated iconoclasm in 815 and the Triumph of Orthodoxy, the final restoration of icon veneration in 843. What is still hotly debated is when iconoclasm actually began and more specifically whether Leo III was actually responsible for inaugurating it, as the later, iconophile accounts (all written after 800) state. The evidence for the early period is quite straightforward, if accepted at face value, but many scholars argue that it represents a massive rewriting of history after 843 that did not shy away from changing texts to fit a specific (iconophile) agenda.

In the 720s some Anatolian bishops objected to the use of religious images and occasionally removed them from their churches. The Patriarch of Constantinople, Germanos II, tried to resolve the issue diplomatically. In 730 he resigned, an extremely unusual action, which suggests that he was reacting to some significant pressure: iconophile sources suggest this was the adoption of iconoclasm by the Emperor Leo III, but it could well have been (also) a reaction to the emperor's fiscal policies against church property exemptions. The strong papal reaction to Leo III outlined above is equally seen as a response to imperial anti-image policy. The sources provide numerous reasons for Leo's iconoclasm: the emperor's reaction to a terrifying volcanic eruption in 726 at the island of Santorini (seen as a sign of God's wrath), the fact that he came from the East and was influenced by Jews and Muslims against the use of images – it all boils down to Leo searching for a reason why the Empire had been suffering defeats for almost a century, while the Arabs were triumphant. The worship shown to images was singled out as the reason, since it could be interpreted as contravening the second commandment that forbids the veneration of images of living things. In short, the Byzantines were being punished for having lapsed into idolatry. Some of the measures that Leo reportedly took included removing a large image of Christ from the Chalke gate of the imperial palace in Constantinople (now widely believed to be a myth), and sending an order to the Church of Rome (and we can assume, to the churches throughout the Empire) to demand the removal of images, prompting a defiant synod in Rome in 731 which condemned such meddling with Christian practice. Although most sources that record these actions were written much later and may well have been tampered with, it is unlikely that all of this is pure invention (Figure 4.1).

Figure 4.1 Apse of Hagia Eirene in Constantinople. It was commonly believed that the church was rebuilt under Constantine V in the 750s, but it may date to the end of the century; its only figural decoration is this large monumental cross, a central tenet of Isaurian piety.

While the nature and extent of Leo's measures against images may be contested, this is not the case with his son Constantine V. He wrote theological treatises to condemn images and summoned a well-attended council in 754 that declared the veneration of images equal to various, long-condemned heresies; the synod's pronouncements on the faith were supported by long patristic florilegia (collections of relevant passages). The 760s saw purges and executions – the iconophile side suggests they were directed mostly against monks and nuns, who were ridiculed and forced to drop the habit and marry – as well as against monasteries and their property, carried out by some of Constantine's *strategoi*. Again, it is difficult to distinguish facts from later iconophile propaganda, but it seems clear that the emperor did not have an anti-monastic bias as such: some monastic leaders were persecuted for dissent against the imperial majesty and for being involved in a plot to oust him, while there may have been other reasons for being critical of monks as individuals who removed themselves from agricultural production and thus from two vital areas for the state: taxation and military service.

By the time of Constantine's death in 775 the Empire was for the first time in a century in a territorially reduced but stable condition. The succession of his son, Leo IV, went smoothly, but his reign was a very short five years. His successor, Constantine VI, was a child of nine years and so his mother, Eirene, a native of Athens, ruled beside him. Eirene invested in diplomacy (e.g. she instigated a marriage alliance between Constantine and one of Charlemagne's daughters that was agreed in 781) and favoured eunuch officials who could not directly threaten hers and her son's power. In the following years one of her eunuch generals consolidated Byzantine authority over the Slavs in Greece all the way to the Peloponnese. Such success was both short-lived and limited as the late 780s and 790s brought a string of serious defeats by the Arabs within the core Byzantine territories in Anatolia. Relations with Rome and the West were fraught as Byzantium viewed with suspicion the Frankish encroachment of the Lombard duchy of Benevento, so close to its own holdings in the south of Italy.

Eirene's policy towards religious images made her prominent. She first had her own candidate elected to the patriarchate (Tarasios, a learned aristocrat and layman), then liaised with the pope – the Church of Rome had staunchly supported images throughout this period – and in 786 she summoned an ecumenical council. Despite opposition by iconoclast bishops and parts of the army, the council took place in Nicaea in the following year. To the iconoclast florilegia the assembled bishops offered even lengthier collections of evidence containing patristic rebuke. A theology of icons was outlined and has since become a distinct part of orthodoxy: contrary to what the detractors claimed, venerating (but never worshipping) an image did not mean honouring the actual object, but through it conveying honour to the prototype it portrays.

As Constantine VI came of age, he had his mother removed from power. His sole reign which began in 790 was not successful, especially a disastrous campaign against the Bulgars in 792. Eirene gradually came back to share power until 797 when a series of events precipitated her son's removal and blinding – he died shortly thereafter. This was connected to the emperor's personal life: he had scandalously separated himself from his first wife and married another, causing a great reaction from monastic cycles headed by two influential aristocratic abbots, Theodore and his uncle Plato. Constantine's harsh efforts to silence them, combined with his flagging military presence, facilitated the regime change. From 797 to 802 Eirene reigned alone – the first time that an empress occupied the throne not as a mother or wife, but independently of her male relatives (Figure 4.2). Despite efforts to consolidate her position both inside the Empire (by granting a remission of taxes and distributing gifts to the population of Constantinople, and also by inviting Theodore to take

Figure 4.2 A&B Solidus of Eirene from her sole reign (797–802), remarkably showing the Empress on both sides of the coin.

over one of the most ancient monasteries of the city, the Stoudios) and outside (there was now a marriage proposal to Charlemagne himself) she remained quite vulnerable. A symbolic blow came in 800, when Pope Leo III crowned Charlemagne Emperor of the Romans on Christmas day. To the Byzantines, this was perceived as the repayment of a debt: Leo had fled to Charles' court to escape rival parties in Rome; Charles had helped reinstate him, just a short time before the coronation. For the pope – who innovated by crowning an emperor, since there was nothing to suggest that to do so was in his gift – this was not only a means to secure the protection that had been offered by the Carolingians for a generation, but also a way of driving a wedge between any prospects of a Byzantine–Frankish alliance that would have necessarily resulted in the weakening of his grip over Rome and its resources. Frankish sources emphasize Charles' reluctance and surprise, but also the fact that since a woman occupied the throne in the Roman Empire, the seat of power could be seen as vacant.

It was not coincidental that Eirene was overthrown in a coup in 802 when Charlemagne's envoys were in the city to negotiate the marriage project. The new emperor, Nikephoros I, had been the general *logothetes* (chief finance minister) and his short reign (802–11) is marked by a number of far-reaching reforms in the administration of the Empire that will be discussed below. In the East the Arabs continued to be victorious. In Italy Carolingian power was growing and came to threaten Byzantine lordship over Venice, but the dispatch of a Byzantine fleet and the dynamic resistance of the Venetians secured the allegiance of the city to Byzantium. The major and immediate danger to the Empire, however, came from the Bulgars under their new leader (khan) Krum

(802–14). From 807 onwards he aimed to expand Bulgar territory and inflicted a number of defeats on the Byzantines. Nikephoros headed a substantial campaign against him in 811. Despite initial success against the capital, Pliska, the Byzantines were ambushed: the emperor and his commanders were killed, his heir, Stavrakios, severely wounded. Krum is said to have beheaded the emperor and turned his skull into a ceremonial drinking cup. Stavrakios had been left paralyzed and support for him was waning; Michael I Rhangabe, his brother-in-law, was proclaimed emperor by the Senate and the army some months after the defeat by the Bulgarians. It was in this critical period that Charlemagne's title – treated with silence for a decade – was officially recognized: the Byzantine envoys heralded Charles as *basileus* (though not of the Romans) in Aachen in 812. The world had once more de facto two Roman emperors in East (the coinage of which began after 812 to bear the title *basileus* of the Romans) and West – unseen since the fifth century and obviously awkward.

Michael's reign was very short: he rejected a rather conciliatory offer of peace by Krum and prepared to campaign against the Bulgars; despite putting together a large force, the Byzantine army was soundly defeated and Michael abdicated in 813 in favour of a friend and colleague, Leo V, *strategos* of the Anatolikon, who had already enjoyed a successful military career under Nikephoros. The death of khan Krum in 814 while planning to attack Constantinople ended the Bulgar threat for the time being. Two years later and after a Byzantine victory the Empire signed a thirty-year peace treaty with his successor, Omurtag.

In the meantime, Leo had pushed for the reintroduction of iconoclasm, officially adopted again by a church synod in 815, inaugurating a second phase that seems almost devoid of doctrinal content. Leo was perhaps hoping to emulate the military victories of Leo III and Constantine V and thus to avoid the taint of the defeats associated with iconophile emperors. Leo's rather uneventful reign was cut short by the successful plot of another military commander, Michael II, head of one of the imperial guard units at Constantinople, who had him murdered in 820. This prompted one of the most successful rebellions in Byzantine history, that of a high-ranking officer from Anatolia, Thomas, nicknamed 'the Slav', who rose to allegedly avenge Leo. Most of the Anatolian armies joined him, including, later, the fleets, but his attempt to take Constantinople in 822 failed, despite mounting a year-long siege. His fleet was destroyed by Greek fire and then the rebel forces were hounded and dispersed by a Bulgar army. Thomas' rebellion was seen by some modern scholars as having an important social component, suggesting that the peasants of Anatolia sided with him as a protector against the high taxation imposed on them from the imperial government, but this view is no longer current.

Michael II would reign until 829, his son Theophilos succeeding him until 842. The second half of the 820s and the 830s were again a low point in military terms: between 826 and 828 Crete was conquered by Arab pirates from Spain; from 827 onwards the Arab conquest of Sicily by the Aghlabids of Africa began: Palermo fell in 830, Messina in 843. The presence of Arab pirates on the two major Mediterranean islands made large tracts of the Aegean, Tyrrhenian and Ionian seas, unsafe. On the eastern front, Theophilos campaigned personally in Anatolia, but despite some victories, he was defeated in Cappadocia in 831. Even more importantly, in 838 the Arabs captured and destroyed the important city of Amorion, the headquarters of the Anatolikon army, capturing and executing forty-two officers, who were later venerated as martyrs. Appeals to the last Umayyad ruler, the Emir of Al-Andalus, in Cordoba for help against the Abbasids were fruitless, as had been the case some two decades before, when Michael and Theophilos addressed a letter to the Carolingian king of Italy to request aid against the Arab raids in Sicily and southern Italy.

Upon Theophilos' death in 842 the situation became once more precarious, as his heir, Michael III, was only an infant. Michael's mother, Theodora, along with her two brothers, Bardas and Petronas, acted as regents. Theodora is remembered to this day in the Orthodox Church for permanently bringing back icon veneration. The Triumph of Orthodoxy, as the event is known, was sealed with church approval in 843 and was fixed in a document produced in the following year, the Synodikon of Orthodoxy, which succinctly sets out the true faith by celebrating heroes of the Church and condemning the heretics who opposed it. The document, which was updated in various instances until the mid-fourteenth century, is still read out today in the Orthodox Church on the first Sunday of Lent.

During Michael III's reign the Empire became more confident. In the early 850s Byzantium supported an Armenian uprising against the Arabs, and although it was put down by 855, this highlights the links between Byzantines and Armenians and makes the presence of a number of Armenians with important careers at the Byzantine court in this period easier to understand. In the same period the supporters of a dualist sect in Anatolia, the Paulicians, who had been tolerated earlier in the century, were now targeted and persecuted as dangerous and subversive.

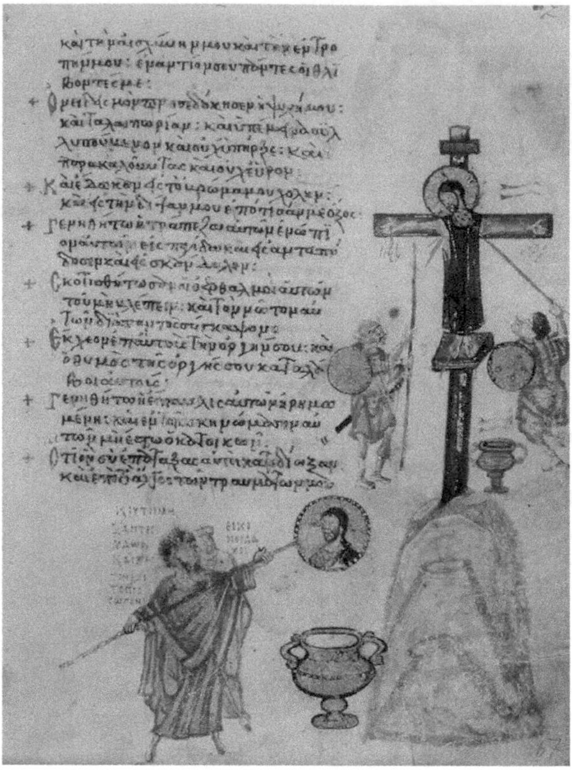

Figure 4.3 Visual propaganda against the iconoclasts from the Khludov Psalter produced after 843. The iconoclasts white-washing the image of Christ parallels the soldiers piercing Christ's side.

Numerous Paulicians were organized in armed militia; there were conflicts with the Byzantines, but despite heavy losses many Paulicians retreated to a fortress in Tefrike, near the Byzantine–Arab border, which would become their last stand in the coming decades (Figure 4.3).

As Michael reached adulthood around 856, there was a change in the setting of power: Theodora was removed from court, but her brothers remained powerful. In 863 the combined Anatolian armies, headed by Petronas, inflicted a crushing defeat on the Arab invaders in Paphlagonia. Bardas, who now more or less controlled the emperor, had the Patriarch Ignatios (the castrated son of Michael I) removed and introduced a talented man of aristocratic stock to the patriarchal throne in 858: Photios, a layman and relative of the former Patriarch Tarasios, a man of great learning, who was to dominate the political and intellectual life of the Empire for more than a generation. In contrast to Photios and his prominent background, the same period also saw the emergence of a social climber: a certain Basil, a young man of peasant stock, whose family had been moved to the Balkans in one of the many ethnic transfers of population. Basil was handsome and wily, he was good with horses and an excellent wrestler; he caught young Michael III's eye and was taken into his entourage. Soon Basil and Michael became inseparable and the former was given the high office of *parakoimomenos* (grand chamberlain) in 862, an office that was actually reserved for eunuchs, as it put its holder into a potentially dangerous proximity to the emperor when he was most vulnerable – during his sleep. The close relationship between the two men became the platform for one of the oddest tangles in Byzantine history: Michael had Basil marry his own mistress (but the emperor continued to sleep with her), while Michael was married to another woman and Basil took Michael's sister as a lover.

The appointment of Photios – uncanonical, since he had been hurried through all ranks in the clergy within a week – and the dismissal of Ignatios were not without repercussions. The latter appealed to Rome and Pope Nicholas I summoned a synod which demanded the return of Eastern Illyricum to his see, but also condemned Photios' elevation; when he did not back down, Nicholas anathematized him, prompting Photios some years later to pronounce the pope himself excommunicated. By 867, the churches of Rome and Constantinople were once more in schism.

In the same year things came to a head at the top of the state as well. Basil had a powerful grip on Michael, but his authority depended on the emperor's good grace. After succeeding in having Bardas removed and murdered in 866, Basil felt threatened by Michael's supposed shift away from him and so had him murdered in 867 and assumed the throne himself, a sign that talent and shrewdness could still win the imperial throne despite lowly social origins.

RECOVERY AND RECONFIGURATION

The eighth and ninth centuries constituted an era of relative stability in the Empire after a century of traumatic defeats and formed the background for a number of important and far-reaching changes and reforms.

Demographically, the last wave of the plague in 750 ushered in a period of recovery; it took around a century for the population levels to pick up. The increased population was moved around to achieve a more homogenous density in areas that had been particularly afflicted. The re-imposition of imperial rule in the Balkans and the increased safety in the core regions in Anatolia (a result of the buffer zone that absorbed most raids) meant that agricultural production was much more regular, which translated into more and more steady revenues. Already in the 760s there were indications of a more positive economic trend, especially discernible in Constantinople, now the only major city in the Empire since the other key urban centres of Late Antiquity had been either lost to Islam or had declined. As a result, the capital profited from the concentration of resources and economic activity. Constantine V made large-scale repairs in Constantinople (which included the aqueduct of Valens, destroyed since the Avar siege of 626) and repopulated the city by importing people from Greece. Eirene is connected to the construction of workshops and a palace near the harbour of Theodosius. More importantly, Nikephoros I took a number of measures (our chief source, Theophanes, calls them vexations) that aimed to reverse most of the popular, but damaging fiscal policies of Eirene and increase state income. Exemptions were largely abolished, taxation was applied in a much more generalized way and significant tracts of highly valued and productive land were confiscated. Furthermore, Nikephoros seems to have fostered maritime trade and encouraged – at times with coercive measures – the growth of a Constantinople-based group of merchants and shipowners.

Although the period from the 660s to c. 800 is characterized by a low monetary output by the state – both the gold coinage and the bronze coins necessary for smaller transactions – this does not mean that the economy had been completely demonetized. The capital and the army were the two major areas for which money was in evidence. In the case of the latter for example, the sources record successful raids by Bulgars and Arabs that managed to rob the payment transports of certain armies in the early 800s, the number of coins they removed amounting to several tens of thousands. The state that had managed to survive the Arab and Bulgar onslaught in the seventh century clearly was very different from the late antique empire of Justinian. This was now mostly a rural state run centrally from a very large city, compared to the rather modest provincial towns which had taken the place of the poleis that peppered the landscapes of Late Antiquity.

The survival of Byzantium had been a result of two main factors: the preservation of the capital with its resources, from which centralized efforts to manage the remaining state radiated, and changes in the military apparatus which enabled the state to hold back the invasions at a reduced, but relatively stable frontier and from that position to gradually regain lost ground. The new system, which was not in place before the Islamic conquests, appears quite confident and stable in the late ninth and tenth centuries when we reach a time of more source material. Its transformation, therefore, took place in the period in between, but its chronology is still a hotly debated issue. In the grand scheme of things chronology might not be the most crucial element, as these developments were gradual and suggest adaptation to changing circumstances and needs rather than the fully worked out plan of one individual emperor.

The system of the *strategiai* spread across Anatolia that had helped stabilize the Empire's frontiers was at the same time fraught with potential dangers for the imperial office, as the constant rebellions by *strategoi* clearly showed. In the fight for survival the state had granted too much power to too few individuals, the five major commanders (of Anatolikon, Opsikion, Armeniakon, Thrakesion and the newly emerged naval command of the Kibyrrhaiotai in southern Anatolia), in control of important resources and geographically removed from the easy grip of the capital. Constantine V took a number of measures to balance it: the Opsikion was divided into smaller units and more importantly Constantine introduced a new professional, elite army corps, the *tagmata*, stationed near the capital, paid directly by the court and thus loyal to the emperor. Other changes followed under Nikephoros I: a large number of people were settled from Anatolia into the newly recovered areas in the Balkans, many of them as soldiers. These had had to sell off their lands and would receive new lands in the places they had been moved to as well as fiscal privileges. By the beginning of the ninth century armies began to be called *themata* (singular: *thema*, from the Greek word for place/placement) rather than *strategiai*. This change obviously suggests structural developments: each army now became much more rooted in and identified with the particular area where it was stationed. Furthermore, the soldiers were recruited locally, and the local communities were tied to this system by being made responsible for the financing of soldiers who could not afford to pay for their own equipment. This was beneficial for the state as a part of the cost of the armies in the provinces would now be financed by the rural communities they were embedded in. Although payments to soldiers in cash continued, overall the state would now have access to a steady number of equipped troops for a much lighter financial load. The *strategos* had also gradually become not only the army's commander, but also the governor of the *thema*, which now became fiscally independent and had its own administration headed by a *protonotarios*, responsible among other things for provisioning the armies while on campaign.

The general trend is one of proliferation: from the initial four military *strategiai* of Anatolikon, Armeniakon, Thrakesion and Opsikion along with the fleet of the Karabisianoi – all in place by 687, at the latest – the eighth and ninth centuries saw several new ones emerge. The Opsikion was split into three *themata* by the 770s, the Armeniakon was divided into two, while the new theme of Cappadocia was carved out of the Thrakesion by 830. Furthermore, as the Empire extended its control over territories, it established more commands in order to integrate them, such as Hellas (central Greece and Peloponnese, by the end of the seventh century), Kephalenia, an island in western Greece (under Constantine V, to guard the Adriatic and the Dalmatian coast) and Macedonia, Thessaloniki and Cherson (on the Crimea at the Black Sea) by the 830s.

A general degree of militarization pervaded all aspects of the Empire's existence and shaped its social and to an extent, cultural values. By the early eighth century social stratification had undergone some major changes as the old senatorial elites had more or less vanished – whatever remained of them joined the only two stable structures: the court and the Church. Especially the latter had been less weakened as an economic institution, as its vast property up to then had been protected by more or less complete tax exemptions from the time of Justinian. In this critical period, some emperors – notably Leo III and later Nikephoros I – chose to disregard this protected status and taxed church properties or the dependent peasants who worked on them. In the military there were still some commanders of aristocratic stock, but the majority were new men. The gradual rise in the status, both social and economic, of the *strategoi* and some other high commanders created a new elite, a military aristocracy, who would dominate political life from the late ninth century onwards. Though offices were not hereditary, the gradual emergence of family names – often attested in the clans of military commanders – would suggest the growing importance of lineage. It is also noteworthy that some members of the high clergy in this period, especially those that came to the office from a secular career, were from wealthy, aristocratic backgrounds and in some cases – as with Photios – had close contacts with the nascent military aristocracy. Relatively speaking, if the seventh-century countryside was characterized by a proliferation of free peasant smallholders and the decline of large estates, this process began to be reversed by the ascent of military aristocrats in the late eighth and ninth centuries.

EMPEROR AND PRIEST

There were two dominant themes in the eighth century: on the one hand, taking stock and planning a longer-term strategy of unavoidable coexistence with Islam, on the other reflecting and trying to identify what had gone wrong, because – so much was clear – the Islamic conquests could only be palatable as signs of divine chastisement. The response to this reflection was a drive to reform, both at the practical and administrative level, as we have seen above, and also at an ideological and spiritual one.

In 741 Leo III and Constantine V promulgated a new book of laws, the *Ekloga* (selection). Where Justinian had made legal history through bulk, this book did the opposite: covering some fifty pages of modern printed text it aimed to put together the most useful parts of existing legislation and to make it accessible to judges. There were distinct accents: family law occupies an important position (the emperors appear as protectors of widows and orphans, for example), but there is also a change in punishments from capital punishment to mutilation 'in order to be more charitable' – a person with a hacked-off limb could live and repent. In the foreword to the *Ekloga* the emperors made clear what they saw as their role in the cosmic order: they had been entrusted with the office of emperor by God and it was their duty to shepherd their flock to the path of righteousness.

On the one hand were the emperors, victorious in battle, guarantors of the state's survival by running a tight ship and demanding complete submission in all areas – including on matters of faith. On the other hand were some leading church figures who resisted what they saw as the infringement of the secular authority in the sacred world of God. The conflict was played out in a number of ways in this period. Up to Tarasios in the 780s, patriarchs in the eighth century had been weak, appointed and removed by emperors more or less at will. But Tarasios inaugurated a period of important patriarchs – more often than not intellectuals with a lay background such as Nikephoros or Photios –

who asserted their authority. In this context iconoclasm was presented as an imperially sponsored heresy that was doomed to fail; its end spelled victory for the patriarchate. Regardless of the lofty pronouncements at the council of Nicaea in 787, which owed a lot to John of Damascus' intricate theology of the icon, the tradition of religious images was too strong to be successfully uprooted with theological or political arguments. Seen in the overall context of the transformations that the Empire went through in the eighth and ninth centuries and given that these were not smooth transitions but the results of conflict and negotiation, iconoclasm seems a characteristic trait, rather than the central preoccupation of this turbulent era.

CULTURAL REVIVAL

Picking up again on the theme of taking stock, the production of extensive florilegia from either side of the iconoclast controversy suggests the existence of well-stocked libraries in the city. Besides their actual function as ammunition for the debate, the act of surveying texts sparked an impulse that was to bear fruit in the tenth century.

Another stimulus in the period came from the engagement with Islam. Already in the eighth century some Byzantine authors (such as John of Damascus and the Arab Christian bishop Theodore Abu Qurrah) were aware of the Qur'an and were referring to it in the spirit of a serious enquiry. In the ninth century a partial translation of a substantial part of the Qur'an into Greek was produced, probably in Syria, and a little later, in the late 860s, the first refutation of the Qur'an was written by Niketas of Byzantium. It is telling that Christians living under Islamic rule were key in expressing their distance from the new religion. But there was more than just polemic. From the second half of the eighth century a cultural flourishing was taking place in the Abbasid Caliphate: supported by extensive royal and elite patronage, hundreds of works of Ancient Greek philosophy, medicine and science were translated into Arabic. No doubt the Byzantines were aware of these processes, as Islamic rulers sent embassies asking for specific manuscripts, or looted libraries whenever they had the opportunity. Byzantine interest in the same texts that were being translated and appropriated by the Muslims is manifest in the ninth century and this timing cannot have been coincidental. The figure of Leo the Mathematician, a Byzantine scholar, teacher and later bishop who lived at the time of Theophilos, is an indicative example.

He was a man with strong interests in science who allegedly invented the system of fire beacons whose signals from Anatolia would warn the court at Constantinople of imminent Arab attacks. A little later Leo would teach at the school of higher learning at the Magnaura Palace in Constantinople supported by Bardas, at which philosophy, geometry, astronomy and grammar were taught. Important figures of the period such as the last iconoclast Patriarch John the Grammarian (a relative of Leo the Mathematician and Theophilos' teacher) and Photios were linked to this revival. The latter left a vast *oeuvre* that spanned various genres from homilies and letters to exegetical and theological works. But perhaps the clearest expression of this cultural revival is his *Bibliotheca*, a collection of – mostly short – reviews of some 380 texts, both secular and ecclesiastical, that he had read before becoming patriarch. Many of the texts stem from Ancient Greece and Rome and a large part of them no longer survive – for Photios to have read them means, however, that they were still extant in ninth-century Constantinopolitan libraries or private collections. There was a practical aspect that operated in the background to this renewed interest in texts: in the early ninth-century manuscripts began to be written in the minuscule script which used small-case letters joined together with ligatures, as opposed to the beautiful, but less practical majuscule script (which used capital letters). The new script meant that more text could be packed onto each parchment page and at a faster pace – two aspects that resulted in making more texts available.

MISSION

The project of imperially sponsored conversion of non-Christians had not been actively pursued after the sixth century, when Justinian and Theodora had sent missionaries to Lower Nubia. However, during Michael III's last decade and the first patriarchate of Photios there was a frenzy of activity in this field. The ambition, intellectual standing and dynamism of the patriarchal office under Photios were certainly crucial to this development, but competition with Islam equally played an important part, spurring the Byzantines to extend their influence as Christian rulers. Byzantium did not practice conversion by sword (as Charlemagne, for example, had done with the Saxons) but instead viewed it as cultural process. The key figure on the ground was Constantine (monastic name: Cyril), the son of a high-ranking military officer from Thessalonica who spoke the Slavonic language. A kind of *wunderkind*, he came to Constantinople and entered the intellectual circles of Leo the Mathematician and Photios. By the early 860s he was an experienced missionary, having already (unsuccessfully) operated at the Khazar and the Moravian courts. He had devised an alphabet (a precursor to the Cyrillic alphabet named in his honour) in which Slavonic could be written; this was used by Constantine and his brother Methodios to translate a number of key texts – including the Bible and the *Ekloga*. Success came around 864 when the ruler of Bulgaria, Boris, converted to Christianity, although his conversion was the result of political pressure: when it became known that he was in close contact with Louis the German, the King of East Francia (roughly equivalent to modern Germany) and was considering converting to Christianity through Rome, the Byzantines marched to the Bulgarian border to show that they would not tolerate it. Photios sent a long and complicated text to Boris to introduce him to the faith, but Boris was still not utterly convinced or committed; he kept his options open and requested instruction on the faith from Rome. Pope Nicholas I sent him an equally long, but much simpler text, replying to the now lost questions of the Bulgar ruler and Boris seemed to favour the Roman option: the Byzantine missionaries were expelled, prompting a vigorous reaction from Photios. In a letter to the Eastern patriarchs he condemned Rome's meddling in Bulgaria. The objection with the more lasting impact, however, concerned the adoption of the phrase *filioque* ('and from the son') by the Roman Church. The term had first been added by Frankish theologians to the creed to explain the Holy Spirit's procession from the Father *and* the son. The Byzantine Church opposed this vehemently – perhaps less for its dogmatic implications and more for the audacity to tamper with a central statement of faith that had been agreed at the first two ecumenical councils. Although the Roman Church had not adopted the *filioque* in the early ninth century, it seemed to have tolerated its use by Frankish missionaries in Bulgaria.

It was clear that the sees of Rome and Constantinople had been growing dangerously apart. Photios was the first patriarch to be successful in making orthodoxy radiate to the outside world through mission and dynamic interventions. Rome's primacy of honour, which was gradually being understood as the supreme authority over the Universal Church, was pitted against the conciliar structure based upon the Pentarchy, favoured by Constantinople, secure in the knowledge that in practice this meant its domination, since the Eastern patriarchates had been marginalized after their absorption into the Islamic polity.

5

EXPANSION AND RADIANCE, 867–1056

Basil I became the founder of the Macedonian dynasty, one of the most long-lasting ruling houses in Byzantine history and ushered in an era of military expansion, economic boom and cultural revival. For many this represented the apogee of medieval Byzantium. The two centuries of Macedonian rule, however, were replete with violent upheavals, usurpations and the murders of emperors. To navigate through this tangled web a brief overview of the imperial reigns in the period will be useful.

When he ascended to the throne Basil already had two sons; two more were to follow shortly and thus a secure succession: however, the designated heir, Constantine, died in 879, while another son, Stephen, had been castrated and was thus barred from the throne. The two remaining sons, Leo and Alexander, succeeded him jointly in 886, but Alexander was sidetracked. Leo VI, known as the Wise, had a turbulent private life. For almost two decades a procession of three wives failed to grant him a surviving male heir. His son, Constantine, by his mistress Zoe Karbonopsina ('Eyes of Coal') was finally born in 905. It was imperative to marry Zoe and thus make Constantine legitimate, but it seemed impossible given that in canon law even a second marriage was viewed as unseemly, while a third was barely tolerated, and a fourth (tetragamy) was out of the question. The patriarch, Nicholas I Mystikos, a companion from Leo's schooldays, refused to grant him his wish, and so Leo removed him to attain his goal.

Shortly before the emperor's death in 912, Nicholas returned to the patriarchate and became a regent for the young Constantine, banishing his mother Zoe. She returned to power with the help of the Phokas, a clan of military commanders who had been promoted by Basil I and ruled in her son's name until 919 when the throne was usurped by Romanos I Lekapenos, the *droungarios* (commander of the imperial fleet). He quickly removed Zoe, married Constantine to his daughter and proclaimed himself first basileopator (Father of the Emperor) and then emperor in 920; three of his sons were crowned co-emperors in the following years. Constantine's chances of ever ascending the throne seemed slim as Romanos I enjoyed a long and quite successful reign. It is debatable whether Romanos actually intended for Constantine to succeed him; his own sons seemed to have thought so and unseated him in a palace coup in 944, only to find themselves likewise deposed a year later by Constantine VII (actual reign 945–59). Barred from power for over a generation and with the stigma of illegitimate birth, Constantine is known by the epithet Porphyrogennetos (born-in-the-purple), which served to emphasize his pedigree as the true heir of the Macedonian dynasty: it meant that he was born while his father ruled as emperor in a special part of the palace covered with this imperial colour. Constantine was not a military man, but he entrusted the military affairs of his reign to some very able generals – mostly from the Phokas clan. The greatest military expansion in Byzantine history after the trauma of the seventh century took place from the mid-tenth century onwards.

The succession of Constantine's son Romanos II (959–63) went smoothly, but it was to prove the exception rather than the rule. Romanos died unexpectedly in 963 – some thought he had been poisoned. His widow, the beautiful Theophano, who was another Byzantine rags-to-riches story as she had been the daughter of an innkeeper, acted as regent for her two young sons, Basil and Constantine, until power was seized by Nikephoros Phokas (963–9), the triumphant military commander who had brought great glory to the Empire. Theophano supported him (as did the powerful eunuch minister Basil, an illegitimate son of Romanos I), and Nikephoros Phokas married the widowed empress. His reign was cut short as a result of another coup: he was murdered in 969 by a group of military aristocrats headed by John Tzimiskes, his nephew and former protégé as well as the lover of his wife. But the Patriarch of Constantinople made John sacrifice Theophano for the imperial crown; she was exiled and John married a daughter of Constantine VII. Tzimiskes' reign was equally cut short for he died in 976 – again there were rumours of foul play.

It was once more the time for a member of the Macedonian dynasty to return to the throne: Basil II (976–1025). Although officially he reigned together with his brother Constantine, the latter was excluded from the actual running of the Empire. Basil had the longest reign of any Byzantine emperor and though his authority was repeatedly challenged by powerful rebellions, he managed to hold on to power. During the first decade of his reign he faced a very serious challenge from Bardas Skleros, a relative of Tzimiskes, who rebelled against him and was initially quite successful. Basil was forced to use a member of the Phokas clan (another Bardas) against Skleros, but the two commanders not only fought against each other, they occasionally joined forces, prolonging the civil war, draining resources and bringing Basil to a critical point: the emperor could not count on the loyalties of his own armies. This was solved in a drastic fashion. In 988 Basil had his sister, Anna, marry Vladimir, the Rus leader of Kiev, who then agreed to convert to Christianity and, more importantly for Basil's war effort, dispatched a large military unit (what came to be called the Varangian guard) with the help of which the emperor crushed his rebellious military aristocrats.

Basil never married, nor did he regulate his succession, which passed to his elderly brother Constantine, himself the father of unmarried daughters. It was only at the end of the latter's reign in 1028 that his daughter Zoe married Romanos III Argyros (1028–34), who succeeded her father.

The last two decades of Macedonian rule read like pages out of a novel, a feeling that is strengthened by the fact that the major source for this period, the *Chronographia* of Michael Psellos, was the work of undoubtedly the most talented and innovative of Byzantine authors. The story has it all: a powerful eunuch, who cannot rule on his own and thus summons his handsome brother to court. Zoe, the middle-aged empress who falls madly in love with him and arranges for her husband to be drowned in his bath, then marrying her young lover Michael IV (1034–41), who turns out to be quite different than she expected: he suffers from epilepsy and is tormented by guilt. He decides to step down and have his nephew, Michael V (1041–2) nicknamed Kalaphates ('the Caulker'), who had been already adopted by Zoe, proclaimed the new emperor. But Michael V overestimates his hold on power, for he banishes Zoe to a monastery. An uprising breaks out in Constantinople, the mob besieges the palace and manages to catch Michael and blind him. Zoe and her sister Theodora assume power on their own for a short time in 1042, when the elder sister takes a third husband, Constantine IX Monomachos (1042–55). Zoe and Monomachos ruled together until her death in 1050; he did not remarry and left no heir (Figure 5.1). Upon

Figure 5.1 A much-photographed mosaic panel in the gallery of the Hagia Sophia depicts the Empress Zoe together with Constantine IX Monomachos flanking Christ. Upon closer inspection one can see that the faces of all three figures as well as the inscription bearing Monomachos' name had all been altered – they had probably depicted one of Zoe's previous husbands and were modified.

his death the throne returned to Theodora for a year (1055–6); with her passing the Macedonian period came to an end.

THE EMPIRE FIGHTS BACK

The territorial expansion of the Byzantine Empire from the late ninth to the early eleventh century is one of the main reasons for the positive historiographical assessment of the Macedonian dynasty. Byzantium successfully faced enemies on three fronts, Italy and the Adriatic in the West, the Balkans and the Black Sea in the North, and Anatolia, Syria and the Caucasus in the East. This success had a number of reasons. It was based on a positive demographic and economic trend as well as on administrative changes that harnessed the momentum. Another important factor was timing: the waning of strong states that had threatened Byzantine territories coincided with this period and facilitated Byzantine expansion. The revival and extension of the Byzantine presence in Italy, for example, profited from the chaotic political circumstances that accompanied the end of Carolingian rule in Francia; Frankish priorities were certainly not focused upon Italy at the time, while Rome and the papacy were embroiled in local power struggles between aristocratic families from the city and its hinterland. Similarly, in the East the Macedonian period more or less coincided with the fragmentation of the Abbasid Caliphate from the mid-ninth century onwards. The emergence of regional states – still nominally loyal to the Abbasids, but in reality politically independent – meant that Byzantium no longer had to face an opponent as formidable and in control of vast resources as in the previous centuries. The situation was less clear-cut in the North. The emergence of Bulgaria as a strong rival state represented the most dangerous development vis-à-vis Byzantine expansion, requiring a century to subdue it. Farther north, the Empire had to constantly adapt its policies to react to the ever-changing political landscape that was the result of the continuous Eurasian migrations. There, the key question was never one of expansion, but of neutralizing new threats and safeguarding the Empire's own territories while fostering ties of commercial, diplomatic and cultural exchange.

The earliest phase of expansion occurred in Italy. The Arab menace from Sicily threatened Byzantine interests in Calabria and Dalmatia; the Empire intervened by dynamically ousting both the Arabs and the Carolingians from the region of Bari by 876. In the 880s Basil sent the commander Nikephoros Phokas the Elder (the future emperor's grandfather) to Italy, where he considerably expanded and secured Byzantine control over large parts of Calabria. Bari became the centre of Byzantine administration in the South from the late 880s as the capital of the *thema* of Langobardia. Byzantium was the only power that could oppose the Arabs in the South and this was acknowledged by all parties in the area, including the papacy.

The balance of power changed only with the advent of the Saxon king of East Francia Otto I in Italy. The first ruler after a generation who managed to impose order on the disjointed political landscape, he defeated the Magyars in 955 and became the new powerful figure in the West. After his coronation in Rome in 962, the German emperor began to meddle more seriously in Italian politics. Following the initially successful, but ultimately disastrous Byzantine campaign against Sicily in 964–5, Otto marched towards the South, received the submission of the Lombard principalities and threatened Byzantine territories in Calabria. This was the background to a diplomatic feat: after numerous rebuttals, a Byzantine lady was offered in marriage to Otto II, already the crowned co-emperor alongside his father. The marriage of Otto and Theophanu – not quite a princess born-in-the-purple, but the niece of John Tzimiskes – was celebrated with pomp in Rome in 972. Otto I died in the following year and his son continued his father's aggressive Italian policy, but failed spectacularly, suffering a humiliating defeat by the Arabs in 982, from which he barely escaped with his life. His heir, Otto III, would later try to control Rome and the north of Italy, but never attempted again to interfere in the Byzantine south. Relations with Byzantium were fairly cordial. In fact, when Otto III died in Rome in 1002, a Byzantine delegation including the Princess Zoe had just arrived in Italy in preparation for an upcoming marriage.

The Byzantine presence in Italy was obviously a costly enterprise, as it required a naval presence in the Adriatic. A possible solution was to delegate this task to a friendly state with common goals. Venice emerged in this period as the ideal candidate. Veneto–Byzantine relations had not always been rosy: in 971, for example, John Tzimiskes severely reprimanded it for supplying the Arabs with timber and iron that was used for the construction of ships and weapons. In 992, however, the first document that links the two states emerged. Coined in the language of a unilateral grant to deserving subjects, the document offered Venetian merchants favourable, reduced tariffs for trade and offered a privileged administrative treatment. The Venetians were expected to come to the Empire's aid, for example, by transporting troops to Italy.

While Calabria with its numerous Greek communities responded well to Byzantine rule, Apulia, whose population was overwhelmingly Latin and its church oriented to the papacy, was plagued by constant rebellions. A Lombard insurgent, Melo, kick-started the Norman engagement in Italian affairs by recruiting some Normans to help against the Byzantines around 1014 after he had failed to take Bari. This joint force was soundly defeated in 1018, but the Normans had witnessed the fragile power dynamics in the region and saw it as a valuable opportunity. Sicily had not been forgotten: just before his death in 1025 Basil II had begun preparations to retake the island and in the late 1030s Byzantium came close to reconquering it. Under the leadership of the brilliant general George Maniakes a series of victories brought hope until he was recalled in 1040 for fear of becoming too successful.

Melo's son, Argyros, went to Italy and in 1042 was supported by both the Lombards and the Normans, who since 1029 had established their first permanent base in Aversa. Maniakes was dispatched again to Italy and tried to put down the rebellions with brute force – his success would again be cut short as he was recalled in 1043 (prompting him to rebel himself, unsuccessfully, against the emperor). Argyros switched sides and was named commander of Italy (*katepano*), but the Norman expansion was impossible to check. Around the middle of the century Norman control over parts of Italy was acknowledged by the German emperor. The papacy saw Byzantium as its only chance of stopping the Normans and a group of prominent envoys was sent to Constantinople to negotiate it, but nothing came of it.

In the north the conversion of the Bulgars in 864/65 bought some decades of peace but did not ultimately deter them from attacking the Empire, especially under the most dynamic and ambitious of its rulers in the period, Symeon (893–927). Having grown up as a hostage in Constantinople he was groomed as an ally. However, as early as 894 he invaded Thrace and Macedonia; the Byzantines appealed to the Magyars, the Bulgars to the Pechenegs, but the latter were ultimately victorious. Up to Symeon's death in 927 the Bulgars launched regular successful raids and even threatened Constantinople in 913 and the 920s, prompting a series of peace treaties in which Byzantium was made to pay substantial sums in tribute. Symeon's achievement was impressive: he built his capital Preslav in the image of Constantinople, forced his coronation as tsar (emperor) by the Patriarch Nicholas I outside the walls of Constantinople in 913 and pushed for the wider recognition of his title by the Byzantines. He supported the growth of the Church in his lands, insisting on a native clergy, and even negotiated the marriage of his daughter to the young heir, Constantine VII, although this union never materialized. Upon succeeding his father in 927, his son, Peter, launched a major campaign against Byzantium. He ultimately withdrew his troops, having secured more than his father had ever managed to: the creation of a patriarchate in Preslav, a sizeable tribute and his marriage to the granddaughter of the then ruling emperor, Romanos I. The frontier with Bulgaria consequently remained peaceful for the whole of Peter's reign (927–67).

The Byzantine victories in the East secured during the decades that followed (see below), however, gave them the confidence to revisit relations with Bulgaria. Another important factor was the forging of an alliance with the Rus, since the main Byzantine allies in the area, the

Khazars, had turned from trusted partners in the eighth century to the number one enemy in the late ninth and tenth – the conversion of their elites to Judaism in the 860s seems to have functioned as a watershed. The trajectory of Byzantine–Rus relations is not a straightforwardly positive one: there were early raids in the 860s, followed by commercial treaties in the early tenth century and the baptism of Olga, the leader's widow, in 957. When Nikephoros Phokas stopped the payment of tribute to Bulgaria in 966 he had the Kievan Rus under Svyatoslav raid Bulgaria in the following year. The plan backfired, however, as the Rus returned to the area with Magyar and Pecheneg allies, determined to occupy Bulgaria for themselves. Under Nikephoros Phokas' successor, John Tzimiskes, the Rus were first pushed back north of the Haemus mountains, before the emperor led the army to capture Preslav and defeat Svyatoslav in 971, when he imposed a truce. Large parts of Bulgaria were annexed to the Empire and its patriarchate was demoted to a metropolis under the jurisdiction of Constantinople. After Tzimiskes' death, however, a rebellion broke out, headed by the Kometopouloi, the four sons of a high official from the area of modern Sofia. Of the four brothers Samuel prevailed, and as his grip on Bulgaria grew, Basil II marched against him and was defeated.

The marriage of Anna and Vladimir and his conversion in 989 brought stability in the Byzantine–Rus relations for about two generations. The alliance brought the destruction of the Khazar state by the Rus with Byzantine naval support. Nevertheless, the northern frontier was far from peaceful as the 990s saw a string of Bulgarian victories and expansion towards the South that was only checked in 997. Samuel was confident enough to have himself acclaimed emperor of the Bulgarians. The last phase of the conflict with Bulgaria took place in the early eleventh century. After securing peace in the East in 1001 Basil led a number of campaigns against the state up to 1005, seizing eastern Bulgaria and reorganizing its military and civil administration. After a decade's break the final and decisive campaign began in 1014; the Bulgarian forces were crushed at Kleidion (modern North Macedonia, near the Bulgarian border). Basil is said to have blinded some 15,000 prisoners, leaving 1 man out of every 100 with one eye to lead the troops back home; upon seeing them Samuel suffered a heart attack and died. Leaving aside the logistics of such a massive mutilation, Bulgarian resistance did not stop, but went on for the following four years, which suggests that we should take this information with a pinch of salt. Nevertheless, Basil has gone down in posterity as the Bulgarslayer ('Boulgaroktonos'). Bulgaria was once more annexed to the Empire, its territories organized in *themata*; peace was kept through the presence of troops. The patriarchate was dissolved and relegated to the archbishopric of Ohrid under direct control of the emperor.

Peace would not last very long: from the late 1020s to 1036 a series of Pecheneg raids from the North reached the area down to Thessalonica. Tribute was paid, the most exposed settlements abandoned and their populations resettled in fortified towns, while the area between the Danube and the Balkan Mountains was left as a no-man's land. After a string of bloody Byzantine defeats a 30-year peace treaty was signed in 1053 and the Pechenegs were allowed to settle in the area between the Danube and the Balkan Mountains.

In the East, Byzantine expansion brought territories under its rule that had been lost to the caliphate for centuries. This success was not sudden: under Basil I the major victories were against the Paulician strongholds on the border with the Arabs. These were destroyed in the early 870s and numerous captives were transferred to the Balkans. There were some important Byzantine victories in Cilicia in 900 and successful efforts to bring parts of Armenia into a more active alliance with the Empire. But some serious setbacks also occurred in this period, such as when an Arab fleet sacked Thessalonica in 904 or when a Byzantine naval expedition to liberate Crete was defeated in 911. When peace was established in the Balkans in 927 the Empire's resources became focused on the East and started reaping results. More timidly in the 930s, but much more resolutely from the 940s to the late 960s, Byzantine commanders invaded Syria and pushed further into Mesopotamia. The Hamdanids, lords of a territory between Aleppo and Mosul, put up a staunch resistance and managed to score some victories, but overall the Byzantine momentum could not be halted. Crete was taken by Nikephoros Phokas in 961 after numerous failed attempts; Cyprus was reconquered in the following year as were Adana and Tarsos and later Nisibis and Dara. Perhaps more spectacularly Antioch was captured in 969 after more than three centuries of Arab rule. John Tzimiskes pushed to the south of Antioch and was ready to campaign against Jerusalem before he died. Basil II consolidated these territorial gains and through frequent peace treaties with the Fatimids (in 1001, 1011 and 1023) managed to speed up the decline of the Hamdanids in Syria, who were enemies of both states. He was also particularly successful in the Caucasus, securing parts of Georgia and Armenia both through diplomacy and military campaigns in the first two decades of the eleventh century. By the 1050s most of

Armenia had been incorporated into the Empire with the surrender of Ani, the capital of the Bagratuni kingdom, in 1045, an event that serves as an important symbolic date. The previous decades had seen some further Byzantine successes in Syria, notably the capture of Edessa in 1032 and a ten-year truce with the Fatimids in Syria that was concluded in 1036. The new danger in the East, however, came from another Turkic people from the steppes, the Seljuqs, who appeared on the scene in the 1040s, threatening the Armenian border. Although repelled at the time, they would mount a formidable return and change Byzantine borders for good within the next generation.

LAND AND GLORY

There is ample evidence of demographic expansion in this period. In many rural areas, for example, the study of pollen in excavations has revealed a decline of forests in favour of fields for agricultural production after 850. Archaeological surveys in several areas in Greece and Turkey have revealed the gradual proliferation of villages and later hamlets, while numerous urban centres expanded. The most telling example is Constantinople, whose population was now steadily rising and would reach levels similar to its pre-plague population by the twelfth century. The city's aqueduct, for example, was repaired twice in the early decades of the eleventh century, suggesting a growing population in need of functioning infrastructures.

This demographic expansion was coupled with increased security to produce the basis for a growing economy. For example, the recapture of Crete from the Arabs in 961 had a positive effect on coastal settlements in Greece and southern Anatolia that had been abandoned due to the constant threat of piracy. Furthermore, the period saw the gradual incorporation of significant areas into the imperial realms: *themata* increased in number (though decreased in size) from eleven in 775 to twenty-two in 867 and more than forty by the late tenth century. The Empire now had access to greater volumes of agricultural production and tax income, especially since it held on to the most productive of the newly conquered areas, classifying them as crown lands and administering them directly from the court. In addition, there is evidence for the flowering of urban trade and manufacture in the early eleventh century. Cities in Greece such as Athens, Thebes and Corinth were on their way to becoming important centres for the production of silk. Italian merchants from Amalfi and Venice acted as go-betweens linking East and West; they bought commodities in Constantinople and Trebizond, and also established direct links to Egypt and North Africa. Venetian merchants would push long-distance trade between the regions of Byzantium, importing, for example, expensive Cretan cheese to Constantinople, while also exporting the much-coveted Byzantine silk to the West. The Rus also traded directly with the Byzantines, exporting furs and slaves by using the riverine system that linked the far north to the Black Sea. Byzantine merchants were likewise involved in trade, but their radius was often more local and regional.

The *Book of the Eparch* (the governor of Constantinople), datable to 912, is a unique text that contains regulations of some major guilds in Constantinople, ranging from grocers, bakers and chandlers to money changers. It makes clear that the state regulated the production and sale of important commodities and services and imposed specific margins for maximum profit. There is a particular emphasis on silk textiles, some types of which were forbidden to export, although there is also evidence that they occasionally did find their way out of the Empire. The overall image of the Byzantine economy is one in which the state played a crucial, defining role, but there were also elements of dynamism through trade.

In contrast to the previous period where, roughly speaking, there was an abundance of land for too few people (a result of the plague and flight due to warfare), now the opposite was true: since there was no shortage of manpower the key aspect was the control and exploitation of (more) land. The state needed to collect revenues to fund the army, infrastructure, the salaries of its officials and its costly diplomacy. It therefore required taxes to be paid, especially by the bulk of the population, who were peasants in rural communities. There was, however, competition for the appropriation of this surplus and the state found itself antagonizing its own elites. This cannot have been a new development overall, but in the tenth century it reached a critical stage. We are informed about this largely through a collection of novels (new laws) issued by a number of Macedonian emperors who seem to have one target: the *dynatoi* (powerful magnates). A natural catastrophe functioned as the tipping point: after a particularly harsh winter in 927/28 (the earth was supposedly frozen for over 100 days), a severe famine broke out in the Empire and forced a number of people to sell their lands – at low prices – to survive. Those who could afford to buy land in such adverse conditions were singled out by the novels: senators, officials of the *themata*, high civil and military officers, bishops, abbots and other members of the elite. The first novel by Romanos I in 934 decreed that all those who had acquired land from those in need would be driven away from the village communities they had encroached on and would receive no compensation, unless they had paid a just price. To prevent this from happening again, outsiders were barred from buying land in village communities: if someone needed to sell or lease land, the community had the first right of purchase. This kind of legislation was taken up by later emperors such as Constantine VII and Nikephoros Phokas. The former introduced another important clause, that of prescription: if a peasant had sold off his land under duress or untoward conditions, he had the right to reclaim it within the next 40 years. The legislation reached its peak (and end) with the draconian measures of Basil II, who removed the time limit of prescription and ordered those who had purchased land in village communities since the famine of 928 to return it without compensation. Basil's particularly harsh measures are certainly connected to his decade-long civil wars against the powerful military clans of Phokas and Skleros that ended in 988 with their defeat and the confiscation of their estates.

In all these novels, the emperors present themselves as the champions and protectors of the poor and weak, which was undoubtedly a key imperial virtue. But there is more to this than a moral stance. The village communities represented the basic fiscal unit of the state around which tax was calculated and collected. In the diverse village communities lived, among others, those who held military lands, that is, those properties whose now hereditary ownership was connected to military service. At some point in the tenth century, the obligation to serve was passed from the actual person registered in the military lists to the land. This had a very positive effect for the state: the gradual fiscalization of military service, or in other words the commutation of the obligation to serve into cash, which the state collected and could use to recruit and pay professional soldiers. Although the thematic armies of peasant-soldiers still existed in this period, it is safe to say that the more ambitious offensive campaigns were not primarily waged by them. Instead, these thematic armies were used for defensive warfare (as had been the case from the seventh century onwards), raids and skirmishes, while the professional troops, including mercenaries, would be primarily employed in pitched battles and sieges. By alienating land from the village communities the *dynatoi* therefore endangered the state's ability to extract revenue and services. This occurred because those powerful elites had lobbying power: they could gain exemptions and privileges. The fact that the anti-magnate legislation was renewed through two generations suggests that it was not easy to impose. The *dynatoi* found ways to circumvent the restrictions; neither did the state ever generally suspend the privileges and exemptions that made them so dangerous. The state confiscated lands with the one hand and made generous land grants to key officials and institutions with the other.

Ultimately the ascent of the military aristocracy could not be stopped. The Phokas family, for example, rose to prominence under Basil I while some generations later one member of the family became emperor himself. From the late ninth century onwards, this group becomes more visible: the emergence and proliferation of family names preserved both in texts and on lead seals (used to validate and authenticate documents) testify to the consolidation of aristocratic networks and alliances and a growing emphasis on lineage as a social virtue. The Macedonian emperors had an ambiguous approach to this emerging social power. On the one hand they needed able military leaders, but more often than not, success, which was coupled with landed wealth and power, led many military aristocrats to challenge imperial power and vie for the throne themselves. The state would make (and at times try to break) aristocratic clans; neither was it loathe to engineer divisions and competition between such aristocrats, for example, the strong antagonism between the Armeno-Paphlagonian commanders (such as the Skleros) and the Cappadocian aristocracy (such as the Phokas). And yet, there were marriages between the two clans (Otto II's bride, Theophanu, was the product of a union between a Phokas and a Skleros) and even cases where the two enemies joined powers against the imperial government, as when Bardas Phokas and Bardas Skleros fought against Basil II. These military aristocrats were not independent warlords; they were officers of a state and their power stemmed largely from the holding of office. A look at the numerous aristocratic rebellions makes this clear: the rebels were most dangerous when they commanded over state armies and not when they fought with only their personal retinues. The period also saw the proliferation of mercenaries in the Byzantine army. Large numbers of them came from the West and North. Serving in Byzantium became a kind of Viking Grand Tour, as made clear by the case of Harald Hardradi, who fought alongside George Maniakes in Sicily and the East and would later become king of Norway (Figure 5.2).

Figure 5.2 Ivory plaque depicting Otto II and Theophanu crowned by Christ dated to 982–3. The imagery closely replicates Byzantine imperial ivories.

EMPERORS, PATRIARCHS AND POPES

Relations between emperors and the Church in this period, though less dramatic than before, were characterized by the latter's efforts to break the tight embrace of secular authority. Some church leaders proved particularly stalwart, Photios being a characteristic example. After his removal in 867, he quickly returned to favour: first he was summoned back to court as a tutor to the two young princes, then reinstalled as patriarch in 877, after which he exerted strong influence on Basil I's last years. He provided the emperor with elaborate tools of ideological propaganda, presenting him as a new David, a new Constantine or a new Justinian, while subtly undermining his position. In an important new collection of laws issued in 885/86, the *Eisagoge* (Introduction) Photios placed particular emphasis on the patriarch – and not the emperor – being the 'living icon of Christ'. When Leo VI ascended the throne in 886 he had Photios removed once more, as he later did with the Patriarch Nicholas Mystikos when the latter vehemently opposed his fourth marriage. Emperors had a monopoly on the legitimate use of violence and were able to have an immediate impact on church affairs, but this does not mean they could get their way with everything. When Nikephoros Phokas, for example, demanded that soldiers who had fallen while fighting the enemy should be venerated as martyrs, the Patriarch Polyeuktos sternly refused and the matter was never taken up again. The Church as an institution was able to withstand secular pressure in the long term.

The period began and ended with mutual excommunications between Rome and Constantinople. The schism under Photios was patched, but tensions and differences remained. Perhaps the only reason for this matter coming to a head again as late as the 1050s was the long period of papal decline in the tenth and early eleventh centuries. Emerging from this period of crisis, the papacy embraced the spirit of reform that emanated from the Abbey of Cluny in Burgundy. A return to a purer Church, untainted by clerical marriage and the sale of office (simony), with a focus on the liturgy and the practice of charity but above all the freedom to practice these without interference by either local lords or bishops – these were some of the Cluniac ideals. Pope Leo IX (1049–55) became the first important figurehead of papal reform. He and his advisors laid particular stress on the primacy of the Roman see: the Pope was above all other bishops and above all secular leaders as well. It was perhaps inevitable that a clash with the Constantinopolitan patriarchate would ensue within such ideological parameters. This occurred in 1054 when a papal delegation in the city (whose actual task was to broker an alliance against the Normans), headed by Cardinal Humbert of Silva Candida, one of the chief supporters of the reform, brought these new ideas to the fore. The Latins met the forceful opposition of the popular patriarch Michael Keroularios, who resented, among other things, the imposition of the Latin rite on the populations of southern Italy that had until very recently been under Byzantine rule. The differences between the two sees – the *filioque*, the use of unleavened bread in the liturgy (the azymes, which the Byzantines thought was a remnant of Jewish customs), the celibacy of the clergy – were debated, but both sides were intransigent and Keroularios seems to have deliberately provoked the Latin party.

The result was a mutual excommunication. This may have seemed to be nothing new at the time – as we have seen, such cases had occurred before – but in the long term, the schism of 1054 proved a definite rift, not least in the way it was used by both sides after the traumatic events of 1204 (see Chapter 6). The lifting of the mutual excommunication only occurred in 1964.

ART AND IDEOLOGY FOR A POWERFUL EMPIRE

The end of iconoclasm coincided with a positive economic trend. The increased revenues of the state and its elites were now channelled, among other things, into buildings and works of art. Basil I was a prolific builder, with a focus on his capital. Not only did he sponsor major reparations and decorations for important landmarks in Constantinople (such as the Hagia Sophia or the Holy Apostles) but he also extended his care to numerous existing churches and founded a number of new churches and monasteries. 'New' is the key word here, as it was used to designate both his lavish five-domed New Church and the New Monastery, which functioned as a burial place for much of his family – none of these survives today. The emphasis placed by the adjective 'new' was meant to stress that his reign represented a departure from the era of iconoclasm.

The trend towards monumental imperial buildings continued throughout the Macedonian period and saw the emergence of vast monastic complexes in the city such as the Myrelaion of Romanos I, the Peribleptos of Romanos III and the Mangana of Constantine IX. Although most of these do not survive today, our sources inform us that their imperial founders used existing structures which they enlarged and adapted. Their main churches were domed, cross-in-square buildings, the form that became dominant from this period until the end of the Byzantine Empire. Gradually, a common programme emerged on the decoration of these churches, dominated by the image of Christ Pantokrator (ruler of all) on the dome, the Mother of God on the apse and images from Christ's life and passion as well as various saints on the walls of the main nave. New churches were built in this period in other parts of the Empire and still survive. Some of the most important can be found in Greece (such as Daphni in Athens, Hosios Loukas in Boetia, Nea Moni on Chios or Panagia Chalkeon in Thessalonica). The lavish decoration of churches harked back to late antique models and celebrated the new-found prosperity with an over-the-top concentration of images and colour. The same traits can be found in more private art objects of the period, such as a number of celebrated manuscripts of the tenth century or contemporary ivories in which figures and motifs appear in classicizing ways (Figure 5.3).

Many of the churches mentioned above were part of monasteries. It is indeed one of the most striking and long-lasting developments of the period that saw the flourishing of new monastic foundations throughout the Empire. They became the major focus of imperial and elite investments and offered a twofold benefit: the communities of monks or nuns that dwelt in them were entrusted with charitable donations to the poor and with the liturgical commemoration of the founders. Their growing numbers were so

Figure 5.3 Miniature from the highly classicizing Paris Psalter (Constantinople, second half of the tenth century). The image shows David surrounded by personifications of Wisdom and Prophecy.

evident that in 964 Nikephoros Phokas issued a novel in which he banned the foundation and endowment of new monasteries (a sign of vanity, in his eyes) and instead urged those willing to do good to assist already-existing monasteries, especially those fallen on hard times. But Nikephoros was not averse to all kinds of monastic foundations: in the same law he praised a type of monastic community, the lavra, built in deserted places and populated by ascetic monks. He put his money where his heart lay by providing substantial means to his friend and spiritual father Athanasios, who founded the first important monastery on the remote peninsula of Athos, not far from Thessalonica. Athanasios' lavra (known to this day as the Great Lavra) inaugurated a monastic community on Athos that came to include some twenty major monasteries with thousands of monks and would come to dominate Byzantine spirituality and ecclesiastical affairs in the last centuries of the Empire (see Chapters 8 and 9).

Another key cultural feature of the Macedonian period is the vast body of texts produced under imperial but also patriarchal sponsorship. Their common trait is that they are compilations of earlier material, but there the similarities end. Some works were merely copied, while others were much more actively redacted (often to attain a higher stylistic register). It seems as if the Empire was taking stock of its heritage in the most varied realms of knowledge: encyclopaedias on medicine and agriculture, a vast collection of saints' lives, of poems, a hard-to-categorize immense dictionary of noteworthy general knowledge (the *Souda*), or texts on military strategy. These emerged alongside important imperial projects such as the translation of the Justinianic Corpus into Greek in sixty books (the *Basilika*), the collection of texts on imperial ceremonies or a treatise on the peoples surrounding the Empire and how they could be managed (the *De Administrando Imperio*). The tenth century produced comparably fewer works of original literature, although the act of compilation, of putting together material by establishing criteria that suggest that it forms a unity of meaning, should not be offhandedly dismissed as derivative and inferior. Perhaps today with the endless amount of available information and the proliferation of lists, remakes and remixes we can be more appreciative of such efforts. But there is another important aspect of this revival: a significant portion of Ancient Greek texts that survive today go back to manuscripts copied in the tenth century. Although the Byzantines certainly used their own aesthetic and perhaps even political criteria to select and preserve Greek literature, without them it is a simple fact that very little of what survives today would have been extant. Preserving texts did not always mean engaging with them critically, although the most original Byzantine thinkers certainly did that. Michael Psellos, who played an important part in the court of the late Macedonian emperors after the 1040s, was certainly one of the most unique cultural figures; he will be discussed in the following chapter.

The context for this revival is made up from different strands: the creation of florilegia during iconoclasm, the revitalization of education in the city under Bardas (see Chapter 4) and the conscious efforts of the Macedonian emperors to present the Iconoclastic period and its emperors as suppressing culture and ushering the Empire into a dark age from which their efforts had freed it. Furthermore – although this is very hard to prove – it is difficult to imagine that the Carolingian Renaissance with its networks of schools and scholars, beautiful manuscripts and rediscovery of ancient texts failed to make an impression on the Byzantines. Perhaps a function of this Macedonian revival was to show – both to themselves and to those outside – that the new and confident Empire was able to challenge Westerners at the heart of their intellectual achievements. Ideologically this was certainly the case. Michael III had allegedly called Latin a barbarian tongue, prompting Pope Nicholas I to suggest that since Latin equalled Roman, then the Byzantines were ridiculous to call themselves Romans without speaking the Roman tongue. It was clear that the question of who had the right to call themselves the inhabitants of the Roman Empire was far from settled from the Byzantine point of view. It is also obvious that attitudes of both East and West were hardening. A key witness to this is the account of a failed Ottonian embassy to Nikephoros Phokas, written by the seasoned diplomat Liudprand of Cremona. The narrative is certainly biased, but reading about the heated arguments over whether Otto was a king or an emperor, as well as Liudprand's offhand dismissal of the imperial court as shabby and the Greeks (as he calls them) as perfidious and weak, is a revealing testimony to the tensions that lay ahead. Such antagonism fuelled the projection of power of the two empires, the Byzantine and the Ottonian, through the means of conversion. The efforts of the Macedonian emperors focused on the Magyars and the Rus. The former, along with the Poles in the East and the Danes in the North, were drawn into the German orbit and thus accepted Rome as their spiritual centre. The Byzantines, on the other hand, were successful in converting the Rus. This was the beginning of what has been termed the 'Byzantine Commonwealth', a number of states in Eastern Europe that looked to Constantinople as their political and cultural ideal – which did not, however, prevent them from attacking the Empire.

6

THE APPEARANCE OF STRENGTH, 1056–1204

Theodora's chosen successor, the elderly Michael VI, barely reigned – he was challenged by an uprising headed by Isaac Komnenos, a military aristocrat from Paphlagonia, in northern Anatolia, who was himself crowned emperor in 1057. Isaac came from one of the minor aristocratic clans favoured by Basil II in his effort to curb the domination of the powerful clans of the Phokas, the Skleros and others (see Chapter 5). His reign, though very short (1057–9), introduced the domination of provincial military aristocrats after the prevalence of families with a Constantinopolitan focus (roughly from 1028 with Zoe's first husband, Romanos III). This would last until the end of the Byzantine period. To navigate the murky waters at court Isaac relied on the Patriarch Michael Keroularios and Michael Psellos in his role as a high civil official. Isaac projected a military image, but ultimately his opposition to too many elite interests brought his downfall. It was Psellos who persuaded him to abdicate and enter the monastery of Stoudios, in favour of his new patrons, the Doukas, another aristocratic clan from Paphlagonia. In 1059 Constantine X Doukas became emperor and elevated his brother, John, to the high office of caesar. Constantine reversed Isaac's anti-aristocratic policy and took measures to attract support in Constantinople. Outside of the imperial borders, however, it became clear that there was a major political reconfiguration of power: in Anatolia the Seljuqs, now rulers of Baghdad, began their conquest of the Byzantine heartland, targeting both south-west Anatolia and Armenia, either directly or through the Turkish warlords they (more or less) controlled. In Italy the Normans, having had their conquests recognized by the papacy which was unable to oppose them, set out after 1059 to conquer the South: Calabria fell by 1060, opening the way for Apulia to the North and Sicily in the South. The brothers Roger I and Robert Guiscard spearheaded the conquest. The Balkans, meanwhile, suffered from Pecheneg raids.

Constantine's death in 1067 produced a crisis, as his heirs were still minors. His widow, Eudokia Makrembolitissa, who was Keroularios' niece, was placed under oath to never remarry in order to ensure the throne would pass to the legitimate heir, Michael Doukas. Shortly afterwards, however, she married Romanos IV Diogenes, an important military commander from a prominent aristocratic family, thus elevating him to the throne. Romanos could easily see that fighting on two fronts at the same time was impossible given the state of the Byzantine army. This consisted for the most part of mercenaries at this point, as the thematic armies had been neglected for over a generation – a repercussion of the civil wars, but also of the offensive warfare of the tenth and early eleventh centuries that had little use for them. Priority was given to Anatolia – not least because this was where both the emperor and his supporters came from and held estates in. This meant that the Norman expansion was left unchecked, leading to the gradual loss of all Byzantine possessions in Italy, with Bari, its last stronghold, falling in 1071. Romanos did enjoy some minor successes against the Seljuqs in Anatolia, which gave him the confidence to tackle the problem head-on: he would mobilize all the forces he could muster and push the Turks back from Armenia. The campaign was launched in 1071 and ended in disaster: at the battle of Manzikert near Lake Van the imperial army was defeated and Romanos captured. It was claimed that Andronikos Doukas, Caesar John's son, spread false rumours at the rear of the formation that the emperor had been caught, causing panic to ensue. Although the actual casualties of the battle were not very high, Manzikert has been perceived as spelling the beginning of the end for Byzantine Anatolia; in reality, however, it was rather the aftermath of the battle and its results that proved decisive. Once the news reached Constantinople, there was a resurgence of Doukas power and upon Romanos' release civil war ensued, fought largely through Armenian and Norman mercenaries. Romanos was defeated and blinded, dying shortly afterwards in 1072. Michael VII Doukas became emperor in 1071.

The decade that followed brought the Empire to the brink of ruin. The great military feats of the previous century had made the Byzantine elites complacent; the military tactics that had proven so successful in the tenth century were obviously no match for the swift and flexibly executed Seljuq raids. The decline of the *themata*, which might have provided some much-needed buffer, was sorely felt. Now, to counter the raids in Anatolia, a mercenary army consisting mostly of Normans was dispatched against them in 1073; its leader, Roussell Balliol, later deserted and managed to carve out a small lordship in the North-east. He was finally defeated in 1075 by the young Alexios Komnenos, a nephew of the Emperor Isaac, again with the help of Turkish mercenaries. Michael VII was facing serious difficulties – the payment of all these mercenaries spelled economic hardships as taxes were raised, prices soared (earning him the nickname *Parapinakes*, 'Minus-a-quarter', linked to the rise in the price of grain) and the *nomisma* further devalued. It was inevitable that his clearly weakened position would move others to challenge his authority. The period 1077–8 saw two main rebellions by notable aristocratic military commanders, Nikephoros Bryennios from Thrace and Nikephoros Botaneiates from Anatolia, both relying on Norman and Turkish mercenaries. Botaneiates prevailed, forcing Michael to abdicate and enter a monastery, and married his widow Maria, a princess from Georgia, in 1078. At almost eighty years old, Botaneiates could only offer a temporary solution and indeed it was not long before a bloody coup unseated him. In April 1081 Alexios Komnenos took control of Constantinople by force, supported by his brothers, the empress Maria and the Doukas (three years earlier Alexios had married Eirene Doukaina, who was a cousin of Constantine, Maria's son and designated heir).

If Alexios had emerged as the most able of the young military aristocrats, his reign began inauspiciously. The neglected Normans, led by Robert Guiscard, crossed over the Adriatic in 1081, captured the crucial port of Dyrrachium at the head of the Via Egnatia, the road that connected the Balkan coast to Constantinople, and began their incursion into Greece. Alexios had to rush to confront them, leaving his mother as governor in his stead. The first encounter with the Normans signalled a serious defeat for Alexios and left them advancing into central Greece. With the help of Turkish mercenaries, largely paid by the confiscation of church plate, Alexios later just about managed to dislodge them, but it was obvious that the Norman threat had to be taken more seriously in the future. It is in this context that Alexios, continuing what Basil II had begun, granted a new set of privileges to Venice in 1082 (or, according to some scholars, in 1092). This grant was much more far-reaching as it exempted Venetian traders from all taxes and provided them with the freedom to trade in all areas of the Empire as well as granting them a residential and commercial quarter in Constantinople.

Alexios' fortunes continued to wane. In 1087, he suffered another devastating defeat while trying to stop a Pecheneg invasion south of the Danube. It was only by securing the alliance of another Turkic people new to the area, the Cumans, that the Pecheneg threat was actually removed in the early years of the 1090s. The fact that Alexios managed to hold on to the throne despite his very poor track record during the first decade of his rule must be attributed to various factors: his mother's efficient administration of the court in his absence and the fact that Alexios based his power on an alliance between some key aristocratic families, of which his own and the Doukas lay at the heart, while a number of other notable families joined in through marriage alliances.

The 1090s gradually brought a more positive turn of affairs: the situation in the Balkans stabilized and conflicts over succession among both the Seljuqs and the Fatimids in Egypt meant that the danger from the East was less acute; in fact in the early 1090s, the Byzantines had managed to re-establish some control at sea and make some first forays into north-western Anatolia. But the decade was marked by another event that originated in the West and came to have tremendous repercussions in the East, both in the Islamic and the Byzantine world: the Crusades. This is a topic with a vast, ever-expanding scholarship and many of its aspects fall outside the scope of this book. As such, in this chapter and subsequent chapters the focus will be on events and developments that have a direct bearing on Byzantine history – such a presentation is necessarily limited and one-sided. Two key, interconnected questions must be dealt with first: what role did Byzantium have in the emergence of the Crusades (especially the First Crusade) and how did Byzantium perceive and therefore react to the reality of the Crusades? The Byzantine Empire needed troops to counter the Seljuqs in Anatolia; it was common practice to recruit a large part of its mercenaries from the West: particularly the Normans and Anglo-Saxons (especially after the Norman conquest of England in 1066 and the souring of Byzantine–Rus relations after an unexpected attack in 1043), but also anyone else that might respond to the frequent and lucrative calls of the Byzantine court. Alexios merely continued a trend that had been tried and tested for at least a generation before him: he attracted mercenaries through letters and embassies. It is in this context that his deputation to Pope Urban II in 1095 must also be understood, wherein he asked for help against the infidels while emphasizing the suffering of Christian populations and the dire state of the holiest places of Christian pilgrimage, the Church of the Holy Sepulchre and the Holy Land more generally. How this call was transformed into what became the First Crusade can never have been envisaged or desired in Byzantium; it was much more than Alexios had bargained for and, as it turned out, almost too much for him to handle.

The first wave, the Crusade of Peter the Hermit, reached Constantinople in the summer of 1096; Alexios had the participants transported as quickly as possible to Anatolia, where the bulk of them were slaughtered by the Turks. Some months later, the actual leaders of the Crusade began to arrive in Constantinople and Alexios, no doubt on the advice of his many Western counsellors, more or less successfully tied them to his person with various oaths: they promised to return to the Empire those areas and cities that had formerly belonged to Byzantium (a hazy concept, at best) in return for military and logistical support by the emperor. It all went very well at first: in 1097 the Seljuqs surrendered Nicaea to the Byzantines in the face of the Frankish menace and Alexios followed through with a successful campaign in which he secured Byzantine control over large parts of western and northern Anatolia. Antioch, a strategically very important city that had fallen to the Seljuqs only about a decade before, brought the first real test of strength, as the Crusaders found it very hard to take the city. Here the opinions of our sources diverge: the Byzantine sources suggest that the imperial troops retreated only upon hearing that the Crusader army had perished; the Frankish sources, on the contrary, suggest that the Byzantines broke their part of the agreement by abandoning them. However, Antioch was ultimately taken and Bohemond, the Norman lord and son of Alexius' archenemy, Robert Guiscard, proclaimed himself its master. The Crusaders continued to Jerusalem and the city was taken in 1099; a bloodbath ensued that would always be remembered by the Muslim populations in the East – evoked, in fact, to this day.

Unexpectedly, the First Crusade was widely and rapidly successful and established a number of colonial Latin states in the Levant; the most long-lasting would survive for centuries. These Crusader states and Byzantium had now to find ways to coexist; given that most Crusaders returned to Europe and that the amount of help required from the West was never quite forthcoming, Byzantium was ultimately the stronger partner in this context and despite the warfare and negative propaganda between them, real exchange – political, economic and cultural – did take place in the centuries that followed. The pressing problem of Bohemond and Antioch for the Byzantines found a first solution in 1107, when Bohemond launched, as his father before him, an attack against the Empire from Italy, but this time Alexios was well prepared and the campaign ended quickly in his favour. Bohemond was forced to capitulate and sign a peace treaty in which he renounced his claims over Antioch, but his death in 1111 prevented its actual transfer to Byzantine control.

Alexios' last years made it clear that the status quo was hard to change: Antioch – and therefore access to the Crusader states – was out of his reach and his efforts to extend Byzantine holdings in central Anatolia bore little fruit. In light of this he signed a peace treaty with the Seljuqs in 1115 in which the emperor agreed to evacuate the Byzantine populations of the area, probably in the hope of at least securing the safety of the coastal regions.

Despite the rhetoric of family harmony on the surface, Alexios' succession was not as smooth as intended: his son and preferred heir, John, had to fight his way to the throne against his mother, who held the reins of power during her husband's final illness. Eirene is said to have favoured her eldest child Anna and her husband, Nikephoros Bryennios, a son (or grandson) of the aristocratic rebel of the 1070s. The plots continued even after John's ascension to the throne in 1118. John, who was married to a Hungarian princess, Piroska (renamed Eirene in Constantinople), enjoyed a rather successful reign – he was fortunate enough not to have to deal with another Crusade in his lifetime – and he could build on the accomplishments of his father, extending Byzantine territories in the East. He warded off a Cuman threat in the 1120s, pushed back a Hungarian invasion in the same decade and managed to keep Serbia and Dalmatia under Byzantine control; in the 1130s he fought successfully in Anatolia both against the Danishmendids in the North and against the Armenian principalities in Cilicia and the Crusader states – Antioch above all, though he did not quite manage to retake the city. When Norman power re-emerged dynamically in the 1130s under Roger II, John made a number of preemptive alliances, the most important of which was with the German emperor Conrad III and sealed it with the engagement of the emperor's sister-in-law, Bertha, to John's youngest son, Manuel. John's policy of territorial consolidation and modest expansion was cut short by his death as a result of a hunting accident in 1143 in Cilicia (Figure 6.1).

Manuel, John's youngest surviving son, succeeded him. The emperor continued his father's policy in Syria and Cilicia with success, though without a major breakthrough. When news of the coming of the Second Crusade (1145–9), whose main goal was to recapture the county of Edessa, reached Byzantium, Manuel succeeded in excluding Roger II from taking part. Conrad III arrived in Constantinople with his army, crossed

Figure 6.1 Mosaic panel from the Gallery of the Hagia Sophia showing John II Komnenos and his wife Eirene (the Hungarian princess Piroska) flanking the Mother of God, dated to the 1120s.

over to Anatolia, suffered defeat and returned to Byzantium. Manuel organized the transfer of the Crusaders (the joint armies of the Germans and the French King) to Syria by sea, but once there, they were defeated and did not meet their goal. Militarily Byzantium was unharmed, but the failure of the Crusade was blamed on the Empire and its reluctance to offer substantial help, or to truly endorse the Crusade and what it meant for Latin Christendom.

During the Crusade Roger II raided a number of islands and coastal areas in Greece in 1147, while also abducting specialized silk weavers from Thebes and taking them back to Sicily. Manuel's alliance with Venice and Conrad III proved effective as the Normans were not able to sustain their presence in the Byzantine lands, but until Roger's death in 1154, the Norman threat continued to be a destabilizing factor. There was increased unrest in the region, with revolts in Serbia in the early 1150s (and again in the 1160s and early 1170s) and a change of emperor in Germany: Frederick Barbarossa was crowned in 1155. Manuel moved quickly to exploit Norman weakness after the change in leadership (to Roger's son, William I) and managed to capture Bari in 1155, but was unable to press on. In a complex web of political and diplomatic relations surrounding Italian affairs, Byzantium tried a number of alliances: with Venice and the papacy against Barbarossa, with Barbarossa against the Normans, then with the Normans against Barbarossa. The principle was well known: no Italian power wished one single state to dominate its affairs and so alliances switched quickly when it seemed as if the balance was tipping dangerously to one side. Ultimately however, by the 1160s it should have been clear to the Byzantines that, contrary to what they might have been hoping or expecting, no Western power was prepared to tolerate their presence in Italy.

Manuel was much more successful in the East, where his military might secured the domination of Cilician Armenia and the submission of the surviving Crusader states in the late 1150s. When he entered Antioch in triumph in 1159, he had finally accomplished what his father and grandfather had failed to achieve. There were common military efforts with Western rulers, such as the (failed) attack against the Egyptian port of Damietta in 1169. The rising star of Saladin, a former vizier and, as of 1171, ruler of Egypt, who began to seriously threaten the Crusader holdings in Syria and Palestine, however, could not be opposed.

The same decade also saw Venetian–Byzantine relations come to a head. Venice was pursuing its own interests, which often ran contrary to those of its supposed major ally despite the ever-growing grant of privileges. When Byzantium chose to spread its strategic focus by favouring Pisa and Genoa as well, Venice retaliated with violence. Manuel reacted with an astute stratagem: in 1171 all Venetian goods and assets were seized at the same time throughout the Empire, highlighting the effectiveness of the Byzantine state machinery. The Venetian reaction was strong but did not manage to reverse the situation in Manuel's lifetime.

Manuel's last years were less successful: his effort to remove the Seljuq threat to central Anatolia ended with disaster at the battle of Myriokephalon in 1176. There were heavy losses and from that point on Byzantium would not be able to check the Seljuq advance towards the coast. When Manuel died in 1180, the situation was again critical, as his designated heir, Alexios, was still a minor. The regency of Manuel's second wife Maria (daughter of the Crusader prince of Antioch), supported by one of his nephews, proved fragile and allowed another family member to ascend the throne in 1183: Andronikos Komnenos, son of Isaac, a brother and one of the major opponents of John II. Just before Andronikos entered Constantinople, a revolt broke out which resulted in the massacre of Latins in the city – at that point mostly Pisans and Genoese, as the Venetians were still reeling from Manuel's expulsion a decade earlier. Andronikos' reign began with yet more bloodshed as ultimately both the young prince Alexios and his mother were killed, while the young widowed Empress Agnes, daughter of the King of France, became Andronikos' wife. Furthermore, he tried to reverse the majority of Manuel's policies, both within the Empire and internationally, and very soon managed to squander the little support he had initially enjoyed, mostly from those who had been excluded from the Komnenian arrangement between the major aristocratic families. Neighbours and enemies of the Empire found it a suitable moment to attack: the Normans raided and captured Thessalonica in 1185, while the Hungarians helped the Serbs wrestle free from Byzantium under their new leader, Stefan Nemanja. In the same year there was a major insurrection in the capital that ended with the lynching of Andronikos, ending a century of Komnenian rule.

The two decades that followed showed that the Komnenian period and its central traits – a strong centralized state based on aristocratic alliances, alongside a clear effort to connect with and tap into the political resources of the West – was but a façade that quickly collapsed. The ruler who ascended the throne in 1185 was Isaac II Angelos (1185–95), whose grandmother had been Alexios I's youngest daughter. The affairs of the state soon took a turn for the worse. The Third Crusade (1189–92) was called after the disastrous defeat of the princes of the Crusader states in 1187 at Hattin by Saladin and the subsequent loss of Jerusalem. Led by Barbarossa, who came by land, and the English king Richard the Lionheart and the French king Philip II, who came by sea, ultimately failed to recover Jerusalem, but had a harmful effect on Byzantine affairs. Barbarossa threatened Constantinople when it emerged that Isaac had negotiated with Saladin. Constantinople was spared, and Barbarossa drowned long before he could reach the Holy Land in 1190, but diplomatically the Byzantine Empire was left isolated. This was one of the reasons why Richard captured Cyprus in 1191, then under the rule of a rebel of Komnenian descent; eventually, the kingdom of Cyprus passed into the hands of the Lusignan, the deposed kings of Jerusalem, and remained in their power until 1489.

The weakness of the Empire was apparent, and as its neighbours realized it, they rushed to emancipate themselves from its grip: this was true for both Serbia under Nemanja and Bulgaria under Kalojan. The removal and blinding of Isaac by his brother Alexios III (1195–1203), if anything, made matters worse. The son of Isaac II, Alexios IV, travelled to Italy to seek help in restoring his father's rule. He tried to lure the Pope with promises of the submission of the Byzantine Church and the return to Union and Western rulers by pledging huge sums of money. Unfortunately for Byzantium, this offer coincided with the preparations for another Crusade, a maritime enterprise directed against Egypt, perceived as the only way to break the Ayyubid stranglehold over the rest of the Crusader domains. Venice, for a lucrative price, would provide the vessels to transport the Crusade. As it turns out, the armies that gathered in Venice were not as numerous as required, nor did they dispose of the money to pay Venice. These shortcomings, Byzantine weakness and Alexios' promises, as well as the dynamics of the Crusade once it set off, produced a 'diversion' towards Constantinople. Upon the Crusaders' arrival Alexios III fled, but Alexios IV and his father Isaac were unable to meet the promises they had made. Amid the tension of having a sizeable army outside the walls, riots broke out in the city, resulting in their deaths and the proclamation of another ruler, Alexios V Doukas Mourtzouphlos, who called for resistance to the Latins. Disillusionment was great among the Crusaders and with the consent of its (mostly French) commanders and the Venetians, but without papal approval, the Crusaders carved out the Byzantine territories among themselves and after a failed attempt, managed to capture Constantinople in April 1204, laying waste to it, looting and massacring its inhabitants for days. The queen of cities that was seen as protected by the Virgin and thus impregnable was taken.

RECONFIGURING THE ECONOMY

It is remarkable how the strong Empire at the end of Basil II's reign in 1025 was brought to the verge of collapse in less than two generations; it is equally remarkable how the successful revival under the first three Komnenoi emperors could disintegrate so easily less than a generation after the death of Manuel I. Obviously there were external factors that were beyond the power of the Empire itself, but it would be imprudent not to seek some of the blame for what happened within Byzantium's own structures.

The rising demographic trend continued: there were no major epidemics, while the core regions of the Empire were fairly safe from warfare. Cities in Greece and the west coast of Anatolia continued to flourish, as did Constantinople: the construction of churches and the widespread use of more expensive, glazed tableware found in surveys and excavations throughout the Empire testify to this. On the whole this would suggest a thriving economy – and indeed this was the case in a number of its sectors. And yet the state encountered serious problems, as is evident by the constant devaluation of its coinage, which began to be noticeable from the 1040s onwards and reached its apogee in the first decade of Alexios I (1081–92): the gold content of the *nomisma* had sunk to around 2 carats and this showed in its colour which was no longer golden. It is a hotly debated issue what the causes of this debasement were; some scholars believe it was the combination of a shortage of bullion and the need to pump more money into the market economy and trade, while others think that it was a desperate effort to create more money needed to pay off enemies. Until 1071 the debasement was controlled and would support the first interpretation. After 1071, however, it became catastrophic and reflects an economy in disarray. Whatever the actual immediate cause, it is important to stress that the state had to find ways to function without the same reliance on gold.

The monetary and fiscal reforms under Alexios I (put into action between the early 1090s and 1109) halted the process and produced stability – at least for around a century. There were several types of coins, but the main currency (the *hyperpyron*) was a gold coin with a reduced gold content of around 20.5 carats (roughly the same as at the beginning of the debasement). The system of coins provided clarity in exchanges and the lower gold content made the state significant savings. Furthermore, Alexios simplified fiscal structures as well as the methods by which taxes were calculated. All this bolstered confidence in the currency and the economic system which was expected to produce a higher monetization of the economy, but there were other measures at hand that countered this trend. Alexios was equally responsible for the restructuring of the Byzantine system of honours. This much-maligned system by which high dignities (but rarely offices) could be purchased in return for an annual yield of around 10 per cent had been excessively used in the generation before him. While it had supplied the state with fast cash, allowing it to tap into the wealth reserves of individuals who were otherwise not members of the traditional elites (such as merchants and artisans), its inflationary use made the returns for the individuals constantly decline and ultimately the state was unable to pay back the investments made. Under Alexios the system was discontinued. Instead, there was a general overhaul of offices and titles, with Alexios creating some new and elaborate ones with the term *sebastos* (august) exclusively for members of his family. For example, his brother Isaac was named *sebastokrator*, *sebastos* and *autokrator* (emperor), which was the highest of these titles. The bearers of such titles now formed the top echelon of Byzantine society, a kind of uber-aristocracy and they were also rewarded with extensive grants and concessions of lands. This was facilitated by large-scale confiscations subsumed under the principle of *epibole*, according to which if an owner was found with more land than the tax he paid entitled him to, the excessive land was confiscated. This freed up land that was redistributed to kin and allies. Alexios, who was later criticized for running the Empire as his own household, was perhaps signalling in this way that it was more profitable to join this inner circle, rather than oppose it. It is telling, in any case, that the reigns of the first three Komnenian emperors were relatively free of the political uprisings which had been endemic from the tenth century onwards, while any challenges came from members of the Komnenian family itself. It is also noteworthy that all subsequent Byzantine emperors until 1453 were descended from Alexios by blood or marriage.

The Komnenian era may seem to stand at the beginning of the important late Byzantine trend towards more and substantial donations, grants and exemptions, but this is undoubtedly also a result of the increasing availability of documentary sources from this period. Those closest to the emperor, obviously, attracted the greatest gains: entire regions and their fiscal revenues were given as concessions and were often accompanied by generous tax exemptions. Major monasteries were endowed in similar ways as well. But more modest individuals did also profit from the state. This period marks the beginning of *pronoia*, the concession of fiscal revenues to individuals in return for service – often military – for the duration of the recipients' lifetime. This system meant that the state did not have to move money around – extracting it in taxes to distribute it in salaries and thus withdrawing money from circulation – but that large segments of the economy were taken out of this equation. One side effect – and it is debatable how much this was intended or not – was that there was more money freed for the market and its economic transactions. The state could and did profit from this through custom duties and taxes on transactions. But the major winners, especially in the long term, were not Byzantine merchants, but Italian ones, Venetian above all. Venice had received important concessions in 992, and even more favourable ones under Alexios (see above). Venetian merchants settled in various parts of the Empire and contributed considerably to the economic boom of the countryside both by stimulating demand from local producers and by making significant investments for the production of various commodities – this is attested, for example, in Cyprus and Lakonia in the Peloponnese in the twelfth century, from where Venetian agents agreed the price for olive oil in advance with local magnates and then exported it to Alexandria. The state lost revenues (although it charged those trading with Venetians the full amount of duties in an effort to get around the privileges they had conferred), but many landowners made good profits from this connection. Other Italian maritime city states (such as Pisa and Genoa) lobbied and often received such privileges as well (the former in 1111, the latter in 1155) – though never at the level of the Venetian freedom from taxes – but Venice itself began to aggressively seek first to confirm and then to expand its privileges, at times with the threat or use of violence. Ultimately, Byzantium always conceded, and the Venetian privileges were confirmed in 1126, 1147, 1187, 1189 and 1198 – until in 1204 Venice became one of the conquerors of the Empire.

BREAKING AWAY FROM THE CENTRE

The Komnenian system was effective under the strong and dynamic leadership of the first three emperors. The economy was flourishing, since the accumulation of land and the creation of huge estates encouraged productivity, not least because of the ability of wealthy landowners to invest in infrastructure and to create new outlets for the surplus they produced. Despite the actual debasement of the coinage, prices remained stable. But there were downsides as well. The state since at least the 1060s increasingly made use of tax farming, that is determining the amount of tax revenue requested from a specific region and assigning the task to collect it to private individuals. The basic land tax was fixed, but secondary taxes and instances of imposed labour were not and this obviously opened the way to corruption, especially during the troubled period of the Angeloi. Furthermore, the growth of regional economies and the great demands of Constantinople as the major centre of consumption that it placed upon them in the form, for example, of heavy taxation, fanned resentment.

After the death of Manuel I in 1180 the dynamic and often heavy-handed and centralized exercise of power by the imperial centre on the provinces was disturbed: emperors with a weaker claim to the throne either attempted to wrest back control or allowed provincial magnates free rein; in both cases it created a backlash. The military administration of the Empire into *themata* had more or less lapsed by the twelfth century, thus removing another factor by which the periphery was tied to the centre (through the *strategoi* and administrators of each *thema* appointed by Constantinople). This role was taken up in some instances by bishops, often educated Constantinopolitans with an elite background, tied to the patriarchate and thus operating within networks of power and patronage linked to the capital. The dynamic emergence of a class of local elites (the *archontes*) in provincial cities – sometimes with ties to Constantinopolitan families – was another characteristic trait of this period and the strengthening of regional identities as a result of economic and social ascent may also have encouraged centrifugal trends. All these reasons gave rise to a significant number of rebellions in the provinces. By 1204 large areas in various parts of the Empire were no longer under the direct rule of the emperors at Constantinople: it will suffice to mention here the creation of lordships in Cyprus (Isaac Komnenos), Trebizond (David Komnenos), Philadelphia (Theodore Mangaphas), Rhodes (Leo Gabalas), and central Greece and Peloponnese (Leo Sgouros). While some of these may have aimed at usurping the throne (as emphasized by the minting of coins in their name), others represent a new phenomenon in Byzantine history. In contrast to the aristocratic rebellions of the tenth century that did not strive to change the political system, but rather wished to place themselves at its centre, these late twelfth-century provincial revolts aimed to carve out independent lordships. Some scholars have seen in these rebellions a Western influence of decentralized rule with the presence of an (often) symbolic centre. This was coupled with the simultaneous eruption of a number of emancipatory moves from hitherto Byzantine-dominated states in the periphery (like Serbia and Bulgaria or Cilician Armenia), and the resurgence of regional enemies (Hungary, for example, which rushed to seize Dalmatia after Manuel's death). Although the reasons for these actions were not the same as the internal Byzantine rebellions, the result was the loss of additional territories and power.

BETWEEN REPRESSION AND HUMANISM

The cultural history of the period has often been framed by the dynamics between the two, seemingly contradictory aspects of repression and Humanism. The relaxation of the constant war footing after Basil II and the weaker state that followed – especially during the period from the 1050s to the late 1070s – enabled a relative opening in social and cultural affairs: there were translations from Arabic, for example, and less agitation over heresies. Education was fostered and the result was a new generation of scholars who began to dominate cultural matters from the late 1040s onwards. The most famous of these was Michael Psellos, undeniably the most talented of Byzantine authors, but equally a highly successful statesman, whose achievements in life were based on his education, talent and remarkable skills of networking. Psellos is best known to a wider audience as the author of work of history, the *Chronographia*, although it does injustice to his ambition to perceive this merely as history: it is a collection of imperial biographies that pays little attention to dates or battles, but instead produces fine and insightful psychological portraits of its protagonists connected with (at times) a none-too-subtle critique not just of imperial persons but of the constitution of monarchy as such. Psellos left hardly a field of knowledge unexplored and his vast body of work is a testimony to his genius. Among his many interests was philosophy – especially the writings of Plato – and his efforts to transcend the traditional Byzantine ways of reading ancient texts (seen as useful and admirable, but potentially also as dangerous and subversive) brought him into conflict with the church establishment and may have contributed to his temporary fall from grace.

The ascent of the Komnenoi placed emphasis on a very different range of cultural values: piety (initially of the monastic persuasion), purity and orthodoxy of faith, nobility of lineage and military ardour were now favoured, and this represented a closing of horizons. Alexios set new accents on the emperor's role as protector of the Christian faith. It was the beginning of show trials against heresy – there would be almost thirty in this period. The first one took place in 1082 against John Italos, a pupil of Psellos, and perhaps a more daring (and less subtle) Platonist, who was condemned as a heretic, exiled and was never heard of again. It is remarkable that the Synodikon of Orthodoxy (see Chapter 4) was updated to include him. The Synodikon would be updated four more times in the Komnenian period to condemn to eternal damnation those that challenged the official orthodoxy. Later in his reign Alexios brought the Bogomils in Constantinople under his control. This dualist sect from the Balkans, which may be linked to previous sects as the Paulicians in Asia Minor (many of which had been transplanted to the Balkans in the 870s, see Chapter 4), and to contemporary and later Western dualists such as the Cathars in France, had become quite popular and therefore dangerous, as it rejected the sacraments and the institutional church. The leader of the Bogomils in Constantinople, Basil, was caught after confessing through a ruse and was publicly burned at the Hippodrome in 1100. Some years later Alexios issued an edict with which he proceeded to reform the clergy – and through it society at large. At this stage in his life he had weakened his ties to monastic leaders – seen as characteristic of the early phase of his reign, still under the dominant gaze of his very pious mother – and had created an alliance with the clergy of the patriarchate: young, educated and ambitious clergymen, who would side with the emperor against any opposition, including that coming from the patriarch himself or provincial bishops. The edict emphasized correct preaching and instigated an order of preachers, who would spread orthodoxy, but also monitor and report any dissent – a moral thought police of sorts. The Church did not always favour this tight embrace of the Komnenian emperors. Disagreement was voiced – for example, against Alexios' seizure of church plate in the 1080s – and several patriarchs tried to oppose the emperor's will, but overall they were pressured into conforming or resigning – this was not a period that produced any particularly strong or vocal patriarchs such as Photios, Nicholas Mystikos or Michael Keroularios in the past (see Chapters 4 and 5).

The Komnenian emperors did support education – perhaps with a particular emphasis on scripture. The court and elites sponsored many scholars (such as Theodore Prodromos) and commissioned works – especially rhetoric and poetry, both performed in public, the former often written to praise the exalted emperors and their kin, especially their prowess in war, the latter also adorning precious objects and other works of art. Literati performed their works publicly in gatherings and salons (the *theatra*) and competed with one another for patronage. The study of Antiquity continued to flourish and this period produced a number of texts that took up and reworked ancient genres such as satires or romances, some of them written in vernacular, rather than the preferred archaizing Greek. Furthermore, there was experimentation with form, producing works mixing prose and verse. Fresh though they may appear, however, these works are on the whole not characterized by the openness of their ideas. The Komnenian period produced, however, at least two particularly accomplished historians. The first, Anna Komnene, was Alexios I's daughter, a highly educated lady who did not wear her learning lightly. She was interested in medicine and Aristotelian philosophy and was an important patron of scholars. She produced an epic history of her father's reign (the *Alexiad*, purposefully evoking Homer's *Iliad*) with a special emphasis on his dealings with the First Crusade. The second, Niketas Choniates, brother of the Archbishop of Athens and a high court official, wrote a commanding history of the twelfth century with particular emphasis on the disaster of 1204. In fact, we now know that he revisited and edited his work a number of times and the trauma of Constantinople's sack made him go back and apportion blame to those he thought had led the Empire to this disaster – Manuel I, above all.

The silencing of Italos did not mean that philosophy was abandoned, although there was a marked turn towards the study of Aristotle, much less transcendental and potentially subversive than Plato. Since Aristotle had also written numerous books on natural history, it is not surprising to see that increased study of his works prompted an appreciation of the natural world in general and of human nature in particular. This is manifested in a clearly discernible trend for detailed descriptions in literature, both of animate and inanimate beings and in a renewed interest in medicine. Perhaps this deep interest in what it meant to be human is what makes Komnenian art and spirituality place such emphasis on provoking emotional responses through images and texts (Figure 6.2).

The defensive orthodoxy of the Komnenians obviously defined itself by contrast to the Other, which in this period was predominately Latin Christianity. East and West had been coming closer – not least as a result of the Crusades – but proximity did not engender a better understanding. The period produced over thirty works of anti-Latin theology and though one can detect that the Byzantine theologians were becoming more aware of the Latin positions and refined their arguments accordingly, the general

Figure 6.2 Wall painting of the Lamentation, St. Panteleimon, Nerezi (North Macedonia) dated to 1164. The image produces a profound emotional response, characteristic of Komnenian art.

attitude towards the West was one of superiority and defiance. This was no longer justified, as the twelfth-century cultural renaissance in Western Europe had produced works that surpassed the mere synthesis of the past and were moving into new, elaborate and exciting creations of their own – no comparable movement occurred in Byzantium.

Visitors in Constantinople before 1204 would marvel at its wealth, which projected the power and authority of its emperors. The splendid appearance of the city in this period owed a lot to the continuing trend towards massive monastic complexes, often with adjacent charitable institutions and designated aristocratic burial places. Alexios, his mother, wife, sons and grandsons were all active as founders in Constantinople. Their monasteries privileged the western part of the city facing the Golden Horn (see Map 5). Two institutions deserve special mention. The first was the Orphanage of Saint Paul on the Acropolis (today the site of the Topkapı palace), restored and enlarged by Alexios I, a city within the city, as Anna describes it, in which orphans, but also other needy and poor individuals were cared for. The second, the monastery

Figure 6.3 View from the west of the three churches of the Pantokrator monastery in Constantinople built by John II Komnenos between the 1120s and early 1130s. It served as an imperial mausoleum in the twelfth century.

of Pantokrator, founded by John II and his wife in the 1130s, combined three monastic churches (still extant today), one of which functioned as a mausoleum for the imperial family, with the most specialized and medicalized hospital that the Middle Ages produced, as well as an old person's home and a leper's asylum (Figure 6.3). These buildings do not survive, but we have ample evidence about them in the foundation document (Typikon) of Pantokrator.

The allure of Constantinople translated from the late eleventh through the twelfth and thirteenth centuries into a craze for Byzantium. From Sicily (the Capella Palatina, and the Martorana in Palermo and the cathedrals at Cefalù and Monreale) to Venice (San Marco), Kiev and Novgorod (both with cathedrals dedicated to Hagia Sophia, as in Constantinople), but also as far north as Iceland and Sweden, important churches were decorated with mosaics (and to a lesser extent, frescoes) that drew upon Byzantine models. It is not crucial whether these mosaics were executed by craftsmen trained in Byzantium, as has been assumed in many cases; the most important aspect is the radiance of the Empire among both allies and enemies. It is ironic that some of these churches are now used to reconstruct the design and splendour of Constantinopolitan monuments which inspired them but have since vanished.

7

THE LEGACY OF FRAGMENTATION, 1204–1341

The conquest and sack of Constantinople in April 1204 was a defining moment in the history of Byzantium. Even though the city was recaptured in 1261, there were lasting changes on the ground that would define the history of the region in political, economic, demographic and cultural terms well beyond the Middle Ages.

Tracking the boundaries of Byzantium becomes a difficult enterprise after 1204 as its area fragmented into over a dozen states and statelets. We can divide them into two broad categories: states headed by Latins, mostly French and Italians who took part in the Fourth Crusade, and those carved out and governed by Byzantines, who drew their legitimacy through their ties to the past imperial dynasties. The aims of these states naturally differed; while all of them attempted to consolidate and expand their territories, the Greek successor states' main aim was the recapture of Constantinople.

With hindsight Nicaea deserves to be treated first, as it was from this state that the capital was regained. Its first leader, Theodore I Laskaris, a son-in-law of Alexios III, had fled to Asia Minor in 1203 and rallied resistance against the Latins in the region of Nicaea. A new patriarch was elected in Nicaea in 1207 and crowned Theodore emperor; his court attracted a number of exiled members of the Constantinopolitan elite. Theodore gradually defeated a number of local Greek lords, who had established quasi-independent lordships in Anatolia but allowed them to govern them in his name. His reign saw the consolidation and expansion of Nicaean territory despite occasional setbacks. Furthermore, it marked the beginning of approaches to the papacy with the aim of Church Union, often with Franciscan friars acting as intermediaries. The reasons were manifold: the protection of Orthodox populations under Latin rule, the need for alliances and genuine theological concerns over the rift in the Universal Church. In 1222, Theodore was succeeded by his son-in-law, John III Vatatzes, who was to rule until 1254. Under Vatatzes, Nicaean troops managed to drive the Latins from Anatolia, gain a foothold in Thrace in 1235, besiege Constantinople (in 1235 and 1236) and capture Thessalonica (1246) as well as extensive areas of Macedonia. John was succeeded by his son, Theodore II.

The second-most important of the Greek successor states was Epiros. Its first ruler was Michael I Komnenos Doukas, a cousin of Isaac II and Alexios III Angelos. After initially serving in the army of Boniface of Montferrat (see below), he fled to Arta and from there carved an independent state in north-western Greece after 1205. Initially as a vassal and ally of the Latin emperor of Constantinople, Michael I went on to conquer territories in north-eastern Greece and Corfu until his death in 1215. He was succeeded by his brother Theodore, who continued the expansion of Epiros, landing his greatest coups in 1217, when he captured Peter of Courtenay, the designated and crowned emperor of Constantinople, and in 1224 when he seized Thessalonica and was crowned emperor by the archbishop of Ochrid (since the patriarch at Nicaea and other Greek bishops refused to comply). Epiros seemed then a serious contender for the recapture of Constantinople, but its hopes were dashed after a crushing defeat by the Bulgarian king John Asen in 1230. Theodore was blinded and Epirote holdings in Macedonia and Thrace collapsed. His nephew, Michael II, emerged as the new leader and was partially successful in recapturing territories and cities lost to Nicaea in Greece.

The third of the Greek successor states was the Empire of Trebizond, set up in 1204 with the help of the Georgian Queen Tamar by Alexios and David Komnenos, grandsons of Andronikos I. Located on the south-eastern coast of the Black Sea and protected at its rear by the Pontic Alps, it was somewhat isolated from Constantinople. Its role in the political developments of the era became quite marginal when, upon David's death in 1212, the ruler of Nicaea annexed Paphlagonia and thus deprived Trebizond of its access to Constantinople. This relative isolation, however, also had a positive effect: Trebizond enjoyed a fairly stable political existence and profited from lively exchange with Georgia and the Seljuq states in Anatolia. After 1258 Trebizond became the Western endpoint of the Silk Road and therefore experienced a flourishing in commercial activities. It outlived the Byzantine Empire by some years and was conquered by the Ottomans in 1461.

On the other side of the linguistic and religious divide were a number of Latin states. Precedence must be given to the Empire of Constantinople, established immediately after the sack of the city. Baldwin I of Flanders was its first emperor, crowned in Hagia Sophia in May 1204. He obtained one-quarter of the Byzantine Empire, comprising Constantinople and its hinterland in Thrace and extensive holdings in Anatolia and some Aegean islands. The rest was divided equally between Venice and the other crusading lords, that is, three-eighths for each party. With the exception of Constantinople, these were rights on paper as the areas needed to be conquered first. Baldwin may have been the suzerain of a number of vassal lords, but the actual control that his state was able to exert was limited. The Latin Empire enjoyed some initial success in capturing territories in Greece and Anatolia but was quickly overshadowed by the expansion of Nicaea and Epiros. After about 1235 the Empire consisted only of the city of Constantinople itself and was in constant demographic and economic hardship. This prompted its rulers to seek aid from the West, which, however, never materialized in any substantial way. Baldwin II (1237–61) had to pledge his county of Namur and later his son Philip to Venice as surety to obtain financial help.

Boniface of Montferrat, who as leader of the Crusade had expected to be crowned emperor, had to content himself with Thessalonica, whose inhabitants welcomed him as king in the summer of 1204. He extended his holdings by capturing large parts of central Greece, including Athens and the island of Euboia, which he handed out as fiefs to the Burgundian Othon de la Roche and James of Avesnes, respectively, but died in 1207 during warfare against Bulgaria. The troubled period that followed ended with the capture of Thessalonica by Epirote forces, and this also spelled the end of the kingdom.

De la Roche controlled large parts of central Greece, conquered without any serious resistance; his state was later termed the Duchy of Athens, although the official residence of the rulers was at nearby Thebes. He also received lordships in the Peloponnese that he had helped capture. He abdicated in 1225 in favour of his nephew Guy. The state remained in the hands of the de la Roche family until 1308, its holdings expanding at times to the North as well as to the Peloponnese. Euboia, called Negroponte in Latin sources, passed to three Lombard lords in 1205. Venice, for which the island was an important strategic point, kept a presence in the capital Chalkis (likewise called Negroponte).

Perhaps the most important of the Latin states in Greece was the principality of Achaia or Morea, largely encompassing the Peloponnese, conquered from the summer of 1204 onwards, initially by Guillaume I de Champlitte and Geoffrey I Villehardouin (but governed solely by the latter after 1209 until his death in 1228). Again, the conquest met with little serious resistance and often with the collaboration of local *archontes*. Geoffrey's heirs continued to rule the principality until 1278. The state was divided into twelve fiefs and was regarded by the Pope 'like a new France'. The principality was defended by a chain of castles in which, for security reasons, the Franks who were always in the minority preferred to reside.

Certainly, the most lasting of the Latin states in the region was that established by Venice, although it did not occupy a continuous territory, but rather comprised a multitude of places connected through political, economic and administrative links to the motherland. Venice obtained a confirmation of its existing trading posts in the East and a number of new possessions that were meant to secure its grip on long-distance trade. Apart from three-eighths of Constantinople (and the right to elect a Venetian as patriarch), Venice received Adrianople, western Greece from Dyrrachium (in Albania) to Lepanto (Naupaktos, in Greece) together with the Ionian islands, a part of Negroponte, the western coast of the Peloponnese down to the important ports of Modon and Coron and some other islands. Furthermore, Venice purchased Crete from Boniface of Montferrat – a strategic coup meant to further exclude its archrival, Genoa, from any participation in the region's trade. Crete had to be conquered and colonized first, but the investment paid off handsomely as Crete remained in Venetian hands until 1669, long after all the Latin states and Byzantium had succumbed to the Ottomans. In the Aegean some Venetian notables, the most prominent of whom was Marco Sanudo, the doge's nephew, captured several islands from the 1210s onwards and established states, for example, Sanudo's Duchy of the Archipelago with its capital at Naxos.

The once centralized Empire was now fragmented into a mosaic of smaller polities. Further parts were carved out by neighbours who took advantage of the turbulent times, especially Bulgaria, which conquered parts of Macedonia and Thrace, especially during the reign of the Tsar John Asen II (1218–41) and Serbia, which proclaimed and defended its independence. In Anatolia the Seljuqs, while successful in capturing lands from the Empire of Trebizond, did not pose a real threat to Nicaea, perhaps as a result of infighting between various contenders to the sultanate. The Mongols only peripherally affected political developments in the area: from the late 1230s onwards they conquered the Kievan Rus, invaded Hungary and made the Bulgarian tsars, some Seljuq emirs as well as Georgia and parts of Armenia their vassals.

The profusion of states with often-conflicting outlooks in the area brought about a voluble configuration of power and shifting alliances at dizzying speed. All the above states were at some point connected through military alliances and marriages but the fight for domination meant that conflicts played out not only between Latin and Greek states, but also between the Greek states themselves. The fierce competition between Nicaea and Epiros expressed both as military conflict and ideological contest for the right to be perceived as the genuine Byzantine Empire allowed the weak Latin Empire of Constantinople to survive until 1261.

THE ASCENT OF THE PALAIOLOGOI

The dynamic balance of power in the region began to shift in 1258. In that year, Theodore II died leaving a seven-year-old son, John IV, as his heir under a regency headed by his most trusted officials, the Mouzalon brothers. These were 'new men' who did not stem from the high aristocracy, which resented them strongly. Shortly after the emperor's funeral they were slaughtered during a coup led by Michael Palaiologos, the son of the Nicaean governor of Thessalonica and a man with blood ties to the Komnenian dynasty. As the supreme commander of the Latin mercenary troops, he quickly established himself as the new power at court, first as guardian of the young heir, and shortly thereafter as Emperor Michael VIII. In the following year, Michael's army inflicted a crushing defeat at the battle of Pelagonia (Macedonia) on a coalition made up of Morea, Epiros, Athens and Sicily. Many knights were killed and William II of Morea was taken prisoner. He was later ransomed by surrendering some key fortresses in the Peloponnese such as Monemvasia, Mystras and Maina, which kick-started the systematic efforts of Byzantium to regain control of the region. As for Epiros, from that period on the state would abandon plans of expansion into Macedonia and Thrace and retreat back to Epiros and Thessaly, increasingly governed as two distinct, but loosely connected states that resembled those of their Frankish neighbours.

The goal of recapturing Constantinople from the Latins now seemed possible. In 1261, to neutralize Venetian naval supremacy, Michael signed the Treaty of Nymphaion with Genoa, conferring privileges previously granted to Venice – including a permanent base in Constantinople – to its rival in exchange for naval support. But this would not be needed after all: alerted by sympathizing Greek inhabitants of Constantinople that the Venetian fleet was away, a Nicaean general took the city with very little resistance in late July 1261. The members of the court fled, but the Latin population, which included numerous offspring of mixed marriages, the Gasmouloi, were allowed to stay on, unharmed. Michael only entered his regained capital on 15 August 1261, on the festival of the Dormition of the Virgin, in a minutely orchestrated ceremony. The emperor walked into the city preceded by the miraculous icon of the Virgin Hodegetria, thought to have been painted by the apostle Luke from life. Shortly thereafter Michael, his wife Theodora, a grandniece of John III Vatatzes, and their young son Andronikos were crowned in Hagia Sophia.

On Christmas Day 1261 Michael had the rightful heir, John IV, blinded and thus permanently removed from succession. The emperor clearly could not have anticipated the implications of his actions: Patriarch Arsenios excommunicated him and this signalled the beginning of a conflict with important religious and political dimensions that was not to be resolved until 1310. Michael had Arsenios deposed and exiled, but the patriarch's supporters, both monks and laypeople, formed a movement that demanded the return to order and in fact antagonized Palaiologan legitimacy. The emperor had the Arsenites, as they were called, persecuted while rallying support for his reign through the large-scale offering of privileges.

Despite the official universalist claims, it was impossible to achieve the reunification of the territories lost in 1204 after two generations of Latin presence. The emperor tried to subjugate Epiros and Thessaly in vain, while his efforts to control the Aegean and especially to neutralize piracy were, by contrast, quite successful.

In his international relations Michael proved a canny political and diplomatic operator. Marriage alliances were used to establish or cement partnerships: his daughters were married to the ruling families of Bulgaria, Epiros and Trebizond, while two illegitimate daughters were married to a Mongol khan of the Golden Horde and an Ilkhanid ruler. The emperor also had to ensure that the Latin population within his domain would support him. Perhaps this is one of the reasons why he sought a rapprochement with the papacy, initiating talks about Union from 1262. This, however, backfired. If debates on the matter during the Nicaean period had not aroused any serious resistance, the opposite was the case now. Resistance to the Union, to which the already disaffected Arsenites equally lent their voice, grew in the following decades and was met with imperial persecution. In the meantime, Michael faced the most serious threat of his reign: Charles of Anjou, younger brother of the French King, Saint Louis IX, conquered Sicily in 1266 and subsequently became the overlord of the deposed Latin emperor of Constantinople. Charles declared himself ready for a Crusade to retake the city. Epiros and Morea joined the alliance, which meant that Michael could not hope to defeat the entire enemy force. To counter the threat, he pursued two different avenues: talks about Union intensified and led to its acceptance by an imperial delegation at the council of Lyon in 1274. This was meant to rob Charles of the argument that he would be launching a crusade against schismatics; the measure worked in that it bought Michael time to pursue the other avenue, covert diplomacy. The emperor incited and financed the Aragonese infiltration and subversion of Angevine (Anjou-ruled) Sicily. As Charles' war efforts intensified, so did Michael's persecution of dissent towards Union. This, however, was strong and encompassed not only common people, but also large segments of the aristocracy – including members of Michael's immediate family. The Sicilian Vespers, the bloody massacre of the French in Sicily in 1282, dashed Angevine hopes on the island. A few months later Michael died, having invested almost a decade in averting the danger from the West. The price proved extremely high, both for the state and for himself. The schism of the Arsenites and the anti-Unionist policies of the Josephites (the supporters of the Patriarch Joseph, who resigned because of his rejection of the Union) continued, state finances were in dire condition – not least because of the volume of bribes that Michael had used to build and sustain his anti-Angevine policy – while the emperor died outside the fold of the Church and was initially even denied a Christian burial.

The long reign of his son, Andronikos II (1282–1321) saw in many ways a reversal of his father's policies. Andronikos immediately repudiated the Union (which he had nevertheless supported while his father lived) and recalled all those persecuted from exile. He invested considerable effort in healing the Arsenite and Josephite schisms; the former was only officially lifted in 1310, while both leading figures were later recognized as saints. Throughout this period the dominant figure at the patriarchate of Constantinople was Athanasios I, a relentless protector of the poor from a deeply ascetic background. His policies of redistribution and rigid principles, directed primarily against the patriarchal clergy and the bishops, made him very popular with the lower socio-economic strata, but deeply resented by the elites, both within and outside the Church, which managed to have him deposed twice (in 1293 and 1309).

Michael had neglected Asia Minor, while its populations, loyal to the memory of the Laskaris, who by now were remembered as heroes, were punished by heavy taxation. Only in the last years of his reign did he try to reverse this trend. Andronikos II made a serious effort to stem the loss of these territories, but the tide could not be turned for a variety of reasons. One of Andronikos' first measures had been to disband the imperial navy and reduce the size of the army as a result for the need for savings. From this point onwards the reliance on mercenary forces grew exponentially, with often disastrous results. Furthermore, some of the initial success that Byzantine campaigns enjoyed in the region in the 1290s were undone by the combined unwillingness of local magnates to use their properties to support the troops and by rebellions of successful military commanders. Another factor was even more decisive: after the Mongols sacked Baghdad in 1258, the demise of the Seljuq sultanate of Rum was effectively complete by 1300, which led to the emergence of a number of beylics, small Turkish emirates, that sprang up in the power vacuum between Mongol and Byzantine Anatolia. Among them was that of Osman in the North-east, destined to produce the dynasty that conquered Byzantium in the following century. The coastal emirate of Aydin with its capital at Smyrna was equally dangerous to the affairs of the Aegean, in which already by the early fourteenth century effective control by the Empire had evaporated.

In the face of Turkish success in 1303 Andronikos hired the services of around 6,500 Catalan soldiers under the leadership of Roger de Flor, who was given a high title and the hand of the emperor's niece in marriage. The Catalan company was initially successful in Anatolia, but very soon began looting the properties of the Greek population in the region. When in 1305 Roger was murdered – allegedly at the instigation of the emperor – the company began to pillage Thrace (to which they had been recalled to deal with a Bulgarian invasion), moving in the following years to Macedonia and Thessaly before annihilating the forces of the Duchy of Athens in 1311 and establishing their own state in the region.

The combined effect of the influx of refugees to Constantinople fleeing Turkish invasions in Anatolia and the destruction of crops in the capital's agricultural hinterland produced shortages in the city, which were aggravated as a result of speculation and profiteering by the wealthy. The Patriarch Athanasios took an active role in the management of the crisis, setting up soup kitchens and castigating corrupt officials and their exploitation of the needy. The grim situation was only alleviated with Bulgarian grain purchased by offering territorial concessions and a marriage alliance with the imperial family in 1307. A similar arrangement had been made some years earlier to deal with the Serbian invasions and conquests in Macedonia. The Serbian *kral* (king) Milutin was given the hand of Andronikos' daughter Simonis in marriage in 1299 recognizing the conquered areas in Macedonia as her dowry; the bride was five years old, the groom about forty-six and the marriage was surrounded by the whiff of scandal.

The last years of Andronikos II's reign were particularly turbulent, characterized by heavy taxation and a climate of corruption by high government officials. In 1320 the heir to the state, Michael IX, died allegedly from grief at the implication that his son Andronikos III's men had accidentally killed his younger son, Manuel. Tensions between grandfather and grandson with the same name were exacerbated. This seemed like an unbridgeable generation gap. The younger Andronikos, surrounded by his close friend and associate John Kantakouzenos, an exceptionally wealthy man with extensive landed property, and other young members of aristocratic families, saw the older Andronikos and his trusted aid Theodore Metochites as men who could not rise to the challenges of their day and should not direct Byzantine affairs. On the other side, Andronikos II and his party regarded the younger emperor as immature and frivolous. The conflict quickly grew into a civil war, the first of many between members of the Palaeologoi that were to have catastrophic results for the Empire down to its last years. After a truce, which actually meant the division of the Empire into two (unequal) parts, the war flared up again in 1323, after which an uneasy peace was kept until 1327. Meanwhile, the Ottomans captured Bursa and made it their capital, some 200 kilometres away from Constantinople. The final phase of the civil war saw the younger Andronikos as victor, deposing his grandfather and sending him to live out his days in a monastery, while a new wave of confiscations and exiles (Theodore Metochites was a prominent victim) ensured that new men occupied the highest positions in the state.

During the relatively short reign of Andronikos III (1328–41) the Ottomans pursued their conquest of Byzantine holdings in Asia Minor, capturing Nicaea in 1331, Nikomedeia and Pergamon in 1336/37 and Chrysopolis (Üsküdar) in 1341. Serbia and Bulgaria formed an alliance under the Serbian kral Stephen Dušan and gradually began the conquest of northern Greece. Andronikos was more successful against Epiros, which he managed to subdue in 1337 with an army consisting largely of Turkish mercenaries from the emirate of Aydin. As various external threats were diminishing Byzantine dominions, a theological debate arose that was to divide the Empire, but also shape its spirituality and identity. This is the controversy surrounding the practice and beliefs conventionally subsumed under the term Hesychasm. The word, which derives from the Greek term *hesychia* (stillness, quiet), was not new, but had been used since Late Antiquity to characterize one of the main aspects of monastic contemplation and prayer. From the thirteenth century onwards, however, it was predominately employed in conjunction with a new emphasis on prayer and meditation with the aim of attaining visions of the divine, especially through the repeated use of the Jesus prayer ('Lord Jesus Christ, son of God, have mercy on me, a sinner'). Furthermore, this mystical practice was positioned by the theologians who supported it as being the opposite pole to the knowledge of the divine gained through intellectual activity and rational means – no doubt, although never explicitly stated, as a contrast to the dominance of the scholastic method in the Western Church, which saw the systematization of theology by the means of Aristotelian logic. The success of Hesychasm was certainly due to the support it received from monastic circles on Athos, by then a centre of undisputed moral and theological authority. Barlaam of Calabria, an exceptionally learned thinker from Italy, became a teacher of philosophy in Constantinople and around 1330 challenged the practices of Hesychasm as heretical. He roused the ire of Gregory Palamas, an Athonite monk who came from an aristocratic Constantinopolitan family and was part of a vast network of patronage as well as enjoying esteem as an Orthodox theologian. Monks had been occupying key positions in the high clergy since 1204 and this, together with the forceful defence of Orthodox practice by Palamas (and others), ensured the success of Hesychasm. Barlaam led the newly resuscitated discussions on Union with Rome (in Constantinople in 1334 and in Avignon, the seat of the popes in this period, in 1339) and in fact attacked scholastic practices while continuing to rebuke Hesychasm. In 1341 a council in Constantinople attended by Andronikos III condemned his ideas and upheld Palamas' views as orthodox. A week later, in June 1341, Andronikos III died, leaving behind him his second wife, Anna of Savoy and a nine-year-old son, John V.

VARIETIES OF SOCIAL AND ECONOMIC CONDITIONS

The political fragmentation after 1204 resulted necessarily in the coexistence of different social and economic practices. The Latin states imported social norms from their place of origin, but also adapted them to fit the local situation. For example, due to the lack of manpower and depending on the process of conquest (with or without resistance) Byzantine *archontes* were accommodated within the system. The rest of the population, however, reverted to the status of unfree individuals – in contrast to the much more variegated picture of the Byzantine countryside in the previous period – a clear trend towards a more rigidly stratified society. The number of slaves increased, a result of conquest and piracy. The mere fact of fragmentation meant an end to the more centralized practices in the area: monopolies were largely abolished while privatization and decentralization of the economy took place. Trade flourished as Venetian holdings in the Aegean were dynamically integrated within commercial networks. New towns emerged (such as Clarentza and Mystras in the Peloponnese), and a new lease of life was granted to some established centres (such as Athens, Patras, Corinth and Monemvasia). However, within this already-established system the Byzantine provinces and their produce were effectively downgraded: instead of manufacturing finished commodities, they were now largely confined to producing raw material that was exported to Italy to be turned into finished products, often to be re-imported back into the area. The Pax Mongolica, the unification of a gigantic territory from China to the Eastern Mediterranean under Mongol rule from the late 1220s onwards, facilitated trade immensely as it made it easier to negotiate agreements and obtain securities for travel. It favoured the penetration of Western commercial interests in inner Asia, while areas such as the Black Sea and the Empire of Trebizond became important points on this route.

As far as the Greek successor states are concerned, our sources mostly allow us to examine developments in Nicaea, which should not, however, be regarded as characteristic. The continuity of structures under reduced economic and political circumstances was certainly the prevalent trend, but Nicaean emperors (especially John III) did put their own accent on social and economic policies. The properties of the Crown had grown as a result of political turmoil and thus land was used to reward faithful servants. The prosperity of agrarian communities was fostered by the state and the elites were compelled to follow their example. The state was strong and exerted policies of economic protectionism: a sumptuary law of John III forbade the import of Italian textiles and seemed to have stimulated local manufacture. Autarky was praised as an ideal, as was a rigid practice of justice mostly focused against the abuse of civil servants and the socially powerful. This brought the rulers into conflict with the aristocracy, accustomed for a generation to a weaker state in which its interests prevailed. John III and, in a much more open and conflictive way, his heir Theodore II showed readiness to curtail the power of the aristocracy by raising 'new men' to important positions at court and by displaying imperial power through punitive actions directed against aristocrats (physical punishments, confiscations, forced marriages with socially inferior individuals). The aristocratic backlash was brewing for some time; it erupted after Theodore's death and brought Michael Palaiologos, a model representative of this social group to power. For the following centuries, the aristocracy was never again challenged in its grip on power as conflicts played out within this ruling elite, more often than not between members of the same family. Through frequent intermarriages – ideally with a member of the Palaiologoi – tangibly manifested in the adoption of a long chain of surnames that made one's pedigree instantly evident (e.g. Angelos Doukas Komnenos Palaiologos), the late Byzantine aristocracy was a closed group that did not care for parvenus.

Once the government returned to Constantinople in 1261, Nicaean policies were abandoned and the state reverted to its traditional centralized mode. The dissolution, however, could not be reversed. Underneath the appearance of centralized rule, authority was being, in effect, shared. Even before the Palaiologan ascent to power, but much more so after 1261, the state conferred a privileged position on a number of important cities such as Thessalonica, Berroia, Monemvasia and Ioannina. This entailed the guarantee of the free possession of land within a specific territory in and around the cities by the state; it promoted the position of urban elites, who did not belong to the highest echelons of society as seen from a Constantinopolitan point of view, but who nevertheless were wealthy and powerful enough within their own communities. In many cases this fostered a growing economic independence and a strong local identity. The state was growing weaker, while some cities and some individuals were growing richer and more powerful. A visible proof of the state's economic downturn is the constant devaluation of the coinage: from 18 carats under the Nicaean emperors to 12 carats around the middle of the fourteenth century. The distrust that such developments caused in economic transactions facilitated the gradual domination of Italian and French coinage in the region.

Relations between the state and the land it owned in the period are defined through the institution of the *pronoia*, originally exceptional, personal and not hereditary. In this period, however, the *pronoia* gradually became a regular fee, as the state found it increasingly difficult to pay its officials in cash. In some exceptional cases a mode of hereditary transmission was granted: for example, under Michael VIII some *pronoias* were granted to two generations of beneficiaries, while later, in the period of the civil war of the two Andronikoi, more and more of them were granted in perpetuity, to attract and sustain loyalties. It would be wrong, however, to assume that in this period the state lost control of this privilege altogether as there was great traffic in *pronoias*: they were in fact revoked, swapped and granted at will, suggesting that the beneficiaries were still largely at the mercy of the state. Confiscations – especially of church and monastic properties – were not uncommon in the quest to free up land for the granting of further *pronoias*.

The peasant population in the period was still expanding. In Macedonia, for which documents from the archives of Athonite monasteries provide most information, populations were growing up to the middle of the fourteenth century, despite localized setbacks – for example, as a result of Catalan raids in the early decades of the century. The tax burden also increased in the period, which suggests that the state recognized the enlarged economic output of the region. Peasant prosperity, however, was diminishing; this was a result of the demographic growth and inheritance patterns: since all children inherited their parents' property equally, land tenure was increasingly fragmented. Equally in the period the reduction in the numbers of free smallholders continued, as peasants sought protection from great landowners and sold their land to them. Especially under Andronikos II it seems that the burden from taxation was unbearable; it was also accompanied by rampant abuse and corruption by state officials and tax collectors as the state increased the widely detested practice of tax farming to ensure revenues. Prominent state officials, like the close associates of Andronikos II, Theodore Metochites and Nikephoros Choumnos, amassed great fortunes from the sale of offices, while Andronikos II was cutting spending by disbanding the fleet, suspending salaries, debasing the coinage and even imposing a tithe on all *pronoias*.

The lion's share of the state's revenues came from land (in the form of both taxation and produce), but trade became an increasingly crucial factor for the general economy in the period. Venice and Genoa above all used their privileged status to pass savings on to their trade partners, for example, by attracting significantly higher volumes of international trade through their port facilities and thus stripping the Byzantine state of potential revenue. In short, while the Italians and later some other

Western merchants fully exploited the economic and strategic position of Constantinople and other important ports, Byzantium as a state lost out. That is not to say that some Byzantines did not profit. In this period we witness the dynamic emergence of a new social group termed the *mesoi* (the middle ones), in our sources. This was an urban group – and it is important to remember that in this period the Byzantine Empire encompassed a number of populous urban centres – whose growing wealth derived from trade (especially in foodstuffs), money lending and manufacture and not, as was the case for traditional elites, from the ownership and exploitation of land. The *mesoi*, not to be confused with the *archontes*, were connected to Italian merchants as their local intermediaries or agents, and equally – unlike the West – to the landed aristocracy, whose agricultural surplus they brought to the markets. This does not mean, however, that the two groups mingled; aristocratic exclusivity was still quite rigidly adhered to. The *mesoi*, as all other social groups in Byzantium, did not develop common interests and goals, and this perhaps was one of the reasons for their swift demise in the decades that followed.

The Church – especially under patriarchs as Athanasios – became an alternative, and much more trustworthy institution than the state, invested with growing judicial powers and mounting a spirited defence of the poor and dispossessed against the demands of the fisc and the growing social and economic inequality between them and the wealthy and powerful. In addition, a group of intellectuals from Thessalonica began to write about economic activities, defending the right to private property against state interventions (confiscations, for example), or castigating those who lent money at interest (a practice that, unlike in the West, was legal in Byzantium), suggesting that economic factors began to raise concerns about the social life of the Empire.

THE EARLY PALAIOLOGAN CULTURAL REVIVAL

Cultural life after 1204 was dictated by the political geography of each region. The French knights and Venetian elites and their families settling in the former territories of the Empire, for example, imported their customs and their books and started erecting both secular and ecclesiastical buildings in the manner fashionable in the West at the time. Some few instances of Mediterranean Gothic survive today in, among other places, mainland Greece, but especially Crete and Cyprus.

In the period that followed the conquest and perhaps as a result of mixed marriages and a more permanent settlement, many of those Latins began to learn, speak and write in Greek. The period also saw the emergence of some highly interesting chronicles in the Greek vernacular, whose heroes are the Latin aristocratic settlers. In the Greek successor states, and especially in Nicaea, the priority was obviously to reconstruct, albeit with much more limited means, the cultural setting of the lost empire and primarily its capital. The Nicaean emperors fostered education, not only for the sake of prestige but also because educated young men were required for the administration. Nikephoros Blemmydes (fl. 1220–70) stands out as the most outstanding product of this era: a prolific author of both secular and theological writings and a rare autobiography, he may not have been a particularly original thinker but he influenced more than one generation of scholars as an outstanding teacher (his pupils included one of the Nicaean emperors) (Figure 7.1).

Figure 7.1 Detail of mosaic panel from the gallery of the Hagia Sophia showing Christ. The work was commissioned by Michael VIII Palaiologos as a sign of gratitude for the reconquest of Constantinople from the Latins in 1261.

It is not surprising that the strong anti-Latin feelings provoked by the sack of Constantinople had an important role in the identity formation of the exiled Byzantines. Orthodoxy, now clearly a category that was more general and more inclusive than each of the states in exile on its own, was at its heart, Latin Christendom its polar opposite and mortal enemy. Furthermore, there is an additional remarkable identity strand, though probably limited in its influence: Hellenism. Wonder and respect for the Greek achievement (visible, for example, in the ruined ancient cities in Asia Minor, in the hinterland of Nicaea) was fused with irredentist ideals and combative orthodoxy to create stirrings of proto-nationalism in the period.

Once Constantinople was retaken in 1261, the focus was initially on restoration and repair of the destroyed city. Despite being hailed as the New Constantine, Michael VIII only focused on what was absolutely essential. Nevertheless, the striking mosaic in the gallery of the Hagia Sophia stems from this period. Under his son Andronikos II building work in the capital flourished: some ten new monasteries were built and twenty-two were restored by aristocratic founders, a sizeable proportion of them women. The churches of some of these monasteries survive to this day, especially the Chora (today Kariye Camii) and the Pammakaristos (Fethiye Camii). The Chora, restored by Theodore Metochites, is seen as a masterpiece of late Byzantine style. Adorned with mosaics and costly marble revetments in the main church and frescoes in the burial chapel, it represents not just a particularly beautiful monument, but also a testament to the great wealth that was invested in producing it. It is difficult to overlook the fact that this flourishing of elite monuments was happening against a backdrop of harrowing fiscal pressure on the peasant population of the Empire. Equally remarkable monuments of the period can be found in Thessalonica (Holy Apostles, funded by the Patriarch Niphon I), and Athos (Chilandar, Vatopedi and Protaton) (Figure 7.2).

The artistic production of the period was not restricted to monumental painting and mosaics, however. Luxurious liturgical objects such as embroidered textiles, gilded icon revetments and portable icons, illuminated manuscripts and micro-mosaics were produced, chiefly in Constantinopolitan workshops and in Thessalonica. The radiance of Byzantine art is visible in the Orthodox monuments in Serbia and Bulgaria, and in the mosaics of San Marco in Venice but also – more unexpectedly – in Siennese painting of the late thirteenth century. Clearly, despite the political disintegration of the state and its growing economic

Figure 7.2 Detail of mosaic panel from the Kariye Camii (formerly the church of the Chora monastery) showing Theodore Metochites, who enlarged it and added lavish decorations in the first decades of the fourteenth century.

hardships, Byzantium was still able to produce coveted objects that were invested with imperial prestige (Figure 7.3).

The revival in the active study of Greek texts continued from Nicaea, despite the fact that Palaiologan scholars wished to suggest that the previous period had been culturally barren. A number of exceptional scholars emerged in this period; they were active in seeking out ancient texts, copying, annotating and using them to teach. Some of them could be termed gentlemen scholars with independent means; others were more dependent on imperial or elite patronage. The bulk of those scholars lived in Constantinople, but Thessalonica had an equally active cultural life. These literati were connected through networks as well as the circles of their pupils and supporters; they read – and often commented – on each other's work. They also often met at *theatra*, imperial and aristocratic literary salons. There, rhetorically ornate works were performed, written in immaculate Attic Greek, flourishing since at least the second half of the thirteenth century. Reputations were made or undone, and promising

Figure 7.3 Icon depicting Saint Demetrios, around 1300.

careers at court were secured. Both the works and their performance have long been perceived as acts of escapism by ivory tower scholars finding refuge in past glories and linguistic and stylistic mannerisms. This view has been challenged, and the scholars can now be seen as a dynamic group who lobbied through their writing for the importance of a secular education. It was a swansong of sorts, as the tide was turning against intellectual pursuits. Some of these scholars were no strangers to day-to-day politics. Thomas Magistros (fl. first half of the fourteenth century) for example, linked his comments on Aeschylus' *Persians* with the Turks who were harassing his city, Thessalonica, at the time. Furthermore, he wrote a number of orations that suggest a strong local civic identity and expressed his concerns over worldly matters such as confiscations of land. Maximos Planoudes (fl. 1260–1300) is perhaps the best known of these literati. Planoudes was a popular teacher in Constantinople and some of his pupils would continue his work, though not match his vast output. There is hardly an area of knowledge that he did not dip into, from Ptolemy's geography (whose rediscovery and dissemination he secured) to mathematics, rhetoric, grammar and poetry. One of his most singular achievements was the translation of Latin texts (philosophy, theology, poetry) for the first time since Late Antiquity. Knowledge of the West was growing, and it was no longer possible to merely dismiss the achievements of Latin Christian authors as irrelevant and barbaric, as had been the tendency in more confident eras. This knowledge extended even to the political developments in the north Italian republics: men like John Kantakouzenos and Theodore Metochites took stock of the running of Venice and Genoa, only to voice their thorough dismissal and disapproval.

8

HEADING FOR THE FALL, 1341–1453

Soon after the death of Andronikos III, in 1341, a conflict arose between two parties vying for power. The first was headed by John Kantakouzenos, the trusted friend of the deceased and the force behind his government. Kantakouzenos expected to be named as regent for the young prince as his father had already specified in 1330 when he believed himself to be dying. A front gradually emerged against Kantakouzenos, consisting of the widowed Empress Anna of Savoy, the Patriarch John Kalekas and perhaps most surprisingly, Alexios Apokaukos, the emperor's *mesazon* (highest civil official) and a man whose career and fortune was largely a result of Kantakouzenos' patronage (see Figure 8.1). This so-called regency did not seem to have any clear political agenda; its purpose was probably to retain and expand its authority away from the shadow of the all-powerful Kantakouzenos. Perhaps the memory of Michael VIII doing away with the Nicaean heir John IV alarmed them. The conflict began in late 1341 when the regency declared Kantakouzenos stripped of his offices while he was encamped at his power base in Thrace, at Didymoteichon. His supporters and relatives were arrested, his mother was imprisoned and the family property confiscated. In response Kantakouzenos was proclaimed emperor by the army under his command and the civil war began. The regency made sure that the conflict was perceived in a social light, as a fight between the high aristocracy and the interests of the lower socio-economic strata, including the increasingly wealthy but politically disenfranchised *mesoi*. Kantakouzenos enjoyed wide support among the aristocracy, the army and the high clergy and equally, through his connection to Palamas, from the Athonite monasteries. Urban populations largely supported Apokaukos. Both sides cultivated a climate that fanned the existing polarization, with grave results. The

Figure 8.1 Manuscript containing the works of Hippocrates dated to the 1330s and dedicated after 1341 to Alexios Apokaukos, who is shown here in the costume of the *megas dux*, the commander of the imperial fleet.

European provinces became theatres of war: agricultural production diminished dramatically, while troops supplied by neighbouring powers such as Serbia and the Ottomans proved almost impossible to get rid of in the long term. The climate of violence and dissension spread in the cities of the Empire on whose control both sides focused. The provinces were largely loyal to Kantakouzenos. The situation in the major cities, however, was different. First in Adrianople and then in Thessalonica aristocrats were targeted. In the latter, on the verge of the city's surrender to Kantakouzenos in 1342, a unique rebellion took place. A motley group consisting of largely common people, urban professionals (sailors and dockworkers are specifically mentioned) and even members of the aristocracy rose to keep Kantakouzenos and his supporters out. The son of Apokaukos, John, became one of the early leaders of the so-called Zealots who held the city until 1349. Aristocrats were slaughtered and their property confiscated; even monastic or church properties were used for common goals such as the strengthening of the city's defences.

As Kantakouzenos was being increasingly recognized as the true emperor, the Serbian king Stephen Dušan marched triumphantly towards the south and was crowned emperor of the Serbs and the Romans: he controlled a territory stretching from the Danube to Corinth and from the Adriatic to Kavala, near Thessalonica – the latter managed to withstand the pressure. The regency realized that there was little room for manoeuvre and invested Apokaukos with more power as the aristocratic backlash against him grew, even within Constantinople. He fell victim to this climate of violence: he was murdered in 1345, after which Kantakouzenos began his march to regain the capital, entering the city in early 1347. Some months earlier the eastern half-dome of the Hagia Sophia collapsed, spreading waves of apocalyptic frenzy; some months later the Black Death reached Constantinople on board Genoese ships from the Black Sea, wreaking havoc before spreading to Italy and from there to the whole of Europe, sparking a global demographic crisis. In Byzantium the plague would return more than ten times until the fall of Constantinople.

With Kantakouzenos' success, Palamas, who had suffered during the regency, was vindicated: councils in 1347 and 1351 reaffirmed his orthodoxy and condemned old and new opponents. He and his followers dominated important church posts for a generation: he was made archbishop of Thessalonica (but could not enter the Zealot-controlled city until 1350), while some of his disciples ascended to the patriarchal throne in Constantinople. During his short reign (1347–54) Kantakouzenos tried to construct a new fleet, but failed due to warfare between Venice and Genoa, whose relentless defence of their privileges and pursuit of their commercial and political interests – especially the lucrative access to the Black Sea – made Byzantium a frequent victim of their antagonism. During the early stage of warfare in the 1350s the Genoese managed to have the new Byzantine fleet captured or destroyed. Kantakouzenos was more successful in the Balkans, where in a number of early campaigns he managed to regain some of the territory lost to Dušan (who at the time was fighting against Hungary in the North) and to oust the Zealots from Thessalonica. Despite efforts at accommodation which included a marriage between Kantakouzenos' daughter and John

V tensions grew between the two men. The elder John gave ample reassurances to the younger emperor, but still pursued a dynastic policy by favouring his own sons. In 1349 Manuel Kantakouzenos was named despot (lord) of Morea and sent to Mystras; under his rule the state prospered until 1380. John V was given Thessalonica, but later exchanged it with Didymoteichon which up to that point had been governed by Kantakouzenos' eldest son, Matthew. Kantakouzenos' move to crown Matthew co-emperor in 1353 pressured John V into action: within a year he had taken control of Constantinople with Genoese assistance and had made Kantakouzenos abdicate and take monastic vows. As the monk Joasaph he would continue to be the grey eminence behind the scenes until his death in 1383, offering political and ideological support to the emperors who were by then all his kinsmen. As for Matthew, he was forced to officially renounce any imperial aspirations and later joined his brother and father at Mystras.

Shortly before John V's coup an earthquake had shattered the important fortress of Gallipoli; the Ottomans under Suleiman, a son of Orhan (one of whose wives was a daughter of Kantakouzenos), crossed the straits and occupied the site that was of great strategic importance, taking hostages along the way (Palamas being the most prominent among them). This establishment of an Ottoman outpost in Gallipoli is conventionally seen as the first step in their conquest of the Balkans that would be completed within roughly a century. As Ottoman power grew, Serbia's diminished: when Dušan died in 1355 his vast state quickly disintegrated into a number of feuding principalities.

The following decades made it clear that the Ottoman advance constituted the biggest danger for all the states in the Eastern Mediterranean, whether Greek, Latin or Slav. Diplomacy was the only way to deal with it as Byzantium no longer had any substantial forces under its command. Help could only be expected from the West and the role of the papacy was crucial in securing it. The question of Church Union became pertinent once more. The ultimate goal was a Crusade against the Ottomans, whose advance seemed unstoppable: Didymoteichon and Adrianople (which soon became the Ottoman capital) were captured by 1362, Plovdiv by 1363. It was at this point that a Crusade was summoned. Headed by Amadeus of Savoy (John V's cousin, on his mother's side), it included Hungarian troops and forces from Genoese Lesbos, and managed to recapture Gallipoli in 1366. It was to remain the only successful military enterprise against the Ottomans.

The Byzantine emperor travelled to Rome in 1369 and converted to the Roman faith – it was a personal act and provoked no reactions in Byzantium. John's return to Byzantium was hindered by Venice, who held him back because of his outstanding debts; he had to leave his younger son Manuel as a hostage before he was allowed to depart. His last two decades unfolded with a backdrop of continuing Ottoman conquests and family feuds. As early as 1372/3 John V became a vassal of the new Ottoman leader, Murad I. This meant not only paying a substantial tribute, but also being obliged to provide military contingents to join Ottoman armies in their campaigns. Andronikos IV, John's eldest son, was excluded from the succession at that time and rebelled against his father in tandem with an Ottoman prince. Having ruled in lieu of his father while the latter travelled abroad, he was perhaps loath to share power. The rebellion was put down, Andronikos imprisoned and his younger brother, Manuel, named co-emperor. Andronikos staged another coup against his father and brother in 1376, capturing Constantinople with Ottoman help and imprisoning them. Gallipoli was returned to the Ottomans as a reward. John and Manuel escaped in 1379 to Murad and promised better terms than Andronikos – among them the surrender of Philadelphia, the last free Christian town in Anatolia; a little later Manuel was forced to take part in the Ottoman campaign to subjugate it. The troubled family managed to come to an agreement in 1381 in which Andronikos was re-established as John's heir and was given Selymbria (in Thrace) as an appanage. Manuel took over Thessalonica in 1382 and enjoyed some small success in capturing several Macedonian towns and administering the city against mounting Ottoman pressure. The communities of Mount Athos made a pact with the Ottomans in 1386, which allowed them to keep an important part of their property. On the eve of Thessalonica's inevitable conquest in 1387 Manuel fled to Lesbos. After the fall of the city the path was opened for further Ottoman advances: Bulgaria was made a tributary state in 1388 and in 1389, after heavy losses from both sides at the battle of Kossovo, the same fate befell Serbia.

In Mystras, Manuel Kantakouzenos died in 1380 and was succeeded by his brother Matthew. A war of succession broke out between the Palaiologoi and the Kantakouzenoi: the former prevailed and established their rule in the Peloponnese with one of John V's sons, Theodore, at the helm of the state until his death in 1407. In his reign the conquest of the peninsula, regaining land from the remains of the principality of Morea, continued successfully.

Andronikos IV died in 1385, followed by his father John V in 1391. Manuel II was crowned emperor in haste, lest the new Ottoman ruler, Bayezid I (1389–1402), object. The latter conceded to this *fait accompli* but demanded a significant raise in tribute and the establishment of a Turkish quarter in the city with its own judge. Bayezid pressed on with his conquests. In the early 1390s Thessaly was conquered and Bulgaria was annexed as an Ottoman province, while Turkish forces began frequent raids against the Morea. Constantinople seemed now ready for the taking and the sultan began what was to be a long siege in 1394. To support his campaign, he built an impressive fortress, Anadolu Hisar, on the Asian side of the Bosporus. The Byzantine capital was not expected to last for long. This realization must have clearly alerted European powers to the grave danger that the conquest of Constantinople would pose, both politically and economically, threatening Western commercial interests in the Levant, although both Venice and Genoa had signed trade agreements with the Ottomans by the late 1380s. It is not surprising that a Crusade against the Ottomans was called by those rulers who felt that the loss of Byzantium as well as Bulgaria and Serbia would pave the way for the conquest of their own territories: Hungary and Wallachia. The call was answered by a contingent of Burgundian nobles headed by John de Nevers (the Fearless) and the marshal John Boucicaut; the Knights Hospitaller based in Rhodes since 1309, and Venice also sent forces. In 1396 the imposing army met Bayezid's troops near Nikopolis on the Danube and suffered a crushing defeat. The Hungarian king Sigismund escaped to Constantinople, but most of the Burgundians were captured and later ransomed for exorbitant sums. The bulk of the crusading army was massacred. Bayezid was now triumphant and returned to the siege of Constantinople. Manuel decided that the desperate situation could only be reversed through Western aid and, as his father before him, he prepared to travel personally to European courts to seek it. Reluctantly he left his nephew John VII in charge of the city, aided by John Boucicaut. He moved his family to Venetian-controlled Modon in the Peloponnese and embarked for Venice in 1400, after having sent an embassy to seek help from the grand duke of Moscow. Manuel spent more than two years in the West; he visited Venice, Padua, Milan, Paris and London and the dignified, but also somewhat exotic appearance of the Eastern emperor and his retinue provoked general sympathy, which was followed by promises of aid that were ultimately to remain empty words. It is revealing that he relied on the aid of high-ranking Hospitallers for his transactions with the Western rulers – these were relationships forged in the East with people who were acutely aware of the gravity of the situation. Byzantium was saved unexpectedly when the powerful Mongol leader Timur rushed to defend the Turkmen principalities in Anatolia that Bayezid was in the process of subduing; he inflicted a crushing defeat on the Ottomans in the battle of Ankara in 1402. The sultan himself was captured and this plunged the Ottoman state into a prolonged state of anarchy for over a decade as his sons attempted to wrestle power from one another, while local warlords in Anatolia rose against the Ottomans.

THE LAST GASP

Manuel returned to Constantinople in the same year. He was now the ruler of a disjointed, small state that encompassed Constantinople and its Thracian hinterland, a few islands in the northern Aegean and the Despotate of Morea in the Peloponnese. 'Empire' was hardly the right designation for it. The decline of Byzantium had not escaped the notice of its neighbours and allies. Around the time of Bayezid's siege of Constantinople, the grand duke of Moscow, Basil I, had claimed that Orthodox Christians had a church, but not an emperor, only to be strongly rebuked by the patriarch: 'it is impossible for Christians to have a Church and no Empire'.

Before departing from the area Timur sacked Smyrna and ejected the Knights Hospitaller, effectively ending Latin presence in Anatolia. The sons of Bayezid, Süleyman, Isa, Mehmed and Musa, competed against each other from Europe and Anatolia for dominance. Manuel initially supported Süleyman from a position of strength and acquired Thessalonica in return. He sent John VII there as a ruler with an imperial title; he died in 1408, preceded by his son Andronikos V in 1407. From this point on, power rested exclusively with Manuel II and his sons. The so-called Ottoman Interregnum ended in 1413 with the victory of Mehmed I (1413–21) over his remaining brothers. The difficult position in which all Christian states in the Mediterranean found themselves in the period must have been apparent. Manuel strengthened the Hexamilion, the protective wall in the entrance to the Peloponnese, and arranged a number of marriages for his children (with the grand dukes of Moscow, the Montferrat and the Malatesta from Italy) that were probably meant to foster protective alliances. When Mehmed I died in 1421, Byzantium yet again backed the losing contender, Mustafa. The prevailing leader Murad II did not take this kindly: already in 1422, he besieged both

Figure 8.2 Monastery of Pantanassa (Queen of All), Mystras, built in the 1420s.
North façade with clear signs of Western elements with ornamental garlands
crowned by *fleur-de-lis*.

Constantinople and Thessalonica. The former resisted successfully, but
Thessalonica's inhabitants surrendered the city to Venice in 1423, who
accepted it, somewhat reluctantly (despite it being an important port,
Venice had never made much use of it in the past); Venice would hold
on to city until 1430 when it was conquered by the Ottomans for good
(Figure 8.2).

John VIII, Manuel II's son, succeeded him in 1425. His younger
brothers were given the remaining Byzantine domains as appanages:
Constantine and Thomas the Morea (where their elder brother Theodore
was already ruling) and Demetrios Selymbria. The Despotate of Morea
extended its territory in this period, annexing the remaining Latin pockets
through military campaigns and marriages: by 1430 the whole of the
Peloponnese was Byzantine again, for the first time since 1204. In the
same year Thessalonica was captured and sacked; on the contrary, the
inhabitants of Ioannina negotiated terms of surrender to the Ottomans
and therefore managed to retain some privileges.

The notion that without outside help the Byzantine state would soon
perish must have been apparent. Such help could only come from the
West, perhaps in the form of a general Crusade. The schism in the Western

Church since 1378 had made it difficult to focus Byzantine attentions on such a project, but this changed with the ending of the rift at the Council of Constance in 1414–17. Byzantine delegates were invited to attend the council, and discussions over Union and military aid from the West resumed. The perpetual Byzantine request for an ecumenical council to debate Union had been rejected for a long time by the papacy, who failed to see the point, since in its view Union meant simply the Byzantine Church returning to the Roman fold. Now, perhaps because of the weakness of both sides, the request was granted and the council was to meet at Ferrara in 1438. The Byzantine deputation was headed by the Emperor John VIII and the Patriarch of Constantinople, Joseph. Numerous bishops and learned Byzantines made up the seven hundred strong party. Differences between Rome and Constantinople manifested themselves immediately, in terms of custom (Joseph would not agree to kiss the Pope's foot, as expected), but primarily on the theological issues they were there to discuss and resolve. After another outbreak of plague, the council moved to Florence in 1439. The endless debates took their toll; material means required to support the impoverished Byzantine delegation were exhausted and intellectual fatigue had set in. In the end Union was agreed, more or less under duress and all but one of the Byzantine delegates signed the required document. Upon their return to Constantinople, most recanted amid a general resistance to the Union, led by the emperor's brother Demetrios.

The hoped-for Crusade was preached in 1443 by Pope Eugene IV. The assembled force consisted mostly of Hungarians, Wallachians and some still independent Serbian lords, with naval support from Venice, Genoa and Burgundy. After some initial victories in Transylvania, however, the crusading army suffered a devastating defeat in 1444 near Varna, on the Bulgarian Black Sea coast. The benefit to Byzantium was nil. Ottoman raids against the remaining Byzantine holdings resumed soon after: during an expedition against the Morea in 1446, the Hexamilion was destroyed and some 60,000 people were captured and enslaved. In the following year, John VIII died and was succeeded by his brother Constantine XI, not without opposition by his remaining brothers. Constantine was to be the last Byzantine emperor and it is remarkable that he was the only one after 1261 not to have been crowned in the Hagia Sophia in Constantinople – where the anti-Unionists held on to their resistance, prompting the Unionist patriarch Gregory to flee to Rome. Constantine's brothers Demetrios and Thomas were left behind to rule the Morea. When Murad II died, he was succeeded by his young son Mehmed II in 1451, who signalled a new determination to take Constantinople. A new fortress, Rumeli Hisar, was erected on the European side of the Bosporus opposite the one built by his great-grandfather. A great number of cannons – including an unwieldy but imposing super-cannon – were positioned against the city's walls, that were not built to withstand cannon fire. To circumvent the boom that blocked the entrance to the Golden Horn, ships were transported over land from the Bosporus, behind Pera, facing the city. The defenders of Constantinople were few despite some small but welcome Western reinforcements. The massive walls of the city were impossible to defend effectively, although all able-bodied citizens helped in any way they could – for example, by carrying rubble to repair breaches in the walls. On Tuesday 29 May 1453, Constantinople was taken and the Byzantine Empire extinguished after a millennium's existence, an event whose significance was recorded in all corners of the known world.

A POOR STATE WITH RICH CITIZENS

The social and economic dimension of the civil war pitted Kantakouzenos, who represented the old aristocracy of landed wealth and noble pedigree, against Apokaukos, a shrewd operator who stood for wealth derived from tax farming and other fiscal manipulations. The discontent of the lower socio-economic classes towards wealthy aristocrats turned into class hatred, as exemplified by the regime of the Zealots in Thessalonica. It is therefore not surprising to see that the victory of Kantakouzenos had implications for this newly formed dynamic social group. Largely speaking, the *mesoi* disappear from our sources after the civil war, although this cannot mean that they also disappeared from the ground. Rather another development took place: the forceful emergence of a new group, whose activities were not entirely new, but who now began to dominate the economic life of Byzantium, the so-called aristocratic entrepreneurs.

Stemming initially from the petty aristocracy of the provinces – especially the Peloponnese, untouched by the civil wars and the Serbian conquests – these were individuals with money and networks who from the 1340s onwards came to Constantinople and invested in trade and business ventures, especially in Italian commercial enterprises. It seems as if these individuals adopted the strategies of the *mesoi* and began to invest capital, rather than hoard it. The closer we get to the fall of

Constantinople, the greater their presence becomes. Some of them became extremely wealthy, for example, Nicholas Notaras and his son Loukas, and George Goudelis, his son John and grandson Francesco Draperio. Some still held offices in the imperial government, but they also acquired Venetian and/or Genoese citizenship and held a part of their capital in Italian banks. The last century of Byzantium may have witnessed the dissolution of the state – especially its ability to manage fiscal revenues and its grip on the provinces – but for some of these aristocratic entrepreneurs it was, literally, a golden age. Income from trade was more significant for the state than had been the case previously, even if the lion's share of these profits actually went into Italian hands.

The signs of an increasingly impoverished state were visible on many levels. When Kantakouzenos was crowned at the end of the civil war, the crowns he and his wife wore were adorned with coloured glass, as the actual crown jewels had been pawned to Venice. Some few years later the Byzantine state ceased to issue gold coins – terminating a tradition that went back to the fourth century. Constantinople was bleeding population; it was now a collection of mostly decrepit, formerly grand buildings surrounded by empty spaces, its vast open cisterns turned into vegetable gardens. Its population was probably as low as it had been in another period of crisis, the late seventh and eighth centuries. Given the importance of trade, Constantinople could well have evolved into a small merchant city state in the fifteenth century, a Venice on the Bosporus. Perhaps it was the realization of such developments that prompted Manuel II to exclaim that the state no longer needed an emperor, but a manager.

The countryside, for centuries the motor of the Empire, was now in a state of disarray. As a result of the civil war of the 1340s and the first outbreak of the plague the demography of the region changed. Some non-Greek populations were present in smaller numbers (e.g. Serbians in Macedonia), while other ethnic groups began to significantly colonize the area. Chief among them were the Albanians (first in northern Greece and Epiros, gradually descending towards central Greece and the Peloponnese) and the Turks (principally settling in Thrace, in the hinterland of Constantinople, but also in Thessaly and then in the last decades before the fall of Byzantium in the Peloponnese as well). The bulk of the population, however, remained Greek. This demographic flux was not only a result of warfare. The civil war and the plague can be seen as a watershed for the prosperity of the agrarian population. The combined effects of plague-induced mortality and flight from marauding armies towards unaffected areas destroyed agricultural production in Macedonia and Thrace, while fear of pirate attacks led to the abandonment of some islands and coastal sites. Large groups of inhabitants were captured and removed from Byzantine areas in the course of military action (e.g. to Anatolia). Furthermore, in those areas that had come under Ottoman dominion the tax system was simplified and contributions were in fact reduced to almost half of that of the Byzantine system, no doubt making accommodation with and reduced resistance to the new overlords appealing.

The centralized element in the government of the state remained the official principle, but in truth political fragmentation was a reality and its implementation was actually fostered by the central government itself. In this period some of the territories that still belonged to the state were given to junior members of the dynasty as appanages to rule in an almost autonomous way. Thessalonica and Mystras were the chief junior courts, with their own elites and cultural production. In addition, the trend towards urban autonomy in various cities (best to be thought of as corporate entities represented by the local *archontes*) continued, most certainly aided by the fact that the direct link to Constantinople was broken: Thessalonica and Mystras, for example, could only be reached by ship. A number of cities negotiated their surrender (or not) to the Ottomans. Those who did (Thessalonica, Serres, Ioannina) were spared and managed to secure a relatively privileged position. Those that did not were captured by force, their citizens enslaved and removed from the cities which were settled with Turkish inhabitants – this is the case for Larissa, for example, whose Turkish population comprised more than eighty per cent according to Ottoman censuses some decades after 1453. Similar documents for the Peloponnese attest that the large Albanian population lived segregated from the Greek inhabitants in newly constructed villages.

The basic structures of Byzantine society did not change, but the gap between rich and poor had grown considerably. There were signs of tension: some wealthy Byzantines in Constantinople built fortified houses with towers, seemingly to protect themselves from the mob.

Following a trend that had already become apparent in the previous period, the Church gained even more ground as the most stable institution compared to the crumbling state. More and more property was transferred to it, in the hope of preserving some parts, as it had become evident that the Ottomans largely respected church property in the areas they conquered. The example of the Athonite monasteries makes a case in point: through accommodation with the Ottomans the major monasteries managed to hold on to a large part of their property and continued to function. Their crucial role in supporting Hesychasm established Athos as a centre of Orthodox identity, radiating from the Balkans to Russia and the Christian East. As such the community attracted sizeable donations not only from Byzantium but also from Serbia, Bulgaria and Wallachia. Those who saw the preservation of orthodoxy as the central concern of the times – more so than survival at the cost of betraying their identity – formed an opposition to the Palaiologan rapprochement with the West. The patriarchal clergy played a key part in fostering this movement as it had become clear to this group that their power and privileges would be endangered by the Union of the churches. At their opposing pole were not only emperors but also the aristocratic entrepreneurs whose economic interests lay in the West, as well as a number of influential intellectuals who converted to the Roman creed and hoped that a Western crusade could still rid Byzantium from the Ottoman menace. They were all proven wrong.

TO CHANGE OR NOT TO CHANGE

The period after the civil war and the first outbreak of the Black Death marks a particularly troubled and difficult time for Byzantine culture. Imperial patronage was no longer sufficient to sustain a significant number of scholars. Naturally there were still opportunities to be had – for example, in producing encomia of emperors and their kin – but they were much more limited. Literati are still visible in the sources, above all through networks made apparent through their extensive correspondence: more than 6,000 letters survive from the entire Palaiologan period. The meteoric rise of the aristocratic entrepreneurs and their great wealth seems to have had an impact on the traditional perception of education. Apparently, young men were no longer encouraged in the same way as before to conquer the wonders of pure Attic Greek through a long and arduous education, but instead were prompted towards business affairs. If in the previous period some of the most powerful and wealthy figures in society were renowned equally for their education and culture (Metochites, Choumnos, even Apokaukos), the learning of a Notaras or a Goudelis was obviously nothing to brag about. Another possible reason for this phenomenon was the absolute prevalence of Hesychasm, or Palamism as some of its opponents chose to see it; this signified a devaluation of secular learning and an almost exclusive focus on a mystical reading of the present and the future. This introspective vision attributed contemporary evils on human transgression but refused to assign blame to particular groups – say, the wealthy for oppressing the weak and not helping the state – as other thinkers were doing. Hesychasm, whether knowingly or not, promoted resignation and was in fact upholding the status quo. The dominant monastic ideals would push all those who opposed this vision into a hardening of attitudes, making alternatives very difficult. This is not to say that there were no distinguished intellectuals in that period or that literary production was exclusively theological. John Chortasmenos (fl. first half of the fifteenth century), for example, was a man of the Church with wide interests in geometry, astronomy, Aristotelian philosophy, rhetoric and poetry, while also being an avid collector and scribe of manuscripts.

The growing desperation provoked some extreme reactions. Some Byzantines found solace in magical practices, prompting a witch hunt from the patriarchate that uncovered a network of practitioners and sympathizers, including members of the elite as well as clergy and monks. There was movement: now that prospects at home were limited and given the constant pressure of enemy incursions, Byzantine intellectuals sought new opportunities for teaching Greek in Italy – in great demand since the mid-fourteenth century. Barlaam had been one of the first teachers of the language, and Boccaccio one of his pupils. Around 1396 the Byzantine aristocrat and diplomat Manuel Chrysoloras was invited to teach Greek in Florence. He composed a new grammar that facilitated the learning of the language and which proved very popular. This trend would become even more dominant with the scholars who attended the Council of Ferrara/Florence in 1438/39. Their learning but also their precious manuscripts full of works unseen in the West for centuries were particularly coveted. It was Plethon's (see below) lectures on Plato in Florence at the time which allegedly moved the Medici to sponsor the Platonic Academy in the city, a gathering that brought together some of the most important scholars of the Italian Renaissance. Many of those who migrated to Italy converted to the Roman Church, from the statesman and scholar Demetrios Kydones in the 1350s to Bessarion in the 1430s (see Chapter 9). They were responsible for a second wave of translations from Latin, this time with particular emphasis on theological texts and particularly the immensely influential writings of Saint Thomas Aquinas, one of the key thinkers of Scholasticism, suggesting an openness to alternative ways of understanding theology.

At the same time, Italians were flocking to Byzantium to learn Greek and to collect manuscripts. In 1423, for example, Giovanni Aurispa brought back to Italy 248 books from Constantinople. Francesco Filelfo (fl. fifteenth century) spent time in Constantinople in the 1420s, learned Greek, married an aristocratic Byzantine lady and began to work as a diplomat and later as a teacher of Greek in Italy. He wrote countless letters, including some in Greek (somewhat surprisingly, he also sent letters in Greek to fellow Italians, which suggests something about the pride and prestige of mastering the language) as well as poems (including a fairly adulatory one to Mehmed II after 1453 – his ulterior motive was to ask for the liberation of his Greek mother-in-law). Filelfo, who became an important political figure in Italy, supported Byzantine émigrés in the West – both before and after 1453, and proclaimed: 'I am entirely Greek'. Another important figure in this cultural traffic was Cyriac of Ancona (fl. first half of the fifteenth century) a merchant-turned-scholar, who learned Greek during his many trips to the East. Cyriac's letters and diaries are an exceptionally important source because he painstakingly recorded (and sometimes even sketched) the inscriptions and antique ruins that he visited – many of which are now lost. The tone of his texts is touchingly pseudo-pagan, full of nymphs and poems to pagan goddesses, but Cyriac was also a tireless lobbyist for an ecumenical council to be followed by a Crusade to rid Byzantium of the Ottomans. By the time of his death both had taken place (without the desired effect), while he did not live to see Constantinople fall to the Turks.

But there was also the flipside of the coin: those who, when faced with increasingly closer contact both with the Latin West and the Islamic Ottomans, chose to define themselves through opposition, constructing an identity on fairly narrow parameters. A major theme in late Palaiologan texts is opposition to the Other, be that Union with the Roman Church or Islam. Manuel II elaborated on an actual dialogue he had conducted with an Islamic scholar in his *Dialogue with a Persian*, and although the work is perhaps less aggressive than previous Byzantine efforts in the genre of anti-Islamic texts, the emperor argued from a position of Christian superiority. The text became quite notorious in recent years when some short passages, taken out of context, were used in 2006 in a speech by Pope Benedict XVI, prompting a spirited defence of Islam by a number of Islamic scholars, thereby making Manuel II known to a much bigger audience.

The artistic production of this period naturally followed the political, social and economic developments in Byzantium. Little remains from

Constantinople. We know of repair works in the Hagia Sophia after the damaging earthquake in the middle of the fourteenth century, but hardly any other building, secular or ecclesiastical, survives. Nevertheless, art of the highest quality, icons and precious objects, was still produced there. Byzantine objects continued to fascinate audiences in the West. Equally, in this period, Byzantines certainly had the opportunity to view Western art – both when they travelled abroad, but also in Western churches within Byzantine territories. Their sparsely recorded reactions to what we now perceive as masterpieces of Renaissance art were vague, if not outright negative. When the Byzantine delegation to Ferrara/Florence visited Venice, for example, they marvelled at the costly objects in San Marco, but could not fail to observe that the most wonderful among them had been looted from Constantinople in 1204. A member of the same delegation, Gregory, the future Unionist last patriarch of Constantinople, also remarked rather drily that he could neither recognize nor venerate images in Western churches. And yet there is evidence to suggest that Western elements were gradually penetrating the Byzantine visual universe: in the monastery of Chora in Constantinople there is one fifteenth-century fresco fragment that shows a figure sitting on a pedestal drawn with perspective, an Italian development at odds with the Byzantine depiction of space. Less surprisingly, in many of the hundreds of tiny village churches built and decorated with wall paintings on Venetian Crete, there are visual loans from the West, as seen, for example, in the iconography of sinners punished in the afterlife with gruesome punishments inflicted on the body parts and with the implements with which the sin was committed (see Figure 8.3).

Some of the most important cultural developments of this period took place in the twin court of Constantinople, at Mystras in the southern Peloponnese, not far away from the site of ancient Sparta. This fortified town, which was originally built by the Crusaders, was by the end of the thirteenth century an established independent court, ruled by younger sons of the Palaiologan dynasty. Mystras experienced a cultural flourishing in the last fifty years of Byzantium, both artistic and intellectual. The site is well preserved and is filled with both churches and secular buildings, including the palace complex of the Palaiologoi. The churches, many dating to the fifteenth century, are beautifully decorated with frescoes – mosaics and the use of polychrome marble were particularly expensive and thus mostly a thing of the past. Intellectually, the court seems to have been somewhat less restrictive than Constantinople, away from the preoccupations of the patriarchate. The most famous scholar to have lived

Figure 8.3 Wall painting of the damned punished in Hell, Hagia Paraskevi, Kitiros (Chania).

and worked there was undoubtedly George Gemistos, known as Plethon, a unique personality if ever there was one, although his approach does tap into the philosophical projects of Psellos and Italos (see Chapter 6). He had studied, among other places, at Adrianople/Edirne, the Ottoman capital at the time. His writings constitute a subversive project that offers an alternative to the pressing problems of the state and society. Plethon was unafraid to attack everything that the Palamite party had established as crucial to the survival of the state, including monasticism and its role in the life of Byzantium. He has been called the 'last of the Hellenes' for his great knowledge and spirited reconfiguration of ancient philosophy (he adopted the nickname Plethon to evoke Plato), but it would be more suitable to see him as a radical thinker whose vision about the future of Byzantium was highly original. Plethon adhered to a cultural construction of Hellenism; this led him, among other things, to produce a project for the renewal of Hellenism based on the reconfiguration of the Despotate of the Morea as a model state, right down to a detailed vision of its social, political and economic organization; needless to say, it was never put into practice, but his radical thought is currently enjoying great popularity in philosophical and political research. His last work, which remained unfinished, *The Laws*, contained such a large number of positive references to paganism that the only manuscript of the text was burned by the first patriarch of Constantinople after the fall of Byzantium. It is then perhaps fitting, that Plethon's remains were removed by one of his great admirers, Sigismondo Pandolfo Malatesta, the great warlord of Rimini and archenemy of the papacy, and placed into his burial church, the Tempio Malatestiano, where they remain to this day.

9

AFTERMATH AND AFTERLIFE

The fall of Constantinople marks the end of the Byzantine state, but not of all things Byzantine. There were still various pockets of unconquered Byzantine territories in 1453, and some Latin-controlled states whose population was predominately Byzantine. To abruptly end with 1453 cannot do justice to the long history of the Empire: both individuals and, more importantly, structures, survived well beyond that date and to pursue their fate can only help us to understand the last phase of Byzantine history and its more lasting legacy, both in the region and in the wider European context.

As a city that was taken by force, Constantinople was, in accordance with Islamic law, given over to looting – traditionally for three days. What actually happened is clouded in the highly emotional extant accounts – quite understandable given the traumatic experience of the besieged: whether the looting lasted three days or was stopped earlier by Mehmed II, the result was devastating. No doubt all those caught up in the fighting were killed, the entire civilian population was enslaved, and the material fabric of the city – especially the walls and the areas adjacent to them – suffered greatly. Immovable property belonged to the state and the sultan made clear that it should be spared. He declared Constantinople the new capital of his empire – although it would only become the official seat of government after 1460. The Hagia Sophia was named the first Friday mosque of the city and Muslim prayers were offered from it as soon as the fighting ceased.

The fate of the last Byzantine emperor is unclear. Most Greek sources record that he died fighting, providing him with a martyr's death. Some even specify that he removed his regalia so as not to be identified in death. Ottoman sources suggest that his dead body was identified and his severed head presented to the sultan. Given his prominence, it is hard to assume that he would have remained unidentified. Whatever the actual circumstances of his death, it is clear that he was not given a public burial; no site for his grave was recorded. This certainly gave rise to legends: an angel was supposed to have lifted Constantine, who was turned to marble, and to have hidden him in a cave. When God wills it, the emperor would come alive again and would free his city.

As far as the Byzantine elites are concerned, the sultan personally ransomed all surviving members of the high aristocracy, especially those that had occupied high office. Among them were the highest civil official Loukas Notaras and his sons. Notaras was assigned the task of compiling a list of aristocratic individuals and their families so that they could be reunited, as families had dispersed as a result of being captured by different Turkish soldiers and officers. For a few days it looked as if Notaras might be entrusted with governing Constantinople for the sultan. But something went awry. Some sources suggest that there were demands from the Ottoman side to which Notaras would not concede; most probably it must have seemed excessive to Ottoman elites (both Turkish and Greek; see below) to grant a person so closely associated with the old order of things such an important post. As a result, together with other adult male members of the high aristocracy, he and his two older sons and sons-in-law were all executed. His wife and his daughters were treated as slaves of the sultan and were transported to the Ottoman capital at Adrianople, while his youngest son entered the Serail and was forced to convert to Islam. Soon the laborious task of trying to ransom the surviving Notaras relatives began – at this point just the sisters, as their mother had died on the way to Adrianople. Their father had deposited substantial sums of money in Venetian and Genoese banks, but in the turmoil of the fall of the city all accounts had been frozen until the rightful heirs could be identified. Ultimately, the particularly high ransom demanded by Mehmed II for the Notaras sisters was paid and they were freed in 1456.

A partially preserved property register dating from the late 1450s suggests that large parts of Constantinople were deserted and ruined. The city needed to be turned back into a functional urban centre; furthermore, the former Byzantine populations needed to be integrated into the new empire. To repopulate the city Mehmed II attracted people with privileges (not dissimilar to the tactic that Constantine I had followed in the fourth century) which included tax remissions. He also compelled refugees to return to the city and guaranteed them residences

– though not necessarily those that had belonged to them originally. These privileged conditions were valid for the first twenty years or so after the fall of Byzantium.

The population of the city was also augmented through compulsory re-settlement (*sürgün*) of inhabitants from Greece and Anatolia: the sources record between 5,000 and 8,000 families that were settled in Constantinople. By the end of Mehmed's rule in 1481, Constantinople had become the largest city in the Ottoman Empire (with a population of around 60,000–70,000); its numbers swelled again after 1492, when it welcomed Jews expelled from Spain, bringing in some 36,000 new citizens. The sultan's main plan was to (re)create an urban environment and to furnish it with the appropriate population. His building programme reflects this: after 1459 he commissioned a new palace complex at the centre of the city at the Forum Tauri (now the Old Serail), his own mosque complex (the Fatih, on the site of Constantine's Holy Apostles, the demolished imperial mausoleum), a covered market (today's Cevahir Bedestan, the oldest part of the Grand Bazaar) as well as roads, bridges, baths and aqueducts, and of course, the repair of the walls and the refortification of the Golden Gate area into a star-shaped citadel, the first in Europe. In addition, Ottoman elites were encouraged to undertake building projects in Constantinople, gradually transforming the city into an Ottoman imperial residence. This early phase was characterized by new building projects and repairs to the city's infrastructure. The conversion of churches and monasteries into mosques – with the exception of the Hagia Sophia – dates to the period after Mehmed's rule. The city's population was mixed, but the Ottoman element was predominant (Figure 9.1).

The year 1453 constituted a watershed date for the Ottoman state too. Owning *the* City (as Constantinople was known) brought home to Mehmed the lessons of Byzantium, which he aimed to surpass. It marked the beginning of a decisive turn towards a centralized state in which the interests and the power of the elites that had spearheaded Ottoman expansion – like the ghazi warlords of the borders – were marginalized and subsumed under the emperor's absolute majesty. The new mosque at Eyüp makes this clear. Built outside the city, on the site of the supposed tomb of a companion of the prophet Muhammad, it was the first new mosque of Constantinople and it marked the reluctance of the old elites to have anything to do with the city itself – Constantinople was supposed to be conquered, looted and abandoned. But for the sultan, Constantinople functioned as both the medium and the message of his new vision for

Figure 9.1 View of the interior of the Hagia Sophia from the Gallery. Three of the six Ottoman medallions can be seen which bear the name of God, Muhammad and the first four caliphs in calligraphic script.

the state. His new elites were to be recruited and effectively created from the ranks of the sultan's slaves; they would thus owe everything to him and their loyalty would be guaranteed. The new state was based on Byzantine, Islamic, Turkish and Iranian traditions.

While Constantinople was being repopulated and transformed, the sultan set out to consolidate his domain. Within two decades of 1453 most of the remaining free pockets of either Byzantine or Latin rule in the area were brought under Ottoman control: Athens in 1456, Serbia in 1459, Mystras in 1460, Trebizond in 1461, Mytilene in 1462, Negroponte in 1470 and Caffa in 1475.

With the Ottomans in power, the Italian republics suffered a dramatic shrinking of the privileged position they had enjoyed under Byzantine rule. All Italian activity in Constantinople was transferred across the water to Galata/Pera, and despite some initial agreements (a treaty with the Genoese, for example, was signed one day after the sack of Constantinople), Venetian and Genoese presence in the area declined. The particularly lucrative role of Genoa in the Black Sea trade dwindled by the end of the century, while Venice fared better in the long run, remaining an important commercial ally of the Ottomans into the seventeenth century despite suffering a number of periodic setbacks. From the mid-1350s to roughly 1500 the fragmentation of political space that had characterized the late Byzantine period was reversed and once more one single power unified the area under its control. This had important repercussions for the fate of some key Byzantine institutions.

Looking for survivors and survivals of the old Byzantine order in this new state, it quickly becomes apparent that there were two main areas in which these were particularly discernible: the Church and the Constantinople-based Greek elites. The two were quite closely connected. As Constantinople already had been an isolated island of Byzantine rule within the Ottoman state for more than fifty years before its fall, the option of cooperating with the new masters had been available to individuals and institutions from the former Byzantine world from at least the last years of the fourteenth century. Submission and accommodation meant holding on to privileges and property (as had been the case with various monasteries and cities) and even offered opportunities for marked social and economic advancement. Immediately after the sack of Constantinople a number of wealthy and powerful individuals emerged on the scene: some belonged to well-known families, others were clearly new. These were individuals who took advantage of the newly established imperial state to invest capital into commercial enterprises. This capital must have existed before the fall, but the turbulent political conditions and also the unchecked competition of Italian merchants had made them reluctant to use it. Now they could flourish, no doubt taking advantage of their knowledge of structures and modes of transactions that must have made them appealing in the eyes of their new lords. Tax farming, the administration of state monopolies (salt, for example) and tolls, provided such individuals with wealth and connections. Some of them were related to prominent converts with power at court, such as the later grand vizier Mesih Ali Pasha, whose father bore the name of Palaiologos. In the first decades after the fall of Constantinople there was no shortage of individuals with family names like Kantakouzenos or Palaiologos in prominent positions. Their ranks increased in the same period as more and more wealthy Constantinopolitans managed to ransom themselves into freedom and return home. In addition, elites from the newly conquered areas (Morea and Trebizond) flocked to the city and attempted to reactivate or recreate their networks of authority. It was from such early winners in the new political situation that the idea was suggested to Mehmed that re-establishing the patriarchate of Constantinople would prove an important motivation for Greek populations to settle once more in the city. Some six months after the conquest, Gennadios Scholarios, a monk who had been the leader of the anti-Unionist faction, was ransomed by the sultan (making him, in a way, his lifelong client); he was chosen by him as the new patriarch only to be duly confirmed by the assembly of the bishops. The sultan conferred certain privileges on the person of the patriarch – not to the patriarchate as an institution, as such a corporate identity was unknown in Ottoman law. Gennadios found himself entrusted with administrative and legal rights over the Orthodox population, initially at least in a fairly privileged position. For the first few decades after 1453, patriarchs were exempt from taxation. Their responsibilities included managing the existing ecclesiastical and monastic property (i.e. the part that had survived extensive Ottoman confiscations) and applying family law within the Orthodox community. The succession of patriarchs in the first two decades after 1453 makes the delicate situation quite clear: there were some eight patriarchs in some twenty years, including, possibly, more than one turn at the office by Scholarios himself and two by Symeon, one of his later successors.

As the first patriarch under Ottoman rule, Gennadios has been invested with a near-legendary aura. In truth, his tenure at the office was destined to fail given the extremely difficult task at hand, involving as it did identifying and constructing a path for the office that navigated the dangerous waters between the sultan's (often changing) wishes and the pressure exerted on the patriarchate by the essential and growing support of the lay *archontes* of the Greek elites, which came at a price. The staunch anti-Unionist Gennadios proved indulgent towards his congregation – an essential step if unity of the Orthodox population was to be secured. This, however, enraged many of his former supporters. He demonstrated his adaptability to the critical circumstances, for example, in tolerating new marriages of those whose spouses were (or were presumed) dead. As the patriarch came to realize, the Church could exist without the Empire – in fact, in some ways, it would have to become a substitute for it in the minds of his congregation and assume the role of a unifying factor. But all this was happening, in the mind of Scholarios and no doubt many of his contemporaries, against the backdrop of the imminent end of times: the year 1492 would signal the end of the seventh millennium and was sure to usher in Judgement Day (see Chapter 2 for the similar circumstances around the year 492). In this light, the preservation of Orthodox purity was more important than ever before and the trauma of the fall of Byzantium could be explained and managed as part of the cosmic plan. The Ottoman state supported this strengthening of Orthodox identity. When former Byzantine territories then under Latin rule were conquered, for example, the Ottomans were quick to re-establish the persecuted Orthodox Church hierarchy in them. The patriarchate, in its turn, duly severed any ties to the Western Church. In 1483 the despised Union of Florence was rejected in a council of all Orthodox Churches in which delegates from the Eastern patriarchates also took part.

The initially positive conditions for the functioning of the patriarchate were gradually limited after the immediate goal of attracting urban populations back to Constantinople was under way, and especially once military campaigns in the 1470s required more resources. Moreover, since relations between the Ottoman state and the patriarchate were not fixed in an institutional way but represented a set of predominately personal arrangements between the patriarch and each new sultan, these changed as well. It became gradually customary and then compulsory for the patriarch to pay an annual tax as well as a fixed sum as a present for the granting of privileges. The revenues from which those sums were to be covered came from the initially optional, but increasingly compulsory contribution of the Orthodox congregation, the *kanonikon*, a survival from Byzantine times. Furthermore, there was the capital generated from the management of church and monastic estates, the taxing of fairs and gifts given on special occasions (e.g. after the celebration of weddings). But as the amounts expected by the Ottomans grew, it became increasingly difficult for the patriarchs to collect them. This is where the influence of the *archontes* became crucial. By lending those sums, they managed to become instrumental in directing the affairs of the Church and often even in choosing their favoured candidates for the patriarchal throne. These were predominately Greek elites and therefore the patriarchate remained a Greek institution (Figure 9.2).

It is obvious that the role of Mehmed II in shaping this early period was crucial. Reared in power from a very young age (his father had initially abdicated in his favour when he was thirteen years old), he conquered Constantinople at the age of twenty-one. He seems to have held Byzantine sacred objects and relics in high regard – he had them collected in his treasury and according to some, probably credulous, accounts he venerated a particular image of the Virgin. Furthermore, he fostered a Greek chancery at the palace (official charters in Greek were produced until 1520) which included the commission of manuscripts to assist the formation of the palace scribes. It is revealing that one of the court historians of the period, Kritoboulos, wrote in Greek what is,

Figure 9.2 Portrait of Mehmed II by Gentile Bellini painted from life in 1480. The crowns refer to the realms (Byzantium, Trebizond, Asia) that the sultan had captured.

in principle, a Byzantine imperial work of history in which, however, the hero is now the Ottoman sultan. Various Greek writers had no difficulty extolling Mehmed's praises in the exact same wording that was customarily addressed to the Byzantine emperor. In his last decade Mehmed asked for a Venetian painter to come to his court. The result of this encounter is his famous portrait by Gentile Bellini, now at the National Gallery in London, a sign of the intersection of the new Ottoman imperial outlook with the world of the European Renaissance. His heir, Bayezid II (1481–1512) did not share his father's appreciation of Byzantine or Western art; in fact, he offered his father's collections for sale (the London portrait, for example, was bought from Venice, where it probably landed in that period). This, however, did not prevent him from commissioning projects from important Renaissance figures: both Leonardo da Vinci and Michelangelo were entrusted with designing bridges in Istanbul – however, these never materialized.

It would nevertheless be false to assume that the relationship between the Ottoman Empire and Christian Europe was as peaceful and harmonious as the above vignettes might suggest. The fall of the Byzantine Empire and the capture of Constantinople sent a shockwave throughout the Christian world. Some, like the Orthodox Russians, interpreted it as divine punishment for apostasy – the Byzantine agreement of Church Union. Humanists lamented the second death of Homer and Plato, alluding to the loss of precious and rare manuscripts. Others, especially those living in areas that now found themselves bordering the expanding Ottoman Empire, for example, Italy or Hungary, would have to watch with increasing trepidation where this expansion might lead next. This would have been particularly true in 1480 when the Ottomans took Otranto. Although this was a very short episode and the city was retaken by Naples in the following year one can imagine the ripples of panic caused by the existence of an Ottoman base just 400 miles or so from Rome.

BYZANTIUM IN EUROPE

Byzantine refugees and other survivors of the fall of Constantinople played a significant part in shaping the perception of the Ottoman threat and in attempting to instrumentalize it. After some Venetian sailors had hacked down the boom across the Golden Horn and managed to break through the blockade in the mayhem of the Ottoman entry into the city, a number of Constantinopolitans swam out to Venetian and Genoese ships. They were taken to Chios and Crete and from there many travelled to Italy; some of them bore prominent names like Palaiologos, Kantakouzenos and Laskaris. Spurred on by the efforts of Bessarion, the former Byzantine archbishop of Nicaea, who had converted to the Roman Church and had become a cardinal after the Council of Ferrara/Florence, the idea of a massive Crusade to retake Constantinople and drive the Ottomans out of the area emerged quickly. The energetic backing of the humanist Pope Pius II produced a lengthy congress at Mantua in 1459. Delegates from all over Europe sojourned over a period of eight months while Bessarion and Pius hammered home the message that unless the Ottomans were checked, Italy and Hungary would soon come under their sway. Despite their efforts, however, the Crusade, whose logistics and details were agreed in principle, never took off. Both Pius and Bessarion did not cease to pursue this enterprise through tireless propaganda – aided now by the new medium of printing that made the dissemination of such calls for a Crusade much easier. In 1461 Pius even wrote a lengthy tractate to Mehmed in the form of a letter; in it he both extolled the sultan's virtues (even comparing him with Constantine the Great) while at the same time castigating the subjugation of Christian peoples and urging him to gain immortal glory by converting to Christianity. It is doubtful whether the letter was ever sent. Pius died in Ancona in 1461 while making preparations to launch a smaller-scale Crusade; these, however, petered out after his passing.

Bessarion supported some of the most prominent Byzantine refugees. He took the children of Thomas Palaiologos, brother of the last emperor and co-ruler of the Morea, under his wing when their father died in Rome in 1465. Andrew, Manuel and Zoe were given a stipend by the popes, and as long as Bessarion lived, their income was secured. He arranged Zoe's marriage to Ivan III, Grand Prince of Moscow (she was renamed Sophia and became the grandmother of Ivan IV, nicknamed the Terrible). Bessarion was much more than a man of the cloth and Crusader propagandist; he was also a distinguished intellectual. From the late 1450s he was embroiled in a bitter struggle with another prominent émigré, George of Trebizond, over the merit of Plato over Aristotle. Bessarion wrote a spirited defence of Plato – in a way he was also defending the work of his beloved teacher, Plethon, and should be seen as the winner in this debate. Bessarion, however, not only produced original and influential works himself, but, perhaps more importantly, supported and fostered a sizeable group of Byzantine émigré scholars and helped to launch their careers in Italy. The demand for Greek teachers of Greek and the precious manuscripts which they could procure had gripped Italy since the late fourteenth century (see Chapter 8). Now, Byzantine scholars would earn their living both as teachers and as scribes – providing wealthy humanists with copies of manuscripts they desired. They would also translate key Greek texts into Latin and later see both translations and editions of Greek texts into printing. Not the earliest, but certainly some of the more prestigious and beautiful early prints were produced in Venice, at the printing house of Aldus Manutius with considerable input by Byzantine émigrés. Chief among them was the tremendous feat of publishing four volumes of the works of Aristotle in Greek between 1495 and 1498.

Venice was termed the new Athens for this new attention to Greek texts, while Bessarion called the city another Byzantium, perhaps because it became also the place where most Byzantine refugees chose to settle. In 1479 the Greek population of the city was calculated at about four thousand. Most of these individuals came from the Venetian-held areas in Greece such as Crete, the Morea or Negroponte. And they were not only scholars. A group of mostly Greek light cavalry soldiers, termed *stradioti*, were first used by Venice against the Ottomans in the Morea. From the late 1470s onwards, they were increasingly mobilized in Venetian warfare in Italy as well. Some of them bore prominent Byzantine surnames such as Palaiologos. Towards the end of the fifteenth century the Greeks of Venice were granted the right to form a confraternity, the Scuola of San Nicolò. Some years later they were allowed to start building a Greek church in the city, San Giorgio dei Greci, which still stands. The cultural landscape of Venice was transformed by two donations made in the fifteenth century, both by Bessarion; in 1463 he bequeathed an important reliquary of the True Cross to the Scuola Grande della Carità (commemorated on his portrait, now in the National Gallery in London) and in 1468 he donated his vast collection of manuscripts, an outstanding 482 Greek and 264 Latin codices, to Venice. They form the core of the collection of the Bibliotheca Marciana to this day.

The search for more Greek manuscripts was fuelled by all these actions. Trips to former Byzantine lands were organized to satisfy this demand. In the early 1490s, for example, Janus Laskaris, one of Bessarion's protégés, travelled to Constantinople to buy Greek manuscripts for the Medici library. And it was not just texts that were sought after. Byzantine icons – especially in the form of miniature mosaics – seem to have been particularly popular. We find them in inventories of fifteenth-century collections such as that of the Medici in Florence, or that of Cardinal Barbo, later Pope Paul II. In Crete, a Venetian dominion with a predominately Orthodox population, painters and workshops were busy producing works not just for the local Orthodox market but for an Italian clientele as well. A single contract from Crete dated to 1499 records the commission of 700 such objects for export. While Byzantine art objects never became as coveted as Ancient Greek and Roman ones, they were nevertheless perceived as precious and worthy of inclusion in prestigious collections.

In the early years of the sixteenth century the Byzantine question was kept alive in Europe by émigrés, their descendants and pupils, for example, by appealing to monarchs with petitions and poems in Greek and Latin – Humanism with a political agenda. At the same time an increasing number of territories in the Christian East were falling into Ottoman hands: Modon and Coron in 1500, Monemvasia in 1540, Chios, Naxos and the Cyclades in 1566. Despite the urgent calls, European powers were much too busy fighting each other to invest in a new Crusade against the Turks. However, when Cyprus was taken in 1571, Venice felt compelled to act. The Sacred League was formed with Spain, and the Papacy and the common fleet inflicted a crushing defeat on the Ottomans at Lepanto in the same year. One of the combatants was Cervantes and the triumphal atmosphere of the day is recorded in his *Don Quixote*: 'all the nations of the earth were disabused of the error under which they lay in imagining the Turks to be invincible on sea.' But the victory did not change the political landscape; by 1573 Venice had already signed a peace treaty with the sultan, but now with Crete as its last important colony in the Aegean, it must have felt that time was running out. On the island itself this was a period of great flourishing of the arts – the term 'Cretan Renaissance' has been applied to it. Literature written in vernacular Greek proliferated. The most famous figure of this era stands somewhat at its margins: the painter Domenikos Theotokopoulos, better known as El Greco (1541–1614), since his most important and mature artistic production did not take place on Crete, but in Italy and even more so in Spain, where he settled after 1577. That this artistic boom was taking place against the backdrop of a grave threat becomes clear by the gigantic fortifications that were repaired or built on Crete in this period and which still dominate the cities of Herakleion, Chania and Rethymno.

STUDYING BYZANTIUM

Although after the Battle of Lepanto a political solution to the Byzantine question never again became current, interest in Byzantium at an intellectual level did not diminish: Greek was being taught in a number of European cities (as confirmed by the thousands of copies of Greek grammars that were printed in the sixteenth century), texts were commissioned, copied or printed and the quest for Byzantine manuscripts to furnish royal and princely libraries was growing. Apart from the long-established humanist interest in Greek texts, two additional reasons fuelled this interest. On the one hand, a veritable Turkophobia stimulated by the recent Ottoman advances drew focus on the fate of the Byzantine Christians. On the other, leading figures of the Reformation that was unfolding in the German lands looked to the Orthodox Church as a potential ally against the Roman Catholic Church and took a particular interest in its traditions. Luther himself was quite sympathetic towards the Orthodox Church, which he credited with being much closer to the traditions of the Ancient Church, while

Melanchthon sought contact with the Patriarch of Constantinople. The two sides exchanged envoys, but soon discovered that despite having a common enemy, their actual differences were irreconcilable. One of the thorniest issues was the veneration of images that the Orthodox Church had painstakingly defined in the age of iconoclasm (see Chapter 4), but which was regarded as idolatry by the Protestants. In the future, relations between the two creeds would remain distant, but overall amicable.

In this context, the figure of Hieronymus Wolf (1516–80) is particularly important. He was a prolific scholar who was commissioned to produce the first printed editions of Byzantine historians while working for the patrician family of Fugger from Augsburg. It was long believed that Wolf had coined the term 'Byzantine' to characterize the culture of the Eastern Roman Empire, as the designation 'Greek' was gradually becoming exclusively used to denote Ancient Greek history and culture. It now seems that it was rather Johannes Oporinus (1507–68), a philologist and printer from Basel, who actually used the term when printing Wolf's editions of Byzantine texts. In the second half of the sixteenth century a number of Byzantine texts were edited and/or translated and printed; the umbrella term 'Byzantine' suggested a distinct era or at least a discrete phase of (Greek) history worthy of study and research on its own and as such may be seen as the conventional beginning of what we understand as Byzantine studies in Europe.

The above editorial enterprise was taken up and pursued in a much more methodical and successful way some generations later in France. At the court of the Sun King, Louis XIV, and with the support of some of the most prominent figures of his reign, such as Cardinal Mazarin and Colbert, patronage of the arts flourished. One of the areas that received support was an edition of Byzantine texts, printed with state funds at the Royal Printing Press at the Louvre. From the 1640s to 1711 some thirty-four volumes were printed (known as *La Byzantine du Louvre*), putting together an unprecedented body of texts from the entire period of Byzantine history. Alongside, Byzantine art objects found their way into the royal collections. The intellectual aspects of the project functioned autonomously – they conferred prestige on the French court and established it as the leading intellectual hub of Europe. An additional reason for this interest in Byzantine matters (although it should not be overstretched) was the somewhat arcane claim of the French kings to the Byzantine throne, leading back both to the Latin Empire of Constantinople after 1204 and to the more recent transferral of rights sold to the French king by the last rightful heir to the Palaiologan throne.

Charles du Fresne, seigneur Du Cange (1610–88) was a key figure in this French Byzantine revival. His studies on Byzantine history, centred on the French presence in the Levant after the Fourth Crusade, which are still consulted, helped to consolidate both the term 'Byzantine' itself and this particular field of historical enterprise.

At around the same time the last Venetian stronghold in the Aegean was lost to the Ottomans: the massive campaign against Crete began in 1645 but was terminated by the surrender of the capital Candia (modern Herakleion) after an almost three-year siege in 1669. Again, there was a wave of refugees, mostly to Corfu and Venice, and again the new émigrés carried works of art and manuscripts and helped renew the interest in the culture of the former Eastern Empire. As Europe entered the Age of Enlightenment attitudes towards Byzantium shifted. The tight embrace of Church and State in the Empire and the imperial style of autocratic rule overshadowed the positive stance of the Humanists and their debt to their Byzantine teachers. Along with everything medieval, key thinkers of the age such as Voltaire and Montesquieu thought of Byzantium as backward and ridiculous – no redeeming quality was granted to its long existence. A genuine product of this era came to be the voice that defined the public perception of the Byzantine Empire not just in his day, but perhaps even in ours: Edward Gibbon. His monumental *Decline and Fall of the Roman Empire* (1776–88), which according to him describes 'the triumph of barbarism and religion', was presented in a combination of impeccable style and authoritative scholarship with an utter rejection of this culture. Although Gibbon only presented an almost comically abridged version of Byzantine history after the sixth century, his vision shaped the way Byzantium was viewed for centuries. It is not coincidental that no work on Byzantine history can do without some critical remarks – of adulation or rejection – about this key figure of the Enlightenment, who perhaps wrote his work as a comment or allegory on the British Empire of his days. The worst damage that Gibbon did to Byzantium is that he made it almost impossible to take it seriously. And how could one take seriously a culture that is characterized as follows:

[The Byzantines] held in their lifeless hands the riches of their fathers, without inheriting the spirit which had created and improved that sacred patrimony: they read, they praised, they compiled, but their languid souls seemed alike incapable of thought and action. In the revolution of ten centuries, not a single discovery was made to exalt the dignity or promote the happiness of mankind.

The nineteenth century brought new developments. The Greek War of Independence (1821–32) focused European interest on both the geographical territory of the former Eastern Empire and the plight of its Christian inhabitants – Byzantium, however, was not part of the equation of Philhellenism, as the movement came to be known. Modern Greeks were connected to their ancient forefathers without the embarrassing middle period, so maligned by Gibbon. It is nevertheless not quite coincidental that at the same time a new intellectual enterprise was gaining momentum: the publication of the Bonn Corpus, an edition of Byzantine texts that was to amass some fifty volumes from 1828 to 1897 and thus become the basis for the formation of a new academic discipline devoted to this culture. Karl Krumbacher occupied the first chair of Byzantine studies at the University of Munich in 1897; other major European centres followed soon thereafter. The young discipline grew with a proliferation of university appointments throughout the world, a profusion of specialist publications and dedicated journals and international meetings. At the last International Congress of Byzantine Studies that took place in Venice and Padua in 2022 over a thousand delegates took part.

Byzantine studies sprang from the philological engagement with texts and seemed for a long time rather conservative and resistant towards new trends and theories that had reshaped the study of Antiquity and the (Western) Middle Ages. Not so anymore. A wave of scholars has been revisiting all aspects of the Byzantine millennium, engaging with critical theory and injecting its study with cutting-edge approaches regarding gender, identity, ideology, cultural exchange (with both the medieval West and the Islamicate world), new literary forms and material culture.

BYZANTIUM TODAY

Outside academia, a number of often-conflicting strands compose the way that Byzantium is perceived in our contemporary world. Probably the key factor is its alleged foreignness, the inability to shoehorn its very long history into the periodization that serves the grand narrative of Western history: it did not, for example, go into decline in the fifth century (rather the contrary), whereas its star was waning, when the West was in the ascendant in the late Middle Ages. As a result, it is often convenient to simply ignore Byzantium, not to include it in discussions, both academic and popular, on issues that touch on the European past. Specialists of Byzantium and more generally intellectuals from countries with an Orthodox heritage often decry this absence, but this has not proved enough to buck the trend. At the same time, its foreignness sometimes works to its advantage. Recent blockbuster exhibitions on Byzantine themes (e.g. those at the Metropolitan Museum in New York in 1997 and 2004 or at the Royal Academy in London in 2008/2009) have been hugely popular. Their emphasis on luxury, exoticism and mysticism may smack of a type of Orientalism, but the public seems to love it. In a way, such a perception is not very different from the world evoked by the most famous use of Byzantium in the English language, W. B. Yeats' 1928 poem 'Sailing to Byzantium' with its opening verse 'That is no country for old men'. Yeats stresses the spiritual aspect of the Empire, but also sets Byzantine craftsmanship in a unique light, stating in a later text that 'in early Byzantium, and maybe never before or since in recorded history, religious, aesthetic and practical life were one, and that architect and artificers . . . spoke to the multitude and the few alike'.

In fiction, Byzantine-themed works have never reached a wide audience. Umberto Eco, who landed a global hit with his medieval novel *The Name of the Rose* (1980), could not repeat his success with *Baudolino* (2000), in which a fictionalized version of the Byzantine historian, Niketas Choniates (see Chapter 6) is one of the key figures. This mirrors, perhaps, the discrepancy between Robert Graves' huge success with *I, Claudius* (1934) set in the familiar world of the early Roman Empire, and the much more modest fortune of his *Count Belisarios* (1938), set in the Justinianic period. A more recent novel by the distinguished linguist and psychoanalyst Julia Kristeva, *Murder in Byzantium* (2004) set the target to reconfigure the European reception of Byzantium ('the blind spot of history') within the genre of crime fiction in which one of the multiple strands revolves around Anna Komnene; the work seems to have been read mostly by specialists, and thus was preaching to the converted.

In visual arts, Byzantium has undergone some very interesting transformations. During the Renaissance the Byzantine art of painting, the *maniera greca*, was deplored by the most famous theoretician of art, Giorgio Vasari, as backward, stiff and rough, lacking in naturalism and, though not expressly stated, not using shadows and perspective. These exact traits, however, would come to be celebrated in the twentieth century as forerunners to the modernist movement: the flatness of space, the preference for the transcendental over the optical – even Byzantine iconoclasm was seen as expressing more general objections to the figurative in artistic representation. In the 1950s the celebrated art critic Clement Greenberg could thus find affinities between Byzantine art and, say Cubism or Abstract Expressionism. This very fruitful trajectory is quite current at the moment, but again it must be noted that its positive connotations have not penetrated the mainstream.

So, where is Byzantium today? It is easier to find in the alleged Orthodox Commonwealth, in the Balkans, Cyprus and Russia, not only because of the extant monuments but also because for both the academic community and the general public in these regions Byzantine history has been integrated into their national historical narrative and serves as part of their identity. In scholarship and the arts, Byzantine themes are present and are negotiated dynamically. It would suffice to point, for example, to the Russian director Andrei Tarkovsky (1932–86), whose 1966 film *Andrei Rublev* about the eponymous fifteenth-century religious painter, is steeped in the imagery of the icons that Rublev painted, or to the Greek painter Stelios Faitakis (1976–), whose work employs the visual language of Byzantine painting but uses it to construct intricate contemporary allegories (Figure 9.3, below). One needs to come

Figure 9.3 Empress Theodora by Stelios Faitakis. The painter combines elements from Byzantine and Japanese painting and street art to produce a new take on Theodora's famous image from Ravenna (see Figure 2.2).

back to the foreignness of the Byzantine Empire to conclude. Since our current hegemonic discourse is centred on the West, it is inevitable that Byzantium is marginalized. As Samuel Huntington controversially put it: 'Where does Europe end? Europe ends where Western Christianity ends and Islam and Orthodoxy begin.' The Eastern Empire, set by its geography and history between Western Christendom and Islam, antagonistic to both and not survived by any national state – and thus effectively indefensible by any single nationalist historiography – remains a vast, but inconvenient, projection space. For some it was a totalitarian and theocratic state, backward and static, whose only redeeming virtue was the preservation of Ancient Greek knowledge and its dissemination to its neighbours. Others view it as an almost utopian Noah's Ark, preserving traditions of the old ways in the Church, its imperial office, its social organization. Despite what the Byzantine sources themselves would want us to believe, Byzantium was far from being an immotile ancient organism: lift the lid of its classicizing archaisms and mannerisms and you will find constant change, resilience and the remarkable ability to adapt to ever-changing circumstances.

But perhaps this was not enough. Like its walls that had been impregnable until the advent of cannons, the slow-changing pace of this state that always had a foot in an ancient world that had long vanished could not keep up with the pace of its shifting environment. As had been predicted in the fourteenth century by the scholar and statesman Theodore Metochites, all empires were born, blossomed, declined and then died.

Appendices

I TIMELINE

The reigns of Byzantine emperors are given in bold; those of Western Roman emperors in bold italics.

306–37	**Constantine I (sole emperor from 324)**
324	Byzantion, renamed Constantinople, is chosen as new imperial residence
325	First general council of the Christian Church at Nicaea (later named Ecumenical)
337–61	**Constantius II [alongside his brothers: Constantine II: 337–40 and Constans I: 337–50]**
361–3	**Julian** – ongoing war with Persia and pagan revival
363–4	**Jovian**
364–75	***Valentinian I***
364–78	**Valens**
367–83	***Gratian***
375–92	***Valentinian II***
379–95	**Theodosius I**
395	Death of Theodosius I – the Empire is divided into two parts
395–408	**Arcadius**
393–423	***Honorius***
408–50	**Theodosius II**
410	Sack of Rome by Alaric
425–55	***Valentinian III***
450–7	**Marcian**

451	Fourth ecumenical council at Chalcedon
453	Attila dies (leader of the Huns since 434; sole leader since 447)
457–74	**Leo I**
467–72	*Anthemius [472 Olybrius; 473–4 Glycerius]*
474	**Leo II**
474–5	*Julius Nepos; 475–6 Romulus Augustulus*
474–91	**Zeno**
476	End of the Western Roman Empire
491–518	**Anastasios**
518–27	**Justin I**
527–65	**Justinian I**
537	The church of Hagia Sophia is dedicated
541	First outbreak of the Justinianic plague
565–78	**Justin II**
578–82	**Tiberios I**
582–602	**Maurice**
602–10	**Phokas**
603–30	Last war between Byzantium and Persia
610–41	**Herakleios**
622	The prophet Muhammad migrates from Mecca to Medina (Hijra)
634	Beginning of Islamic expansion
641	**Constantine III, Herakleios III and Heraklonas**
641–68	**Constans II**
661–80	Caliphate of Muawiya, founder of the Umayyad dynasty
668–85	**Constantine IV**
685–95	**Justinian II (first reign)**
695–8	**Leontios II**
698–705	**Tiberios II**
705–11	**Justinian II (second reign)**
711–13	**Philippikos Bardanes**
713–15	**Anastasios II**
715–17	**Theodosios III**
717–41	**Leo III the Isaurian**
717/18	Last Arab siege of Constantinople
732	Charles Martel defeats Arabs near Poitiers
741–75	**Constantine V**
743–50	Last wave of the Justinianic plague

750	The Abbasids topple the Umayyads – Islamic capital later transferred from Damascus to Baghdad
754	Council of Hiereia establishes iconoclasm as official dogma of the Church
775–80	**Leo IV**
780–97	**Constantine VI and Eirene**
787	Seventh ecumenical council at Nicaea, condemns iconoclasm
797–802	**Eirene, sole reign**
800	Charlemagne, king of the Franks from 768, is crowned emperor of the Romans by Pope Leo III
802–11	**Nikephoros I**
811–13	**Michael I**
813–20	**Leo V**
820–9	**Michael II**
829–42	**Theophilos**
842–67	**Michael III**
843	The 'Triumph of Orthodoxy', the final restoration of images and condemnation of iconoclasm in the Byzantine Church
858–67	Patriarchate of Photios (second term in office, 877–86)
864	The Bulgar leader Boris converts to Christianity
867–86	**Basil I the Macedonian** founder of the Macedonian Dynasty that would rule Byzantium until 1055
912–13	**Alexander**
913–59	**Constantine VII Porphyrogenetos (actual reign from 945)**
920–44	**Romanos I Lekapenos**
959–63	**Romanos II**
961	Nikephoros II Phokas retakes Crete, while Cyprus is reconquered the following year
962	Otto I, the German king, is crowned emperor in Rome
963–9	**Nikephoros II Phokas**
969–76	**John I Tzimiskes**
972	Marriage of Otto II with Theophanu, a Byzantine aristocrat
976–1025	**Basil II, The Bulgar-slayer**
989	Vladimir, leader of the Kievan Rus, marries Basil II's sister Anna and converts to Christianity
992	Basil II grants Venice commercial privileges
1025–8	**Constantine VIII**

1028–34	Romanos III Argyros
1034–41	Michael IV
1041–2	Michael V Kalaphates
1042	Zoe and Theodora
1042–55	Constantine IX Monomachos
1054	Mutual excommunication between papal legates and Michael Keroularios, patriarch of Constantinople (1043–59), results in schism between the churches of Rome and Constantinople
1055–6	Theodora
1056–7	Michael VI
1057–9	Isaac I Komnenos
1059–67	Constantine X Doukas
1068–71	Romanos IV Diogenes
1071	Bari, the last Byzantine stronghold in Italy, is taken by the Normans; later in the year the Byzantine army suffers a crushing defeat by the Seljuqs in Manzikert
1071–8	Michael VII Doukas
1078–81	Nikephoros III Botaneiates
1081–1118	Alexios I Komnenos – founder of the Komnenian dynasty that would rule until 1185
1082	Grant of significant commercial privileges to Venice
1096–9	The First Crusade
1118–43	John II Komnenos
1143–80	Manuel I Komnenos
1145–9	The Second Crusade
1180–3	Alexios II
1183–5	Andronikos I Komnenos
1185–95	Isaac II Angelos
1187	Saladin defeats the Crusader armies at Hattin and Jerusalem surrenders to his rule
1189–92	The Third Crusade
1195–1203	Alexios III Angelos
1203	Alexios IV and Isaac II Angelos
1203–22	Theodore I Laskaris (Empire of Nicaea)
1204	Alexios V Doukas Mourtzouphlos
1204	The armies of the Fourth Crusade capture and sack Constantinople
1222–54	John III Vatatzes (Empire of Nicaea)
1254–8	Theodore II Laskaris (Empire of Nicaea)

1258–61	**John IV Laskaris (Empire of Nicaea)**
1258–82	**Michael VIII Palaiologos**
1261	Constantinople is recaptured by the armies of Michael VIII
1274	Union between the Roman and Byzantine Church established at the Second Council of Lyon
1282–1328	**Andronikos II Palaiologos**
1321–8	Civil war between Andronikos II and Andronikos III
1328–41	**Andronikos III Palaiologos**
1341–7	**John V Palaiologos under the regency of Empress Anna, Patriarch Kalekas and Alexios Apokaukos;** civil war between the regency and John VI Kantakouzenos
1347–54	**John VI Kantakouzenos**
1347	The Black Death breaks out in Constantinople
1354–91	**John V Palaiologos**
1372/73	Byzantine emperors become vassals of the Ottomans
1376–9	**Andronikos IV Palaiologos**
1390	**John VII Palaiologos**
1391–1425	**Manuel II Palaiologos**
1394–1402	Long siege of Constantinople by Bayezid I
1425–48	**John VIII Palaiologos**
1438–9	A Byzantine delegation attends the general council at Ferrara (which then transfers to Florence). Union between the two churches is proclaimed
1448–53	**Constantine XI Palaiologos**
1451–81	Ottoman Sultan Mehmed II
1453	Conquest of Constantinople by the Ottomans
1460–1	Last free pockets of Byzantine rule are conquered by the Ottomans

II PEOPLES AROUND BYZANTIUM

THE NOMADIC STEPPE PEOPLES

Turkic nomads (or semi-nomads) from the Eurasian steppe formed part of migratory movements to the west and south that affected the Byzantine Empire. The first were the **Huns**, who first pushed other peoples westwards in the fourth century, and then expanded into Eastern Europe in the fifth century, forming a vast empire under Attila, which quickly collapsed after his death. The **Avars** appeared in the sixth century north of the Black Sea and, although originally allied to Byzantium, soon posed a grave threat as they formed a confederation with Slavs and launched attacks against the Empire. They were defeated by Charlemagne in the late seventh century. In the East, Byzantium formed an alliance with the **Gökturks**, a nomadic confederation, against the Sasanids under Herakleios. They were later subsumed under the Tang dynasty in China. The **Bulgars** originally moved to the Black Sea area in the sixth century, and gradually divided into two groups, one moving to the area of Bulgaria (together with another Turkic people, the **Kutrigurs**) where they dominated the local Slavic population, the other settling in the Volga region and later converting to Islam. The Volga Bulgars were conquered by the Kievan Rus in the tenth century. The area of the northern Caucasus was dominated from the mid-seventh century by the **Khazars**. Originally allies of Byzantium against the Avars, Persians and Arabs, but once they were established in Crimea and their elites had converted to Judaism, Byzantium turned against them. They were destroyed by the Rus in the late tenth/early eleventh century. The **Pechenegs** moved to the basin of the Volga in the late ninth century and initially fought for the Byzantines against Bulgarians and Rus, but often changed sides and attacked the Empire, especially in the second half of the eleventh century, when they were defeated first by Alexios I and then by John II in 1122. Coming from the East the **Magyars/Hungarians** moved to the basin of the Don in the ninth century and later under Pecheneg pressure settled in the Carpathian basin. The Hungarians frequently made forays into the south and south-west, despite some marriage alliances with Byzantium. In the last century of Byzantium the Hungarians offered military help against the Ottomans. The **Cumans**, a confederation of Eurasian nomadic and semi-nomadic tribes, replaced the Pechenegs in the east European steppe in the mid-eleventh century and were, in turn, subjected by the Mongols in the early thirteenth century. They often served as Byzantine mercenaries in the thirteenth century. From the mid-eleventh century the **Seljuqs** gradually moved from the Aral Sea towards the West. They conquered Persia and then established the Sultanate of Rum (with its capital at Ikonion/Konya) over vast areas in Anatolia. The **Danishmendids** controlled central Anatolia for around a century after 1085. As a result of the Mongol invasions, the Seljuq sultanate state disintegrated by the early fourteenth century. The last major movement in Eurasia occurred when the **Mongols,** under the leadership of Genghis Khan (died 1227) and his successors created an empire stretching from the Baltic to the Pacific Ocean. The vast state was divided into two major parts: the Golden Horde (around the Volga) and the **Ilkhanate** in Persia. The Mongols crushed the Rus by 1240 and captured Baghdad in 1258. The **Ottomans** were a Turkish dynasty ruling first over an emirate in Bithynia that began its expansion under its founder, Osman (around 1300). The Ottomans initially served as mercenaries for Byzantium, but by 1453 they had conquered most of the areas of the Byzantine Empire as well as the Balkans.

THE ARAB WORLD

Byzantium continued the late Roman strategy of employing Arab tribal confederations as allies in the buffer zone between the Roman Empire and Sasanid Persia. The **Ghassanids,** who had migrated from Yemen in the third century, became Byzantium's most powerful and influential allies in modern Syria and Palestine towards the late fifth century. Their main opponents were the **Lakhmids,** allies of Persia who frequently attacked the Byzantine border region from their settlements in modern Iraq. At roughly the same time, the Lakhmids faced threats by the **Kindite** confederation, which made forays into North Arabia and Mesopotamia. Parts of the Ghassanid confederation (especially the ruling classes) had adopted Miaphysite Christianity, which eventually led to the dissolution of the confederation. Despite Herakleios' attempts to restore the alliance with the Ghassanids to its former strength, the defence of the Eastern border was too weakened to withstand the onslaught of the Muslim armies after 634.

Further south, in modern-day Yemen, the **Himyarites** had established their hegemony around 270. Once parts of their elites adopted a form of Judaism, this led to a successful Axumite-Ethiopian military expedition that reinstated Christianity in South Arabia.

Muslim armies had conquered large parts of the Byzantine Near East a decade after Muhammad's death. Internal conflicts broke out over the prophet's succession. When the third of his successors, Uthman, a member of the **Umayyad** clan, was murdered in 656, only parts of the community backed the elected successor, Ali. The first Islamic civil war (*fitna*) broke out between the followers of the Umayyad clan, who presented Muawiya as a counter-caliph, and the party (*shia*) of Ali, eventually resulting in the political-religious schism between Sunnites and Shi'ites. In the shadow of the Umayyad Caliphate, a group of descendants from Muhammad's uncle al-Abbas, the **Abbasids** sought adherents particularly in Khurasan (Persia) and entered in open revolt against the Umayyads in 747. After the fall of Damascus in the spring of 750, the entire Umayyad family elite was killed, with the exception of one single prince, Abd al-Rahman I, who fled to Spain and established the **Umayyad Emirate of Cordoba**. The Abbasid Caliphate ruled the Islamic world first from Baghdad and after 863 from Samarra. The rule of the Abbasids faced various uprisings and a gradual fragmentation. By the mid-tenth century, their power existed only nominally, and several local dynasties ruled independently over formerly Abbasid realms.

In 800, Harun al-Rashid, the most famous Abbasid caliph, had installed Ibrahim ibn al-Aghlab as emir in North Africa. Ibrahim's successors, the **Aghlabids** ruled de facto independently for a century but continued to nominally recognize the Abbasid Caliphate. They started their conquest of Byzantine Sicily in 827. The dynasty went into decline during the last quarter of the ninth century; it lost its possessions in Calabria to Byzantium and was eventually overthrown by the Fatimids of Egypt.

Between 890 and 1003, the **Hamdanids** ruled over parts of northern Syria and Iraq – in the beginning as legally installed governors. Already in the mid-tenth century the Hamdanids came under **Buyid** control, a dynasty ruling from the borderlands between modern Iran and Iraq which effectively held control over the Abbasid Caliphate from 945 until the mid-eleventh century, when they were deposed by the Seljuqs and Shabankara Kurds. A Hamdanid ruler, Sayf al-Dawla, adopted Shi'ite Islam in 969 and sought help from the Fatimids of Egypt, who eventually terminated Hamdanid rule in Aleppo in 1003. The **Fatimids,** originally a Shi'ite sect that originated in the ninth century, was particularly successful among the Berber people in North Africa who facilitated the Fatimid coup against the Aghlabids. Until 978, the dynasty ruled over large parts of Syria and Palestine and controlled the holy cities of Mecca and Medina. From the early twelfth century onwards, however, the Fatimid empire faced serious financial and administrative problems. They lost Syria and Palestine to the Seljuqs and to the Crusader armies. Saladin terminated the Fatimid Caliphate and founded the **Ayyubid** dynasty in Egypt and

Syria. Since the ninth century, the Abbasid caliphs had extensively relied upon their elite guards consisting of royal slaves (arab. *mamalik*, sing. *mamluk*). Similarly, Saladin had introduced this Abbasid model to Egypt. When in 1249 the Ayyubid Sultan al-Salih died, the Mamluk general Aybak married the dowager and founded the **Mamluk Sultanate** that ruled over Egypt and Syria until they were conquered by the Ottomans in 1517. The Mamluks were the only state that successfully withstood the Mongol onslaught.

THE GERMANIC WORLD

The major migratory move of Germanic peoples in the period occurred largely as a result of Hunnic pressure in the second half of the fourth century. From their settlements north of the Black Sea the **Goths** moved westwards in the 370s, crossed the Danube and inaugurated a period of intense exchange with the Empire. One group of Goths, later termed the **Visigoths,** defeated the Roman army at Adrianople and were later settled in Thrace. Under Alaric they would continue to pillage the Balkans, then move to invade Italy, sack Rome (in 410), then proceed through Gaul to Spain. The **Ostrogoths** formed into a group two generations later than the Visigoths under the leadership of Theoderic. He would ally with the Empire and ultimately establish a kingdom in Italy. The Ostrogoths were defeated by the Byzantines in the 550s after two decades of warfare. The **Vandals** entered the Empire by crossing the Rhine at the start of the fifth century; they proceeded through Spain and then crossed into Africa in 429, capturing large parts of the region by 439. They were defeated in 534. The **Gepids** were an eastern Germanic people, who settled in northern Dacia (modern Romania) where they came under Hunnic overlordship. After Attila's death they occupied the region on the left bank of the Danube and allied themselves with the Empire against the Ostrogoths. They were defeated by the Lombards in 567/68. All the above peoples disappear from history by the sixth century. The **Lombards** were a west Germanic people who occupied Pannonia in the early sixth century; they served as allies of the Empire against the Ostrogoths but were pushed westwards into Italy by the Avars in the late 560s. By the end of the seventh century they had conquered the North and established a kingdom, while in the South the Duchy of Benevento captured most of Byzantine holdings in Apulia and Calabria. They captured Ravenna, seat of the Byzantine administration, in 751, but their kingdom was dissolved by Charlemagne in 774. The Lombard principalities in the South were splintered and oscillated between alliances with Byzantium against the Carolingians and later Ottonians and vice versa. From the late ninth century onwards, Byzantium once more became an important power in Italy, but ultimately both the Byzantine and the Lombard areas were conquered by the **Normans** in the late eleventh century. These were Vikings mostly from Scandinavia who settled in northern France (Normandy) in the tenth century. They were quickly assimilated by the local Frankish population and formed a powerful principality in the region. In the eleventh century Norman warlords began to interfere in Italian affairs and by the end of the century they had subjugated the south of Italy and had taken Sicily from the Aghlabids. They established a Norman kingdom over both areas in the early twelfth century. Another Northern people who played an important role in Byzantine affairs were the **Rus,** originally a Viking group from Sweden who raided north-eastern Europe and used rivers to launch raids against, but also engage in trade with Byzantium in the ninth century. In the early tenth century the Rus conquered Kiev and established their lordship over the predominately Slavic population. In a few generations the Vikings had been assimilated by them. The Rus were for the most part allies of Byzantium against the Khazars. They converted to Christianity at the end of the tenth century under Vladimir, who married the sister of Basil II.

INDO-EUROPEANS

The **Alans** were known in the later Roman period as nomadic pastoralists inhabiting the region between the Black Sea and the Caspian Sea. Under pressure by the Huns, large groups of Alans fled westwards in the late fourth century. Some Alans were active as mercenaries and built up important careers in the fourth and fifth centuries. There was an Alan state in the north Caucasus, which was in close contact with Byzantium, to which it was often allied. The **Slavs** first come to the attention of Byzantine sources at the end of the sixth century on the left bank of the Danube. Despite some raids, they were routinely recruited as mercenaries under Justinian. Nevertheless, raids continued to the end of the century; the Slavs were targeted with frequent campaigns under Maurice. The Slavs often came under the leadership of Turkic warrior groups such as the Avars and later the Bulgars. In the early seventh century they migrated to and settled south of the Danube in significant numbers.

Further reading

In putting together this annotated bibliography I had to respect the compact size of the book and keep it fairly short. I have privileged recent scholarship, because it incorporates earlier research; furthermore, the emphasis is clearly on easily accessible works in English.

OUP stands for Oxford University Press, CUP for Cambridge University Press, UP for University Press, *DOP* for *Dumbarton Oaks Papers*, *TM* for *Travaux et Mémoires*; all web links were last accessed on 27 September 2022.

INTRODUCTION

At the moment there is no authoritative and widely accepted single-authored monograph on the entire history of the Byzantine Empire. The classic and very influential *History of the Byzantine State* by George Ostrogorsky (revised English edition Oxford: Blackwell, 1969, but going back to a book originally written in the 1930s) is quite outdated by now. Three books written by authorities on Byzantium treat the topic in very different, but compelling ways: Averil Cameron, *The Byzantines* (Oxford: Wiley, 2007); Judith Herrin, *Byzantium: The Surprising Life of a Medieval Empire* (London: Allan Lane, 2007); and Anthony Kaldellis, *Byzantium Unbound* (Leeds: Arc Humanities Press, Leeds, 2019). A number of edited volumes, though they may lack the unified focus of a single-authored work, provide a more varied approach to each period and its key questions. The most authoritative collections have been produced by CUP. Chronologically, one should start with the last two volumes of *The Cambridge Ancient History*: Vol. 13, *The Late Empire,*

AD 337–425, edited by A. Cameron and P. Garnsey (1998) and Vol. 14, *Late Antiquity: Empire and Successors, AD 425–600*, edited by A. Cameron, B. Ward-Perkins and M. Whitby (2001) and continue with *The Cambridge History of the Byzantine Empire c.500–1492*, edited by J. Shepard (2009). Alongside, it is very profitable to consult *The New Cambridge Medieval History*, Vols 1–7, which cover the period from 500 to 1500 (various editors, published between 1998 and 2005). Equally important are the volumes of *The Cambridge History of Christianity*, Vol. 1, *Origins to Constantine*, edited by M. M. Mitchell and F. M. Young (2006), Vol. 2, *Constantine to c.600*, edited by A. Casiday and F. W. Norris (2007), Vol. 3, *Early Medieval Christianities, c.600–c.1100*, edited by Th. F. X. Noble and J. M. H. Smith (2008) and Vol. 5, *Eastern Christianity*, edited by M. Angold (2006). To these one should also add the three volumes *Le monde byzantin* published by the Presses Universitaires de France (PUF): I, *L'Empire romain d'Orient (330-641)*, edited by C. Morrisson (Paris: PUF, 2004); II, *L'Empire byzantin (641-1204)*, edited J.-C. Cheynet (Paris: PUF, 2006); III, *L'empire grec et ses voisins XIIIe-XVe siècle*, edited by A. Laiou and C. Morrisson (Paris: PUF, 2011), but also the two-volume overview by T. C. Lounghis, *Επισκόπηση Βυζαντινής Ιστορίας* (Athens: Sygchrone Epoche, Vol. I, 2nd edn., 1998, Vol. II, 2011), to which my reconstruction of the social history of Empire owes a lot.

Two edited volumes, *A Companion to Byzantium*, edited by L. James (Chichester: Wiley-Blackwell, 2010) and *The Byzantine World*, edited by P. Stephenson (London: Routledge, 2010) are quite eclectic in their choice of topics, but include a number of important contributions and guide readers towards less-trodden paths. On economic history there is the magisterial *The Economic History of Byzantium*, edited by A. E. Laiou (Washington DC: Dumbarton Oaks Research Library and Collection, 2002) in three volumes which is also available on the web, https://www.doaks.org/resources/publications/books/the-economic -history-of-byzantium. It has a more detailed analysis of the overall problems than any other synthesis. For a more succinct approach see A. E. Laiou and C. Morrisson, *The Byzantine Economy* (Cambridge: CUP, 2007), and also Michael F. Hendy, *Studies in the Byzantine Monetary Economy* (Cambridge: CUP, 1985). Social matters have not yet received the attention they deserve; *A Social History of Byzantium*, edited by J. Haldon (Chichester: Wiley-Blackwell, 2009) is a good place to start. Warfare was obviously a very important aspect of Byzantine history. For a good introduction to this topic see John F. Haldon, *Warfare, State and Society in the Byzantine World, 565–1204* (London: Routledge, 1999).

On Byzantine art see John Lowden, *Early Christian and Byzantine Art* (London: Phaidon, 1997) and on architecture Robert G. Ousterhout, *Eastern Medieval Architecture: The Building Traditions of Byzantium and Neighboring Lands* (Oxford: OUP, 2019). Apart from more specialized studies on Constantinople that will be mentioned in the following, a collection of essays on all aspects of the city's pivotal role and function in Byzantine history can be found in *Constantinople réelle et imaginaire: Autour de l' œuvre de Gilbert Dagron*, edited by C. Morrisson and J. P. Sodini = *TM* 22/1 (2018). For detailed maps on all periods of Byzantine history, the best work is John F. Haldon, *The Palgrave Atlas of Byzantine history* (Houndmills, and Hampshire: Palgrave Macmillan, 2005).

The contested term 'Byzantine' is connected both to the birth and development of Byzantine studies as a discipline (on which see the bibliography for the last chapter of this book) but also to the elusive matter of Byzantine identity. The debate is ongoing and scholarly views have become increasingly polarized. Out of the vast scholarship I suggest three works that stand for three different approaches: Anthony Kaldellis, *Romanland. Ethnicity and Empire in Byzantium* (Cambridge, MA: Harvard UP, 2019), Ioannis Stouraitis, 'Byzantine Romanness: From Geopolitical to Ethnic Conceptions', in *Transformations of Romanness. Early Medieval Regions and Identities*, edited by W. Pohl, et al. (Berlin and Boston: Walter de Gruyter, 2018), 123–39 and Averil Cameron, 'Late Antiquity and Byzantium: An Identity Problem', *Byzantine and Modern Greek Studies* 40 (2016): 27–37.

My very quick overview of the physical world of the Byzantine Empire is greatly indebted to Johannes Koder, *Der Lebensraum der Byzantiner. Historish-geographischer Abriß ihres mittelalterlichen Staates im östlichen Mittelmeerraum* (Vienna: Fassbaender, 2nd edn., 2001).

FROM CRISIS TO CONSTANTINE I

The study of the period owes a lot to Peter Brown and his ground-breaking book *The World of Late Antiquity* (London: Thames and Hudson, 1971). More specifically on the era before Constantine see Simon Corcoran, *The Empire of the Tetrarchs: Imperial Pronouncements and Government, AD 284–324* (Oxford: OUP, 2000). The *Cambridge Companion to the Age of Constantine*, edited by N. Lenski (Cambridge: CUP, 2006) includes a number of chapters dealing with Constantine and his reign, his predecessors and his successors. Of the numerous works by

Timothy Barnes his latest, *Constantine. Dynasty, Religion and Power in the Later Roman Empire* (Chichester: Wiley-Blackwell, 2011) provides an assessment of his reign based on decades of research. Garth Fowden's study, *Empire to Commonwealth: The Consequences of Monotheism in Late Antiquity* (Princeton: Princeton UP, 1993) contextualizes the theological shifts in the period. On Constantine and Christianity see Timothy D. Barnes, *Constantine and Eusebius* (Cambridge, MA: Harvard UP, 1981) and Claudia Rapp, 'Imperial Ideology in the Making: Eusebius of Caesarea on Constantine as "Bishop"', *Journal of Theological Studies* 49 (1998): 685–95.

BECOMING THE EASTERN ROMAN EMPIRE, 330–491

Events. Peter Heather's, *Empires and Barbarians: Migration, Development and the Birth of Europe* (London: Macmillan, 2009) excellently surveys the relationship between the Empire and its barbarian enemies, allies and conquerors. The key study on Theodosius I is Stephen Williams and Gerard Friell, *Theodosius: The Empire at Bay* (London and New Haven: Yale UP, 1994). On Pulcheria see Kenneth G. Holum, *Theodosian Empresses. Women and Imperial Dominion in Late Antiquity* (Berkeley: University of California Press, 1989) and Liz James, *Empresses and Power in Early Byzantium* (London and New York: Continuum, 2001). *Chalcedon in Context: Church Councils 400–700*, edited by R. Price and M. Whitby (Liverpool: Liverpool UP, 2009), discusses the various councils and their impact on dogma and society at large.

Infrastructures. Chris Wickham's imposing and thought-provoking *Framing the Early Middle Ages: Europe and the Mediterranean, 400–800* (Oxford: OUP, 2005) is a crucial study of states, societies and their economies in the period; it should be consulted for the following chapters as well. On the importance of the gold coinage see Jairus Banaji, *Agrarian Change in Late Antiquity: Gold, Labour and Aristocratic Dominance* (Oxford: OUP, 2001); on great estates and their role see Peter Sarris, 'The Early Byzantine Economy in Context: Aristocratic Property and Economic Growth Reconsidered', *Early Medieval Europe* 19.3 (2011): 255–84. On the importance of trade see Mark Whittow, 'How Much Trade was Local, Regional and Inter-Regional? A Comparative Perspective on the Late Antique Economy', in *Local Economies? Production and Exchange of Inland Regions in Late Antiquity*, edited by L. Lavan (Leiden and Boston: Brill, 2015), 131–65.

Environment. On early Constantinople see Sarah Basset, *The Urban Image of Late Antique Constantinople* (Cambridge: CUP, 2004); especially on Constantine's Holy Apostles see *The Holy Apostles: A Lost Monument, a Forgotten Project, and the Presentness of the Past*, edited by M. Mullett and R. G. Ousterhout (Washington, DC: Dumbarton Oaks Research Library and Collection, 2020). Gilbert Dagron's, *Emperor and Priest: The Imperial Office in Byzantium* (Cambridge: CUP, 2003) is an authoritative study of the Byzantine perception of the imperial office; it should be consulted for the entire Byzantine period. On the fate of paganism within the Christian Empire see Alan Cameron, *The Last Pagans of Rome* (Oxford and New York: OUP, 2011). On Christianization and its effects on all aspects of life see Fergus Millar, *A Greek Roman Empire. Power and Belief under Theodosius II (408–450)* (Berkeley: University of California Press, 2007) and Peter Brown, *The Body and Society: Men, Women, and Sexual Renunciation in Early Christianity* (New York: Columbia UP, 1988) as well as the latter's study on charity *Through the Eye of a Needle: Wealth, the Fall of Rome, and the Making of Christianity in the West, 350–550 AD* (Princeton and Oxford: Princeton UP, 2012). On the emergence of monks and monasteries see Samuel Rubenson, 'Asceticism and Monasticism, I: Eastern', in *Cambridge History of Christianity*, Vol. 2 (as above), 637–68 and Derwas Chitty, *The Desert a City: An Introduction to the Study of Egyptian and Palestinian Monasticism under the Christian Empire* (Oxford: Blackwell, 1966). On the creation of charitable institutions see Peregrine Horden, 'The Christian Hospital in Late Antiquity: Break or Bridge?' in *Gesundheit–Krankheit. Kulturtransfer medizinischen Wissens von der Spätantike bis in die frühe Neuzeit*, edited by F. Steger and K. P. Jankrift (Cologne and Weimar: Böhlau, 2004), 2–24. On the cult of Mary see *The Cult of the Mother of God in Byzantium: Texts and Images*, edited by L. Brubaker and M. B. Cunningham (Farnham and Burlington, VT: Ashgate, 2011).

MASTERS OF THE MEDITERRANEAN, 491–602

Events. *The Cambridge Companion to the Age of Justinian*, edited by M. Maas (Cambridge: CUP, 2005) is a useful collection of studies on the period. On Theoderic and Italy see Peter Heather, 'Theoderic, King of the Goths', *Early Medieval Europe* 4 (1995): 145–73, V. Vlysidou, St. Lampakis, M. Leontsini and T. Lounghis, *Βυζαντινά στρατεύματα στη*

Δύση (5ος-11ος αι.) (Athens: National Hellenic Research Foundation, 2008) and Judith Herrin, *Ravenna. Capital of Empire, Crucible of Europe* (Princeton and Oxford: Princeton UP, 2020). On relations with Persia see Beate Dignas and Engelbert Winter, *Rome and Persia in Late Antiquity* (Cambridge: CUP, 2007); on the Arab tribes between Byzantium and Persia see Gregg Fischer, *Between Empires: Arabs, Romans, and Sasanians in Late Antiquity* (Oxford: OUP, 2011). On the empress Theodora see James, *Empresses and Power* (as above) and Leslie Brubaker, 'Sex, Lies and Textuality: The Secret History of Prokopios and the Rhetoric of Gender in Sixth-Century Byzantium', in *Gender in the Early Medieval World, East and West, 300–900*, edited by L. Brubaker and J. Smith (Cambridge: CUP, 2004), 83–101. On Prokopios see the two very different approaches by Averil Cameron, *Procopius and the Sixth Century* (London: Duckworth, 1985) and Anthony Kaldellis, *Procopius of Caesarea: Tyranny, History, and Philosophy at the End of Antiquity* (Philadelphia: University of Pennsylvania Press, 2004). On the ambitious Justinianic codification of legislation as well as his overall approach to law see the chapter 'Law and Legal Practice in the Age of Justinian' by Caroline Humfress in the *Cambridge Companion* (as above) 161–84. On Justinianic wars see the two recent collections *Warfare in Late Antiquity*, edited by L. Lavan, et al. (Leiden and Boston: Brill, 2013) and *War and Warfare in Late Antiquity*, edited by A. Sarantis and M. Christie (Leiden and Boston: Brill, 2013).

Infrastructures. Apart from relevant chapters in the *Economic History of Byzantium* (as above), Michael Decker's *Tilling the Hateful Earth: Agricultural Production and the Late Antique East* (Oxford: OUP, 2009) provides the background to the late antique economic boom; it should be read side by side with Peter Sarris, 'Aristocrats, Peasants and the Transformation of Rural Society, c. 400–800', *Journal of Agrarian Change* 9 (2009): 3–22. On the importance of archaeology for the understanding of the changing landscapes of Late Antiquity see J. H. W. G. Liebeschuetz, *Decline and Fall of the Roman City* (Oxford: OUP, 2001) and the series *Late Antique Archaeology*, edited by Luke Lavan with several volumes already published.

On the plague and its impact see Dionysios Ch. Stathakopoulos, *Famine and Pestilence in the Late Roman and Early Byzantine Empire* (Aldershot: Ashgate, 2004), *Plague and the End of Antiquity: The Pandemic of 541–750*, edited by L. K. Little (Cambridge: CUP, 2007) as well as Peter Sarris, 'New Approaches to the "Plague of Justinian"', *Past and Present*, 2021. https://doi.org/10.1093/pastj/gtab024

Environment. On Justinianic administrative reforms see Michael Maas, 'Roman History and Christian Ideology in Justinianic Reform Legislation', *DOP* 40 (1986): 17–31. The work of Anthony Kaldellis has focused on highlighting the tensions behind the Justinianic façade, especially his 'Identifying Dissident Circles in Sixth-Century Byzantium: The Friendship of Prokopios and Ioannes Lydos', *Florilegium* 21 (2004): 1–17 and his 'Classicism, Barbarism, and Warfare: Prokopios and the Conservative Reaction to Later Roman Military Policy', *American Journal of Ancient History*, new series 3–4 (2004–2005 [2007]): 189–218. On the important, but often overlooked, aspect of eschatology see Paul Magdalino, 'The History of the Future and Its Uses: Prophecy, Policy and Propaganda', in *The Making of Byzantine History. Studies Dedicated to Donald M. Nicol on His Seventieth Birthday*, edited by R. Beaton and C. Roueché (Aldershot: Ashgate, 1993), 3–34. On the Hagia Sophia see Hans Buchwald, 'St. Sophia: Turning Point in the Development of Byzantine Architecture?' in *Die Hagia Sophia in Istanbul*, edited by V. Hoffman (Bern: Peter Lang, 1997), 29–48. On miraculous images not made by human hands see Averil Cameron, 'Images of Authority: Elites and Icons in Late Sixth-Century Byzantium', *Past and Present* 84 (1979): 3–35 and Hans Belting, *Likeness and Presence: A History of the Image before the Era of Art* (Chicago: Chicago UP, 1994). On the chronicle and John Malalas see *Studies in John Malalas*, edited by B. Croke et al. (Sydney: Australian Association for Byzantine Studies, 1990) and Roger D. Scott, 'Malalas, The Secret History, and Justinian's Propaganda', *DOP* 39 (1985): 99–109. On Romanos the Melodist and his connection to Justinian see Johannes Koder, 'Imperial Propaganda in the Kontakia of Romanos the Melode', *DOP* 62 (2008): 275–91.

NEGOTIATING RETRACTION, 602–717

Events. John F. Haldon's *Byzantium in the Seventh Century: The Transformation of a Culture* (Cambridge: CUP, 2nd edn., 1997) is still an important book on the period. Haldon's thinking has changed in his more recent *The Empire That Would Not Die: The Paradox of Eastern Roman Survival, 640–740* (Cambridge, MA and London: Harvard UP, 2016) as well as in the crucial study by Leslie Brubaker and John F. Haldon, *Byzantium in the Iconoclast Era c. 680–850: A History* (Cambridge: CUP, 2011) which will be important for the next chapter as well. On the rise of Islam the authoritative studies are by Robert G.

Hoyland, *In God's Path: The Arab Conquests and the Creation of an Islamic Empire* (Oxford: OUP, 2015) and Fred M. Donner, *Muhammad and the Believers: At the Origins of Islam* (Cambridge, MA and London: Harvard UP, 2010); these should be consulted together with James Howard Johnston, *Witnesses to a World Crisis: Historians and Histories of the Middle East in the Seventh Century* (Oxford: OUP, 2010). The battle of propaganda over coins is discussed most recently in Michael Humphreys, 'The "War of Images" Revisited. Justinian II's Coinage Reform and the Caliphate', *The Numismatic Chronicle* 173 (2013): 229–44. On the other main Byzantine enemy in the period see Florin Curta, *The Making of the Slavs: History and Archaeology of the Lower Danube Region, c.500–700* (Cambridge: CUP, 2001). On Monothelitism see Judith Herrin, *The Formation of Christendom* (Oxford: Basil Blackwell, 1997 and now reissued by Princeton UP in 2021), which is a key work on the period from the sixth to the ninth century, and Phil Booth, *Crisis of Empire: Doctrine and Dissent at the End of Late Antiquity* (Berkeley: University of California Press, 2013). The councils of the seventh century are analysed by Judith Herrin, in 'The Quinisext Council (692) as a Continuation of Chalcedon', in *Chalcedon in Context* (as above), 148–68.

Infrastructures. There is a lively debate on the question of administrative changes in the Byzantine Empire after the Arab conquests. The definitive interpretation can be found in Constantin Zuckerman, 'Learning from the Enemy and More: Studies in "Dark Centuries" Byzantium', *Millenium* 2 (2005): 79–135 and (in much more detail) in Brubaker and Haldon, *Byzantium in the Iconoclast Era* (as above). Both these works should be consulted for the following chapter as well; see also the overview in Mark Whittow, 'Early Medieval Byzantium and the End of the Ancient World', *Journal of Agrarian Change* 9 (2009): 134–53. Petra M. Sijpesteijn, 'Landholding Patterns in Early Egypt', *Journal of Agrarian Change* 9 (2009): 120–33 discusses the key topic of what happened in the areas conquered by the Muslims. On the transformation of cities see Clive Foss, 'Syria in Transition, AD 550–750: An Archaeological Approach', *DOP* 51 (1997): 189–269 and Archibald Dunn, 'The Transition from Polis to Kastron in the Balkans (III–VII cc.): General and Regional Perspectives', *Byzantine and Modern Greek Studies* 18 (1994): 60–81 as well as Marlia Mundell Mango, 'Monumentality Versus Economic Vitality: Was a Balance Struck in the Late Antique City?' in *Proceedings of the 22nd International Congress of Byzantine Studies*, Vol. I (Sofia: Bulgarian Historical Heritage Foundation, 2011), 240–62. The key question of the social developments in the period has been explored by Telemachos Lounghis, 'Some Gaps in a Social Evolution Theory as Research Directions', in *The Dark Centuries of Byzantium (7th–9th c.),* edited by E. Kountoura-Galake (Athens: National Hellenic Research Foundation, 2001), 411–20 and in much more detail in his 'Δοκίμιο για την κοινωνική εξέλιξη στη διάρκεια των λεγόμενων «σκοτεινών αιώνων»', *Symmeikta* 6 (1985): 139–222, which goes up to the ninth century and should be consulted for the following chapter as well. On Constantinople see Paul Magdalino, *Studies on the History and Topography of Byzantine Constantinople* (Aldershot: Ashgate, 2007).

Environment. On the eschatological reading of disasters see Gerrit J. Reinink, 'Pseudo-Methodius: A Concept of History in Response to the Rise of Islam', in *The Byzantine and Early Islamic Near East,* edited by A. Cameron and L. Conrad (Princeton: Princeton UP, 1992), 149–87. On the David Plates see *Byzantium and Islam: Age of Transition* edited by Helen C. Evans (New York: Metropolitan Museum of Art, 2012). On interaction with Islam see Jack Tannous, *The Making of the Medieval Middle East: Religion, Society, and Simple Believers* (Princeton and Oxford: Princeton UP, 2018). On Anastasios of Sinai see Joseph A. Munitiz (trans.), *Anastasios of Sinai: Questions and Answers* (Turnhout: Brepols, 2011) and Yannis Papadogiannakis, 'Christian Identity in the Seventh-Century Byzantium: The Case of Anastasius of Sinai', in *Religion, Politics, and Society from Constantine to Charlemagne: Collected Essays in Honor of Peter Brown,* edited by J. Kreiner and H. Reimitz, (Turnhout: Brepols, 2014).

FROM SURVIVAL TO REVIVAL, 717–867

Events. The key study is Judith Herrin's, *The Formation of Christendom* (as above); it should be read alongside Brubaker and Haldon, *Byzantium in the Iconoclast Era* (as above). Additionally, on iconoclasm see *A Companion to Byzantine Iconoclasm,* edited by M. Humphreys (Leiden and Boston: Brill, 2021). On Leo III's fiscal measures see Vivien Prigent, 'Les empereurs isauriens et la confiscation des patrimoines pontificaux d'Italie du Sud', *Mélanges de l'École française de Rome. Moyen Âge* 116 (2004): 557–94. On the Slavs in the Balkans and their integration into the Byzantine state see Werner Seibt, 'Siegel als Quelle für Slawen und Slawenarchonten in Griechenland', *Studies in Byzantine Sigillography* 6 (1999): 27–36. On the estrangement between Rome and Constantinople see the chapters by Maria Leontsini and Vassiliki Vlysidou in *Byzantine Diplomacy: A Seminar*, edited by T. C. Lounghis et al. (Athens: Ministry of Foreign Affairs, 2007), 83–163. On external relations of the Empire in this period see Panos Sophoulis, *Byzantium and Bulgaria, 775–831* (Leiden and Boston: Brill, 2012) and *Imperial Spheres and the Adriatic: Byzantium, the Carolingians and the Treaty of Aachen (812)*, edited by Mladen Ančić, et al. (Cambridge: CUP, 2018). On the question of the Pentarchy see Judith Herrin, 'The Pentarchy: Theory and Reality in the Ninth Century', in *Margins and Metropolis: Authority across the Byzantine Empire* (Princeton: Princeton UP, 2013), 239–66. On the relationship between Michael III and Basil I see Shaun Tougher, 'Michael III and Basil the Macedonian: Just Good Friends?' in *Desire and denial in Byzantium: Papers from the 31st Spring Symposium of Byzantine Studies*, edited by L. James (Aldershot: Ashgate, 1999) 149–58.

Infrastructures. The book by Brubaker and Haldon and the articles by Dunn and Foss already cited are crucial for this period. On the growth of Constantinople see Paul Magdalino, *Studies on the History and Topography of Byzantine Constantinople* (as above) and also his 'The Merchant of Constantinople', in *Trade in Byzantium: Papers from the Third International Sevgi Gönül Byzantine Studies Symposium*, ed. P. Magdalino and N. Necipoğlu (Istanbul: Koç UP, 2016), 181–91. On the emergence of family names see Werner Seibt, 'Beinamen, "Spitznamen", Herkunftsnamen, Familiennamen bis ins 10. Jahrhundert: Der Beitrag der Sigillographie zu einem prosopographischen Problem', *Studies in Byzantine Sigillography* 7 (2002): 119–36.

Environment. For a more general study of important aspects of ninth-century Byzantium see *Byzantium in the Ninth Century: Dead or Alive?* in *Papers from the Thirtieth Spring Symposium of Byzantine Studies, Birmingham, March 1996*, edited by L. Brubaker (Aldershot: Ashgate, 1998). On Leo III's understanding of the imperial office see Dagron, *Emperor and Priest* (as above); on the Ekloga and imperial authority see M. T. G. Humhreys, *Law, Power, and Imperial Ideology in the Iconoclast Era, c. 680–850* (Oxford: OUP, 2015). On Tarasios and other patriarchs of Constantinople of the period see Dmitry E. Afinogenov, 'Κωνσταντινούπολις ἐπίσκοπον ἔχει. The Rise of the Patriarchal Power in Byzantium from Nicaenum II to Epanagoga', *Erytheia* 15 (1994): 45–65 and *Erytheia* 17 (1996): 43–71. On John of Damascus see Andrew Louth, *St John Damascene* (Oxford: OUP, 2002); on the theology of the icon see Mariamna Fortounatto and Mary Cunningham, 'Theology of the Icon', in *The Cambridge Companion to Orthodox Christian*

Theology, edited by M. B. Cunningham and E. Theokritoff (Cambridge: CUP, 2008), 136–49. On cultural exchange with Islam see Dimitri Gutas, *Greek Thought, Arabic Culture: The Graeco–Arabic Translation Movement in Baghdad and Early 'Abbasid Society* (London: Routledge, 1998), Maria Mavroudi, *A Byzantine Book on Dream Interpretation. The Oneirocriticon of Achmet and Its Arabic Sources* (Leiden: Brill, 2002) and Christos Simelidis, 'The Byzantine Understanding of the Qur'anic Term al-Samad and the Greek Translation of the Qur'an', *Speculum* 86 (2011): 887–913. On cultural developments in the period see Óscar Prieto Domínguez, *Literary Circles in Byzantine Iconoclasm* (Cambridge: CUP, 2020). On mission see Jonathan Shepard, 'Spreading the Word: Byzantine Missions', in *The Oxford History of Byzantium*, edited by C. Mango (Oxford: OUP, 2002), 230–47 and Sergey A. Ivanov, 'Religious Missions', in *The Cambridge History of the Byzantine Empire* (as above) 305–32, which will be relevant for the following chapter as well.

EXPANSION AND RADIANCE, 867–1056

Events. For an overview see Mark Whittow, *The Making of Orthodox Byzantium, 600–1025* (London: Macmillan, 1996), Michael Angold, *The Byzantine Empire, 1025–1204: A Political History* (London and New York: Longman, 2nd edn, 1997) and Anthony Kaldellis, *Streams of Gold, Rivers of Blood. The Rise and Fall of Byzantium, 955 A.D. to the First* Crusade (Oxford: OUP, 2017); the latter two books should be consulted for the next chapter as well. On the wars of expansion, see Catherine Holmes, 'How the East was Won in the Reign of Basil II', in *Eastern Approaches to Byzantium*, edited by A. Eastmond (Aldershort: Ashgate, 2001), 41–56; Paul Stephenson, *Byzantium's Balkan Frontier* (Cambridge: CUP, 2000), and Βυζαντινά στρατεύματα στη Δύση (as above). Two collections of essays on the eleventh century offer valuable insights into all aspects of the entire period (and should be consulted for the following chapter as well) *Byzantium in the Eleventh Century: Being in Between*, edited by M. D. Lauxtermann and M. Whittow (London and New York: Routledge, 2017), especially the chapters by Magdalino, Whittow and Shepard and the issue 21/2 of the journal *TM* (2017), edited by B. Flusin and J.-C. Cheynet, 419–846, especially the chapters by Haldon and Jacoby. On the rise of Venice see Donald M. Nicol, *Byzantium and Venice* (Cambridge: CUP, 1988). On Italy in the

11th century see André Guillou, *Studies on Byzantine Italy* (London: Variorum Reprints, 1970), especially his paper on the expanding society. On the conversion of the Rus see Jonathan Shepard, 'Conversions and Regimes Compared: The Rus' and the Poles, ca. 1000', *in East Central and Eastern Europe in the Early Middle Ages*, edited by F. Curta (Ann Arbor, MI: University of Michigan Press, 2005), 254–82; On Basil II and Bulgaria see Catherine Holmes, *Basil II and the Governance of Empire (976–1025)* (Oxford: OUP, 2005).

Infrastructures. The relevant chapters in the *Economic History of Byzantium* and *Byzantium in the Eleventh Century: Being in Between* (as above) should be consulted together with Alan Harvey, *Economic Expansion in the Byzantine Empire, 900–1200* (Cambridge: CUP, 1989). On the Venetians' role in trade with Byzantium see David Jacoby, 'Venetian Commercial Expansion in the Eastern Mediterranean, 8th–11th Centuries', in *Byzantine Trade*, edited by M. Mundell Mango (Aldershot: Ashgate, 2009), 371–91. On the Book of the Eparch see Johannes Koder, 'The Authority of the Eparchos in the Markets of Constantinople (according to the Book of the Eparch)', in *Authority in Byzantium*, edited by P. Armstrong (Farnham: Ashgate, 2013), 83–108. On the legislation against the powerful magnates see Eric McGeer, *The Land Legislation of the Macedonian Emperors* (Toronto: Pontifical Institute of Mediaeval Studies, 2000). On the social aspects of this conflict see Rosemary Morris, 'The Powerful and the Poor in Tenth Century Byzantium', *Past and Present* 73 (1976): 3–27, the collected studies by Jean-Claude Cheynet, *The Military Aristocracy and its Military Function* (Aldershot: Ashgate, 2006) and his *Pouvoir et contestations à Byzance (963–1210)* (Paris: Publications de la Sorbonne, 1990) on the numerous (mostly) aristocratic rebellions against the imperial power in the period, but also Vasiliki Vlysidou's *Αριστοκρατικές οικογένειες και εξουσία (9ος – 10ος αι.). Έρευνες πάνω στα διαδοχικά στάδια αντιμετώπισης της αρμενο–παφλαγονικής και της καππαδοκικής αριστοκρατίας* (Thessalonica: Banias, 2001) which examines the competition and conflicts between the most powerful military aristocratic clans. On mercenaries from the North see Sverrir Jakobson, *The Varangians: In God's Holy Fire* (Cham: Palgrave Macmillan, 2020).

Environment. On Photios and his role in the period see Óscar Prieto Domínguez, *Literary Circles in Byzantine Iconoclasm* (as above) and Vlada Stanković, 'Living Icon of Christ: Photios' Characterization of the Patriarch in the Introduction of the Eisagoge and its Significance', in *ΣΥΜΜΕΙΚΤΑ*, edited by I. Stevovic´ (Belgrade, 2012), 39–43. On the role of patriarchs and their relationship to imperial power see also Vlada Stanković, 'The Path toward Michael Keroularios: The Power, Self-presentation and Propaganda of the Patriarchs of Constantinople in the Late 10th and Early 11th Century', in *Zwei Sonnen am Goldenen Horn? Kaiserliche und patriarchale Macht im byzantinischen Mittelalter*, Teilband 2, edited by M. Grünbart et al. (Münster: Lit Verlag, 2013), 137–55. On the path to the schism between Rome and Constantinople see Henry Chadwick, *East and West: The Making of a Rift in the Church: From Apostolic Times until the Council of Florence* (Oxford: OUP, 2005) – this study will be useful for all the following chapters of this book. See also the more specialist treatment by Tia M. Kolbaba, *Inventing Latin Heretics: Byzantines and the Filioque in the Ninth Century* (Kalamazoo: Medieval Institute Publications, 2008). On the events of 1054 see J. R. Ryder, 'Changing Perspectives on 1054', *Byzantine and Modern Greek Studies* 35 (2011): 20–37 and the response by Tia Kolbaba in the same volume, pp. 38–44. On art and architecture in the period see *The Glory of Byzantium: Art and Culture of the Middle Byzantine Era, A.D. 843–1261*, edited by H. C. Evans, and W. D. Wixom (New Haven and London: Yale UP, 1997); more specifically on the major churches in Greece in this period see Doula Mouriki, 'Stylistic Trends in Monumental Painting of Greece during the Eleventh and Twelfth Centuries', *DOP* 34/35 (1980/1981): 77–124. On Byzantine monasticism the best overview is given in *Byzantine Monastic Foundation Documents: A Complete Translation of the Surviving Founders' Typika and Testaments*, edited by J. Thomas and A. Constantinides Hero with the assistance of G. Constable, 5 vols (Washington, DC: Dumbarton Oaks Research Library and Collection, 2000). See especially the chapter on 'Athonite Monasteries' and on the early rules of Athanasios for his Lavra as well as the Typika (foundation charters) of John Tzimiskes and Constantine IX Monomachos for the Athonite communities. On literary and intellectual trends see Anthony Kaldellis, *Hellenism in Byzantium: The Transformations of Greek Identity and the Reception of the Classical Tradition* (Cambridge: CUP, 2007). On the hardening of attitudes between East and West see *The Complete Works of Liudprand of Cremona*, translated by P. Squatriti (Washington, DC: Catholic University of America Press, 2007) and Henry Mayr-Harting, 'Liudprand of Cremona's Account of His Legation to Constantinople (968) and Ottonian Imperial Strategy', *English Historical Review* 116 (2001): 539–56. On the workings and the allure of the Byzantine court see *Byzantine Court Culture from 829 to 1204*, edited by H. Maguire (Washington, DC: Dumbarton Oaks Research

Library and Collection, 1997). The notion of an imagined community linking Byzantium and its orthodox neighbours was first put forward by Dimitri Obolensky in *The Byzantine Commonwealth: Eastern Europe 500–1453* (London: Weidenfeld and Nicolson, 1971); the concept has been revisited by Jonathan Shepard, 'Byzantium's Overlapping Circles', in *Proceedings of the 21st International Congress of Byzantine Studies, London 2006*, edited by Elizabeth Jeffreys, Vol. 1 (Aldershot: Ashgate, 2006), 15–56; new concepts of power are explored in *Political Culture in the Latin West, Byzantium and the Islamic World, c.700–c.1500*, edited by C. Holmes, et al. (Cambridge: CUP, 2021).

THE APPEARANCE OF STRENGTH, 1056–1204

Events Michael Angold's *The Byzantine Empire 1025–1204* and Anthony Kaldellis', *Streams of Gold, Rivers of Blood* (as above) are important handbooks on the period. They should be supplemented with more specialist studies devoted to individual emperors as *Alexios I Komnenos*, Vol. 1, Papers, edited by M. Mullett and D. Smythe (Belfast: Queen's University of Belfast Press, 1996), Paul Magdalino, *The Empire of Manuel I Komnenos, 1143–1180* (Cambridge: CUP, 1993) and *Byzantium, 1180–1204: 'The Sad Quarter of a Century'?*, edited by A. Simpson (Athens: National Hellenic Research Foundation, 2015). The impact of the defeat at Manzikert is contextualized in Carole Hillenbrand, *Turkish Myth and Muslim Symbol: The Battle of Manzikert* (Edinburgh: Edinburgh UP, 2007). On the question of the Crusades there is more than ample literature; from the vast output studies that devote sufficient attention to Byzantium include Peter Frankopan's, *The First Crusade: The Call from the East* (Cambridge, MA: Harvard UP, 2012) and *The Crusades from the Perspective of Byzantium and the Muslim World*, edited by A. E. Laiou and R. P. Mottahedeh (Washington DC: Dumbarton Oaks Research Library and Collection, 2001), online https://www.doaks.org /resources/publications/books/the-crusades-from-the-perspective-of -byzantium-and as well as Ralph-Johannes Lilie, *Byzantium and the Crusader States, 1096–1204*, translated by J. C. Morris and J. E. Ridings (Oxford: OUP, 1993). The study by Jonathan Shepard, 'Cross-Purposes: Alexius Comnenus and the First Crusade', in *The First Crusade Origins and Impact*, edited by J. Phillips (Manchester: Manchester UP, 1997), 107–29 is particularly useful; equally important is Michael Angold's, 'The Road to 1204: The Byzantine Background to the Fourth Crusade',

Journal of Medieval History 25 (1999): 257–78 and Angeliki Laiou, 'Byzantium and the Crusades in the Twelfth Century: Why was the Fourth Crusade so Late in Coming?' in *Urbs capta: The Fourth Crusade and its Consequences*, edited by A. E. Laiou (Paris: Lethielleux, 2005), 17–40. On the Byzantine presence in Italy in the period see Βυζαντινά στρ ατεύματα στη Δύση (as above).

Infrastructures Harvey's *Economic Expansion* (as above) provides a general framework for the economy of the period; this should be supplemented with the study of Cécille Morrisson in *TM* 21/2 (2017; as above), 611–25. On *pronoia* see Mark C. Bartusis, *Land and Privilege in Byzantium: The Institution of Pronoia* (Cambridge: CUP, 2013), but see also on the flipside of the coin: Kostis Smyrlis, 'Private Property and State Finances: The Emperor's Right to Donate His Subjects' Land in the Comnenian Period', *Byzantine and Modern Greek Studies* 33 (2009): 115–32. The chapter by Magdalino, 'Innovations in Government', in *Alexios I Komnenos* (as above) is crucial for the understanding of the Komnenian reforms as is the contribution of Smyrlis on 'The Fiscal Revolution of Alexios I Komnenos: Timing, Scope and Motives', in *TM* 21/2 (2017; as above). The rise of the Italian city states and their relations with Byzantium are explored in Nicol's *Byzantium and Venice* (as above), David Jacoby, 'Italian Privileges and Trade in Byzantium before the Fourth Crusade: A Reconsideration', *Anuario de estudi medievales* 24 (1994): 349–69, Tassos Papacostas, 'Secular Landholdings and Venetians in 12th-Century Cyprus', *Byzantinische Zeitschrift* 92 (1999): 479–501 and Pamela Armstrong, 'Merchants of Venice at Sparta in the 12th Century', in *Sparta and Laconia from Prehistory to Pre-modern,* edited by W. G. Cavanagh, et al. (London: British School at Athens, 2009), 313–21. For a very useful collection and discussion of all treaties between Byzantium and the Italian city states until 1198 see Dafni Penna, *The Byzantine Imperial Acts to Venice, Pisa and Genoa, 10th–12th Centuries: A Comparative Legal Study* (The Hague: Eleven International Publishing, 2012). On the centrifugal trends in the twelfth century see Nicholas Oikonomides, 'La décomposition de l'empire byzantin à la veille de 1204 et les origines de l'empire de Nicée: à propos de la *Partitio Romaniae*', in *Actes du XVe Congrès International des Études Byzantines. Rapports* (Athens: Bibliotheke tes en Athenais Archaiologikes Etaireias, 1976), 3–28; Magdalino, *The Empire of Manuel I Komnenos* (as above) and the chapters by Stankovic and Anagnostakis in *Byzantium, 1180–1204: 'The Sad Quarter of a Century'?* (as above).

Environment. The best overview is provided by Michael Angold, *Church and Society in Byzantium under the Comneni, 1081–1261* (Cambridge: CUP, 1995). I have based my presentation of the cultural and intellectual life of the period on Robert Browning, 'Enlightenment and Repression in Byzantium in the Eleventh and Twelfth Centuries', *Past & Present* 69 (1975): 3–23, Kaldellis, *Hellenism* (as above), chapter 5 and Dion Smythe, 'Alexios I and the Heretics: The Account of Anna Komnene's Alexiad', in *Alexios I Komnenos* (as abobe), 232–59. On Paulicians and Bogomils see *Christian Dualist Heresies in the Byzantine World* (as above). On important Byzantine authors in the period see Stratis Papaioannou, *Michael Psellos: Rhetoric and Authorship in Byzantium* (Cambridge: CUP, 2013); *Anna Komnene and Her Times*, edited by Thalia Gouma-Peterson (New York and London: Garland, 2000), Leonora Neville, *Anna Komnene: the Life and Work of a Medieval Historian* (Oxford: OUP, 2016); Alicia Simpson, *Niketas Choniates: A Historiographical Study* (Oxford: OUP, 2013). On new literary genres and experimentation see Roderick Beaton, *The Medieval Greek Romance* (London and New York: Routledge, 2nd edn, 1996); Nikos Zagklas, 'Experimenting with Prose and Verse in Twelfth-Century Byzantium: A Preliminary Study', *DOP* 71 (2017): 229–48 and Panagiotis A. Agapitos, 'The Politics and Practices of Commentary in Komnenian Byzantium', in *Preserving, Commenting, Adapting: Commentaries on Ancient Texts in Byzantium*, edited by B. van den Berg, et al. (Cambridge – forthcoming). On religious debates with the Latin West see Tia M. Kolbaba, 'Byzantine Perceptions of Latin Religious "Errors": Themes and Changes from 850 to 1350', in *The Crusades from the Perspective of Byzantium and the Muslim World* (as above) 117–43. On the Komnenian cult of commemoration see Titos Papamastorakis, 'The Display of Accumulated Wealth in Luxury Icons: Gift-giving from the Byzantine Aristocracy to God in the Twelfth Century', in *Byzantine Icons: Art, Technique and Technology*, edited by M. Vassilaki (Heraklion: Crete UP, 2002), 35–47. On the Pantokrator monastery see *The Pantokrator Monastery in Constantinople*, edited by S. Kotzabassi (Boston and Berlin: De Gruyter, 2013); on the international allure of Byzantium see Ernst Kitzinger, 'The Byzantine Contribution to Western Art of the Twelfth and Thirteenth Centuries', *DOP* 20 (1966): 25–47; Hans Bloemsma, 'Venetian Crossroads: East and West and the Origins of Modernity in Twelfth-Century Mosaics in San Marco', *Journal of Intercultural Studies* 31 (2010): 299–312; Tassos Papacostas, 'The Medieval Progeny of the Holy Apostles: Trails of Architectural Imitation Across the Mediterranean', *The Byzantine World* (as above) 386–405;

and Elena Boeck, 'Simulating the Hippodrome: The Performance of Power in Kiev's St. Sophia', *The Art Bulletin* 91 (2009): 283–301.

THE LEGACY OF FRAGMENTATION, 1204–1341

Events. On the political landscape after the Fourth Crusade see *Urbs capta: The Fourth Crusade and Its Consequences* (as above), *Identities and Allegiances in the Eastern Mediterranean After 1204*, edited by J. Herrin and G. Saint-Guillain (Aldershot: Ashgate, 2011) and *Liquid & Multiple: Individuals & Identities in the Thirteenth-Century Aegean*, edited by G. Saint-Guillain and D. Stathakopoulos (Paris: ACHCByz, 2012). There are numerous specialist studies that deal with each of the states that emerged in the period: Michael Angold, *A Byzantine Government in Exile: Government and Society under the Laskarids of Nicaea, 1204–1261* (London: OUP, 1975); Donald M. Nicol, *The Despotate of Epiros, 1267–1479: A Contribution to the History of Greece in the Middle Ages* (Cambridge: Cambridge UP, 2010); Antony Eastmond, *Art and Identity in Thirteenth-Century Byzantium: Hagia Sophia and the Empire of Trebiz*ond (Aldershot: Ashgate, 2004); Peter Lock, *The Franks in the Aegean, 1204–1500* (London: Longman, 1995); *A Companion to Latin Greece*, edited by N. Tsougarakis and P. Lock (Leiden and Boston: Brill, 2015); Filip Van Tricht, *The Latin Renovatio of Byzantium: The Empire of Constantinople (1204–1228)* (Leiden and Boston: Brill, 2011); Guillaume Saint-Guillain, 'Les conquérants de l'Archipel: l'empire latin de Constantinople, Venise et les premiers seigneurs des Cyclades', in *Quarta crociata. Venezia, Bisanzio, Impero latino*, edited by G. Ortalli, et al. (Venice: IVSLA, 2006), Vol. 1, 125–237 and his 'Seigneuries insulaires: les Cyclades au temps de la domination latine (XIIIe-XVe siècle)', *Médiévales* 47 (2004): 31–45.

Donald M. Nicol's *The Last Centuries of Byzantium, 1261–1453* (Cambridge: CUP, 1993) is a detailed study of the period, but now largely outdated. On the political situation in the Balkans see John V. A. Fine, *The Late Medieval Balkans: A Critical Survey from the Late Twelfth Century to the Ottoman Conquest* (Ann Arbor: University of Michigan Press, 1987). On Anatolia see Gary Leiser, 'The Turks in Anatolia before the Ottomans', in *The New Cambridge History of Islam*, Vol. 2, edited by M. Fierro (Cambridge: CUP, 2010), 301–12 and more generally *The Cambridge History of Turkey*, Vol.1: *Byzantium to Turkey, 1071–1453*, edited by K. Fleet (Cambridge: CUP, 2009). On the question of the army and the use of mercenaries see Savvas Kyriakidis, *Warfare in Late Byzantium, 1204–1453* (Leiden and Boston: Brill, 2011), which should be consulted for the following chapter as well. On the schism of the Arsenites see Franz Tinnefeld, 'Das Schisma zwischen Anhängern und Gegnern des Patriarchen Arsenios in der orthodoxen Kirche von Byzanz (1265–1310)', *Byzantinische Zeitschrift* 105 (2012): 143–66. On Hesychasm see the overview by Dirk Krausmüller, 'The Rise of Hesychasm', in *The Cambridge History of Christianity*, Vol. 5 (as above), 101–26.

Infrastructures. On the economic developments in this period see the chapters by Klaus-Peter Matschke in the *Economic History of Byzantium* (as above). On more specific developments see numerous studies by Kostis Smyrlis, 'Taxation Reform and the Pronoia System in Thirteenth-Century Byzantium', in *Change in the Byzantine World in the Twelfth and Thirteenth Centuries. First International Sevgi Gönül Byzantine Studies Symposium: Proceedings*, edited by A. Ödekan, et al. (Istanbul: Vehbi Koç Vafki, 2010), 211–17; 'The State, the Land and Private Property: Confiscating Church and Monastic Properties in the Palaiologan Period', in *Church and Society in Late Byzantium*, edited by D. Angelov (Kalamazoo: Medieval Institute Publications, 2009), 58–87; 'Financial Crisis and the Limits of Taxation under Andronikos II Palaiologos (1282-1321)', in *Power and Subversion in Byzantium*, edited by D. Angelov and M. Saxby (Farnham: Ashgate, 2013) 71–82. The fate of cities is discussed by Demetrios Kyritses in 'The "common chrysobulls" of Cities and the Notion of Property in Late Byzantium', *Symmeikta* 13 (1999): 229–45 and Tonia Kiousopoulou, *Οι «αόρατες» βυζαντινές πόλεις στον ελλαδικό χώρο (13ος–15ος αιώνας)* (Athens: Polis, 2013). On the *mesoi* see Klaus-Peter Matschke and Franz Tinnefeld, *Die Gesellschaft im späten Byzanz: Gruppen, Strukturen und Lebensformen* (Cologne, Weimar and Vienna: Böhlau, 2001); on the archontes see Michael Angold, 'Archons and Dynasts: Local Aristocracies and the Cities of the Later Byzantine Empire', in *The Byzantine Aristocracy IX to XIII Centuries*, edited by M. Angold (Oxford: B.A.R., 1984), 236–59 and Nevra Necipoğlu, 'The Aristocracy in Late Byzantine Thessalonike: A Case Study of the City's Archontes (late 14th and Early 15th Centuries)', *DOP* 57 (2003): 133–51.

Environment. On cases of Mediterranean Gothic see Maria Georgopoulou, 'Gothic Architecture and Sculpture in Latin Greece and Cyprus', in *Byzance et le monde extérieur, Contacts, relations, échanges*, edited by M. Balard, et al. (Paris: Publications de la Sorbonne, 2005),

225–54. On the mixed society in the Morea see *Viewing the Morea: Land and People in the Late Medieval Peloponnese*, edited by S. E. J. Gerstel (Washington, D.C.: Dumbarton Oaks Research Library and Collection, 2013). Byzantine ideology in the period is the topic of Dimiter Angelov, *Imperial Ideology and Political thought in Byzantium, 1204–1330* (Cambridge: CUP, 2006). On the construction of identity in the period see Gill Page, *Being Byzantine. Greek Identity before the Ottomans* (Cambridge: CUP, 2008). On education in the early Palaiologan period see Costas N. Constantinides' *Higher Education in Byzantium in the Thirteenth and Early Fourteenth Centuries (1204–ca 1310)* (Nicosia: Cyprus Research Centre, 1982). This is connected to the literary and artistic output in the period surveyed by Edmund B. Fryde, *The Early Palaeologan Renaissance 1261–1360* (Leiden: Brill, 2000). The work of Nigel G. Wilson, *Scholars of Byzantium* (Baltimore: Johns Hopkins UP, 1983) is more specifically focused on texts, while the catalogue of the major exhibition *Byzantium: Faith and Power (1261–1557)*, edited by H. C. Evans (New Haven and London: Yale UP, 2004) is dedicated to art. On Theodore Metochites and the Chora see *The Kariye Camii Reconsidered*, edited by H. A. Klein, et al. (Istanbul: Istanbul Research Institute, 2011). On the Byzantine influence on Italian painting see Hans Bloemsma, 'Byzantine Art and Early Italian Painting', in *Byzantine Art and Renaissance Europe*, edited by A. Lymberopoulou and R. Duits (Farnham: Ashgate, 2013), 37–59. A new take on late Byzantine intellectuals can be found in Niels Gaul, 'The Twitching Shroud: Collective Construction of Paideia in the Circle of Thomas Magistros', *Segno e testo 5* (2007): 263–340; for a much more detailed account see his book *Thomas Magistros und die spätbyzantinische Sophistik. Studien zum Humanismus urbaner Eliten in der frühen Palaiologenzeit* (Wiesbaden: Harrasowitz, 2011). On late Byzantine views of Italian political affairs see Vasileios Syros, 'Between Chimera and Charybdis: Byzantine and Post-Byzantine Views on the Political Organization of the Italian City-States', *Journal of Early Modern History* 14 (2010): 451–504.

HEADING FOR THE FALL, 1341–1453

Events. On the career of Alexios Apokaukos, see Georgios Makris, 'Alexios Apokaukos und sein Porträt im Codex Paris. gr. 2144', in *Geschehenes und Geschriebenes. Studien zu Ehren von Günther S. Heinrich und Klaus-Peter Matschke*, edited by S. Kolditz and R. C. Müller (Leipzig:

Eudora Verlag, 2005), 157–79. On his opponent, John Kantakouzenos see Donald M. Nicol, *The Reluctant Emperor: A Biography of John Cantacuzene, Byzantine Emperor and Monk, c.1295–1383* (Cambridge: CUP, 2002). On the Zealots in Thessalonica see *Les Zélotes: une révolte urbaine à Thessalonique au 14ème siècle: le dossier des sources*, traduction des sources sous la direction de M.-H. Congourdeau (Paris: Beauchesne, 2013), which offers a collection and interpretation of all sources on this urban uprising and discusses the previous literature as well as the edited volume *Thessalonique au temps des Zélotes (1342–1350)*, edited by M.-H. Congourdeau (Paris: ACHCByz, 2014). On the Black Death as the backdrop of the last century of Byzantium see Ole J. Benedictow, *The Black Death, 1346–1353: The Complete History* (Woodbridge: Boydell Press, 2004), a study written by one of the authorities on plague in history as well as Kostas P. Kostes, *Στον καιρό της πανώλης* (Herakleion: Crete UP, 1995). On Manuel II see John Barker, *Manuel II Paleologus (1391–1425): A Study in Late Byzantine Statesmanship* (New Brunswick, NJ: Rutgers UP, 1969) and Florin Leonte, *Imperial Visions of Late Byzantium: Manuel II Palaiologos and Rhetoric in Purple* (Edinburgh: Edinburgh UP, 2020); on his journey to the West see *Die letzten Tage von Byzanz. Das Freisinger Lukasbild in Venedig*, edited by C. Kürzleder and C. Roll (Munich: Sieveking, 2018).

The best overview of the last decades of Byzantium is Jonathan Harris', *The End of Byzantium* (New Haven: Yale UP, 2010). On the political turmoil after Bayezid's capture by the Mongols in 1402 see: Dimitris J. Kastritsis, *The Sons of Bayezid: Empire Building and Representation in the Ottoman Civil War of 1402–13* (Leiden and Boston: Brill, 2007). On the Council of Ferrara-Florence apart from Henry Chadwick, East and West: The Making of a Rift in the Church (as above) see also Paris Gounaridis, 'Πολιτικὲς διαστάσεις τῆς συνόδου Φεράρας-Φλωρεντίας', *Thesaurismata* 31 (2001): 107–29 and Judith Herrin and Stuart M. McManus, 'Renaissance Encounters: Byzantium meets the West at the Council of Ferrara-Florence 1438–9', in *Renaissance Encounters: Greek East and Latin West,* edited by D. Gondicas and M. S. Brownlee (Leiden and Boston: Brill, 2012) 35–56. Especially on the fall of Constantinople in 1453 see Marios Philippides and Walter K. Hanak, *Siege and Fall of Constantinople in 1453: Historiography, Topography, and Military Studies* (Farnham: Ashgate, 2011), which is more technical, and the more readable, Roger Crowley, *Constantinople: The Last Great Siege, 1453* (London: Faber and Faber, 2005) as well as Marios Philippides, *Constantine XI Dragaš Palaeologus (1404-1453): The Last Emperor of*

Byzantium (London and New York: Routledge, 2019). A comprehensive collection of annotated sources on the fall of Constantinople is given in *Constantinople 1453: Des Byzantins aux Ottomans*, sous la direction de V. Deroche and N. Vatin (Toulouse: Anacharsis, 2016).

Infrastructures On social developments in the period see Tonia Kiousopoulou, *Emperor or Manager: Power and Political Ideology in Byzantium before 1453* (Geneva: La Pomme d'or, 2011). On the economy the best overviews are again Matchke's chapters in the *Economic History of Byzantium* (as above). More specifically on Constantinople see Nevra Necipoğlu, *Byzantium between the Ottomans and the Latins: Politics and Society in the Late Empire* (Cambridge: CUP, 2009). The most thorough examination of late Byzantine social history is by Klaus-Peter Matschke and Franz Tinnefeld, *Die Gesellschaft im späten Byzanz* (as above). Apart from Matscke's publications on the leading aristocratic entrepreneurs Notaras and Goudelis (whose conclusions are included in his study with Tinnefeld), the most important scholarship on the topic is by Thierry Ganchou. I will refer to some of his most recent relevant publications, as they include his previous scholarship, but readers are encouraged to explore his rich oeuvre in his academia.edu page: 'L'ultime testament de Géôrgios Goudélès, homme d'affaires, mésazôn de Jean V et ktètôr (Constantinople, 4 mars 1421)', in *Mélanges Cécile Morrisson = TM* 16 (2010): 277–359 and 'Autonomie locale et relations avec les Latins à Byzance au XIVe siècle: Iôannès Limpidarios / Libadarios, Ainos et les Draperio de Péra', in *Chemins d'outre-mer. Études d'histoire sur la Méditerranée médiévale offertes à Michel Balard* (Paris: Publications de la Sorbonne, 2004), 353–74. See also Jonathan Harris, 'Constantinople as City-State, c. 1360-1453', in *Byzantines, Latins, and Turks in the Eastern Mediterranean World after 1150*, edited by J. Harris, et al. (Oxford: OUP, 2012), 119–40. On the importance of Athos see *Lire les Archives de l'Athos*, edited by O. Delouis and K. Smyrlis = *TM* 23/2 (2019) devoted to the study of the precious documents preserved in Athonite archives (especially the contributions by Kyritses and Smyrlis on economic and fiscal matters) and Kostis Smyrlis, 'Mount Athos in the Fifteenth Century: Crisis and the Beginning of Recovery', in *Το Άγιον Όρος στον 15ο και 16ο αιώνα* (Thessalonica: Aristoteleio Panepistemio Thessalonikes, 2012), 33–55.

Environment. On Hesychasm see the overview by Dirk Krausmüller, 'The Rise of Hesychasm', in *The Cambridge History of Christianity*, Vol. 5: *Eastern Christianity* (as above), 101–26. On Palaiologan scholars and intellectuals see the studies by N. Wilson and E. Fryde (as above) and also Matschke and Tinnefeld, *Die Gesellschaft im späten Byzanz* (as above) 221–385, which includes a detailed list of 174 such individuals. The case of conversion to the Roman creed is discussed in Claudine Delacroix-Besnier, 'Conversions constantinopolitaines au XIVe siècle', *Mélanges de l'Ecole française de Rome. Moyen-Age, Temps modernes* 105 (1993): 715–61 and Judith R. Ryder, '"Catholics" in the Byzantine Political Elite: The Case of Demetrius Kydones', in *Languages of Love and Hate: Conflict, Communication, and Identity in the Medieval Mediterranean*, edited by S. Lambert and H. Nicholson (Turnhout: Brepols, 2012), 159–74. On the general question of Greek Studies in Italy see Nigel G. Wilson, *From Byzantium to Italy: Greek Studies in the Italian Renaissance* (London: Duckworth, 1992); On Manuel Chrysoloras see Ian Thompson, 'Manuel Chrysoloras and Early Italian Renaissance', *Greek, Roman and Byzantine Studies* 7 (1966): 63–82; on Demerios Kydones, see Judith R. Ryder, *The Career and Writings of Demetrius Kydones: A Study of Fourteenth-Century Byzantine Politics, Religion and Society* (Leiden and Boston: Brill, 2010). On Cyriac of Ancona see *Cyriac of Ancona, Later Travels*, edited and translated by E. W. Bodnar with C. Foss (Cambridge, MA and London: Harvard UP, 2003) and Marina Belozerskaya, *To Wake the Dead: A Renaissance Merchant and the Birth of Archaeology* (New York: W.W. Norton, 2009), which offers a useful overview written for a general audience. On late Byzantine art see Byzantium: Faith and Power (as above). On the material culture of Athos see the catalogues of two exhibitions devoted to it: *Θησαυροί του Αγίου Όρους*, edited by A. A. Karakatsanes (Thessalonica: Greek Ministry of Culture, 1997) and *Le Mont Athos et l'Empire byzantin: Trésors de la Sainte Montagne*, edited by H. Studievic (Paris: Les Éditions Paris Musée, 2009). On Mystras see Manolis Chatzidakis, *Mystras: the Medieval City and the Castle* (Athens: Ekdotike Athenon, 1981). On Plethon, the late, radical thinker see Niketas Siniossoglou, *Radical Platonism in Byzantium: Illumination and Utopia in Gemistos Plethon* (Cambridge: CUP, 2011).

AFTERMATH AND AFTERLIFE

The early Ottoman Empire and Byzantine émigrés
For a general history of the early Ottoman Empire see Elizabeth Zachariadou, 'The Ottoman World', in *The New Cambridge Medieval History*, Vol. 7, c. 1415–c. 1500, edited by C. Allmand (Cambridge: CUP, 1998), 812–30. The question of 1453 as a pivotal event in the transition

from the Middle Ages to the Early Modern period (in the Greek case) is explored in *1453: Η άλωση της Κωνσταντινούπολης και η μετάβαση από τους μεσαιωνικούς στους νεώτερους χρόνους*, edited by T. Kiousopoulou (Herakleion: Crete UP, 2005). On Mehmed II see the classic monograph Franz Babinger, *Mehmed the Conqueror and His Time*, edited by W. C. Hickman (Princeton: Princeton UP, 1978), Julian Raby, 'A Sultan of Paradox: Mehmed the Conqueror as a Patron of the Arts', *Oxford Art Journal* 5 (1982): 3–8 and the more recent collection of essays *Sultan Mehmet II. Eroberer Konstantinopels – Patron der Künste*, edited by N. Asutay-Effenberger and Ulrich Rehm (Cologne: Böhlau, 2009). On the fate of the Notaras family, see the latest contributions by Thierry Ganchou, '"La tour d'Irène" (Eirene Kulesi) à Istanbul: le palais de Loukas Notaras?' in *Mélanges Jean-Claude Cheynet* = TM 21/1 (2017): 169–256 and 'Les tribulations Vénitiennes de la *Ca' Notara* (1460/1490. À la recherche du Plutarque d'Anna', in *Mauscripta Graeca et Orientalia. Mélanges monastiques et patristiques* en l'honneur de Paul Géhin, edited by A. Binggeli, et al. (Leuven, Paris, and Bristol: Peeters, 2016), 383–442. More specifically on developments in Constantinople/Istanbul see Halil Inalcick, 'Istanbul', in *Encyclopedia of Islam*, Vol. 4 (Leiden and New York: Brill, 1971), 224–48 and Çiğdem Kafescioğlu, *Constantinopolis/ Istanbul: Cultural Encounter, Imperial Vision, and the Construction of the Ottoman Capital* (University Park: Pennsylvania State UP, 2009). The question of the emerging Greek elites in the period and their role in the patriarchate of Constantinople is addressed by Thierry Ganchou, 'Le prôtogéros de Constantinople Laskaris Kanabès (1454). À propos d'une institution ottomane méconnue', *Revue des Études Byzantines* 71 (2013): 209–58. On the role of Venice within the Ottoman Empire see Eric R. Dursteler, *Venetians in Constantinople. Nation, Identity, and Coexistence in the Early Modern Mediterranean* (Baltimore: The Johns Hopkins UP, 2006). On the fate of the Church after the Ottoman conquest see Elizabeth Zachariadou, 'The Great Church in Captivity', in *The Cambridge History of Christianity*, Vol. 5 (as above), 169–87. The most complete biography of the first patriarch of Constantinople after 1453 is by Marie-Hélène Blanchet, *Georges-Gennadios Scholarios (vers 1400–vers 1472): un intellectuel orthodoxe face à la disparition de l'empire byzantin* (Paris: Institut Français d'Etudes Byzantines, 2008), see also Nevra Necipoğlu, 'Gennadios Scholarios and the Patriarchate: A Reluctant Patriarch on the "Unhappy Throne"', in *The Holy Apostles* (as above). The place of the Patriarchate of Constantinople in the Ottoman state is analysed in the seminal essay by Benjamin Braude, 'Foundation

Myths of the Millet System', in *Christians and Jews in the Ottoman Empire: The Functioning of a Plural Society*, edited by B. Braude and B. Lewis (Teaneck: Holmes & Meier Publishers, 1982), 69–87.

On the fate of the surviving members of the Palaiologoi see Donald M. Nicol, *The Immortal Emperor: The Life and Legend of Constantine Palaiologos, Last Emperor of the Romans* (Cambridge: CUP, 1992) and Jonathan Harris, 'A Worthless Prince? Andreas Palaeologus in Rome – 1462–1502', *Orientalia Christiana Periodica* 61 (1995): 537–54. The lives and careers of Byzantines in the West after 1453 are explored in James Hankins, 'Renaissance Crusaders: Humanist Crusade Literature in the Age of Mehmed II', *DOP* 49 (1995): 111–46; Jonathan Harris, *Greek Émigrés in the West*, 1400–1520 (Camberley: Porphyrogenitus, 1995); John Monfasani, *Byzantine Scholars in Renaissance Italy: Cardinal Bessarion and Other Emigres* (Aldershot: Ashgate, 1995); and Nigel G. Wilson, *From Byzantium to Italy* (as above). On Greeks in Venice see Chrysa Maltezou, *Η Βενετία των Ελλήνων* (Athens: Miletos, 2005); on the *stradioti* see M. E. Mallett and J. R. Hale, *The Military Organization of a Renaissance State: Venice c. 1400 to 1617* (Cambridge: CUP, 1984). On the printing of Greek books see Martin Davies, *Aldus Manutius: Printer and Publisher of Renaissance Venice* (Tempe: Arizona Center for Medieval and Renaissance Studies, 1999). On Venetian Crete see Maria Georgopoulou, *Venice's Mediterranean Colonies: Architecture and Urbanism* (Cambridge: Cambridge UP, 2001), and *Byzantine Art and Renaissance Europe* (as above), which also includes chapters on the presence of Byzantine art in the West. This is also the topic of Anthony Cutler's 'From Loot to Scholarship: Changing Modes in the Italian Response to Byzantine artifacts, ca. 1200–1750', *DOP* 49 (1995): 237–67. On the role of printing for disseminating news of Ottoman success see Margaret Meserve, 'News from Negroponte: Politics, Popular Opinion, and Information Exchange in the First Decade of the Italian Press', *Renaissance Quarterly* 59 (2006): 440–80.

BYZANTINE STUDIES AND BYZANTIUM IN ART

On the relations between Orthodoxy and Protestantism see Gunnar Herring, 'Orthodoxie und Protestantismus', *Jahrbuch der Österreichischen Byzantinistik* 31 (1981): 823–74; on Hieronymus Wolf and Johannes Oporinus pioneering the edition and publication of Byzantine texts see A. Ben-Tov, *Lutheran Humanists and Greek*

Antiquity: Melanchthonian Scholarship between Universal History and Pedagogy (Leiden and Boston: Brill, 2009), while *The Invention of Byzantium in Early Modern Europe*, edited by N. Aschenbrenner and J. Ransohoff (Cambridge, MA: Harvard UP, 2021), sets the new field of Byzantine studies within the cultural trends that shaped it; the chapter by Kaldellis is an important contribution on the issue of Byzantine as the name for the state and its culture. *Edward Gibbon and Empire*, edited by R. McKitterick and R. Quinault (Cambridge: CUP, 1996), 162–89, is dedicated to the important author who found Byzantium wanting. A. A. Vasiliev, *History of the Byzantine Empire, 324–1453*, Vol. I (Madison: The University of Wisconsin Press, 1952), 3–41 provides an overview of the emergence of Byzantine studies.

It is obviously impossible to offer a comprehensive survey of new trends in Byzantine studies within a short textbook like this. What follows is an eclectic and personal choice meant to highlight various directions and lead readers to further discoveries: Leonora Neville, *Byzantine Gender* (Leeds: ARC Humanities Press, 2019); Roland Betancourt, *Byzantine Intersectionality. Sexuality, Gender, and Race in the Middle Ages* (Princeton and Oxford: Princeton UP, 2020); Sharon E. J. Gerstel, *Rural Lives and Landscapes in Late Byzantium. Art, Archaeology, and Ethnography* (Cambridge: CUP, 2015); Ingela Nilson, *Writer and Occasion in Twelfth-Century Byzantium. The Authorial Voice of Constantine Manasses* (Cambridge: CUP, 2020); Claudia Rapp, *Brother-Making in Late Antiquity and Byzantium. Monks, Laymen, and Christian Ritual* (Oxford: OUP, 2016); *Emotions and Gender in Byzantine Culture*, edited by S. Constantinou and M. Meyer (Cham: Palgrave Macmillan, 2019); *Hybride Kulturen im mittelalterlichen Europa*, edited by M. Borgolte and B. Schneidmüller (Berlin: Akademie Verlag, 2010); Youval Rotman, *Insanity and Sanctity in Byzantium: The Ambiguity of Religious Experience* (Cambridge, MA: Harvard UP, 2016); Anthony Kaldellis, *The Byzantine Republic. People and Power in New Rome* (Cambridge, MA: Harvard UP, 2015).

The following studies deal with the presence (or absence) of Byzantium in art and literature: Anthony T. Aftonomos, *The Stream of Time Irresistible: Byzantine Civilization in the Modern Popular Imagination* (Montreal: Concordia University, 2005); Clement Greenberg, 'Byzantine Parallels' (1958), in *Art and Culture: Critical Essays* (Boston: Beacon Press, 1961), 167–70; Robert Nelson, '"Starlit Dome": The Byzantine Poems of W. B. Yeats', in his *Hagia Sofia 1850–1950: Holy Wisdom Modern Monument* (Chicago: The University of Chicago Press, 2004);

and Stelios Faitakis and Katerina Gregos, *Hell on Earth* (Berlin: Die Gestalten Verlag, 2011). On recent exhibitions devoted to Byzantium see the catalogues already cited above *The Glory of Byzantium* and *Byzantium: Faith and Power* (Metropolitan Museum New York 1997 and 2004), as well as *Byzantium, 330–1453*, edited by R. Cormack and M. Vasilaki (London: Royal Academy of Arts, 2008) [London, Royal Academy of Arts]: *De Byzance à Istanbul: un port pour deux continents*, edited by E. Eldem (Paris: Éditions de la Reunion des musées nationaux, 2009) [Paris, Grand Palais]; *Byzanz: Pracht und Alltag*, edited by F. Daim and R. Fleck (Munich: Hirmer, 2010) [Bonn, Bundeskunsthalle]; *Das goldene Byzanz und der Orient*, edited by F. Daim (Schallaburg, 2012) [Schallaburg, Austria] and *Heaven & Earth: Art of Byzantium from Greek Collections*, edited by A. Drandaki, et al. (Athens: Hellenic Ministry of Culture and Sports and Benaki Museum, 2013) [J. Paul Getty Museum and the National Gallery of Art, Washington, DC]. Johann P. Arnason, 'Approaching Byzantium: Identity, Predicament and Afterlife', *Thesis Eleven* 62 (2000): 39–69 challenges numerous historiographical stereotypes regarding Byzantine history, while Elizabeth Jeffreys, 'We Need to Talk about Byzantium: Or, Byzantium, Its Reception of the Classical World as Discussed in Current Scholarship, and Should Classicists Pay Attention?' *Classical Receptions Journal* 6 (2014): 158–74, explores the Byzantine preservation of Classical texts as well as the reception of the Classical world by Byzantine authors.

For a thought-provoking essay on the place of Byzantium in a more general and global context, consult Averil Cameron, 'Thinking with Byzantium', *Transactions of the Royal Historical Society* 21 (2011): 39–57; it would be profitable for readers to compare her thoughts with Anthony Kaldellis' *Byzantium Unbound* (as above).

Index

Index